# The Journalist of Castro Street

# The Journalist of Castro Street

## The Life of Randy Shilts

ANDREW E. STONER

UNIVERSITY OF
ILLINOIS PRESS
Urbana, Chicago, and Springfield

© 2019 by the Board of Trustees
of the University of Illinois
All rights reserved
Manufactured in the United States of America
1  2  3  4  5  C  P  5  4  3  2  1
♾ This book is printed on acid-free paper.

Cataloging-in-Publication Data available from
the Library of Congress
ISBN 978-0-252-04248-5 (cloth : alk.)
ISBN 978-0-252-08426-3 (paper : alk.)
ISBN 978-0-252-05132-6 (ebook)

*In loving memory of my friends Christopher T. Gonzalez,*
*Jeffrey N. Werner, and Mark J. Goff. Rest in perfect peace.*

# Contents

*Illustrations follow page 110*

# Preface

I remember the winter morning in 1994 when I heard a radio news report about the death of journalist and author Randy Shilts. I was in my tiny graduate student apartment in Muncie, Indiana, getting ready for a cold walk to the bus stop, and I sat down on the bed and listened to the discussion of Shilts and his work. I felt as if I'd lost someone I knew well, though I had never known him personally at all.

His book *And the Band Played On* had made a strong impression on me. Shilts's writing style and his journalistic commitment to detail had impressed me. The day of the announcement of Shilts's death, I went looking for my paperback copy of *The Mayor of Castro Street*, his earlier book about the life and times of gay icon and martyr Harvey Milk. Now that Shilts was gone, reading more of his words seemed to take on an even greater importance.

At the time of Shilts's death, AIDS seemed a troublesome, vexing issue that remained far away. I believed I had never known anyone who was HIV positive or had AIDS. People with AIDS were still distant ghosts on television or in magazines in faraway places like San Francisco and New York City. Nevertheless, I had a rude awakening ahead of me, as Shilts's death from AIDS served as a forerunner to even more personal losses that would follow in the years to come among my own circle of friends.

Randy Shilts represented so much of what I fantasized that I might someday be—a proud, openly gay man who offered the world his words, which could move people and things in positive ways. Shilts was the journalist—the writer—I most wanted to be. It would be many more years before I would take up Shilts's words in any meaningful way, but they remained in my mind always. What Shilts accomplished with his writing, becoming a respected and sought-after expert on once-hidden subjects, shining light in dark places, was what I envisioned it meant to be a journalist and a truly liberated member of this society as a gay man.

The words on the pages that follow here, however, have to move beyond admiration and acclamation and offer a more critical review of Shilts. The necessity to take a more critical look grew not only from the academic requirements of writing a doctoral dissertation that attempted to add meaning to the overall consideration of Shilts's work but also because nothing short of the piercing honesty Shilts brought to his subjects would do. A review of Randy Shilts had to be as honest and uncompromising as Shilts himself had been.

While Shilts was always a man with a thin skin, easily hurt and feeling slighted by the stinging criticism he received, he was sometimes equally determined to give back as good as he got. He knew that some of the things he wrote would incite anger, but he wrote them anyway. He also gladly soaked up praise—and pay—for a controversial story that exposed portions of the still-emerging gay liberation movement that others would have preferred remain unexamined. He learned in his life that a wounded heart stands right next to a determined soul. He discovered that the balm for the pain the world can inflict is sometimes found in immersing one's self in one's work, one's commitment to tell the truth, and a driving desire to change the world and lessen the pain. From an early age, he learned to take whippings and verbal abuse at home, dry his tears, and somehow pull himself together during the daily walk to school, where he presented himself as an able, interesting, and engaged student who had overcome more than anyone could imagine and remained determined to succeed.

Shilts's rock-ribbed intensity and his drive to succeed carried a sense of urgency that put me in awe of him and eluded me for many years. Was it because he understood that the reality of AIDS forced him and the burning beneath his skin for fairness and freedom to bullishly push forward, always? I've attempted to explore these issues here while remaining true to a critical examination of Shilts's work and impact and the meaning behind not only his bulldozer approach to life but also the words he produced.

Shilts has been with me throughout the writing of this work. As education scholar Craig Kridel divined, "I have had company in [the] dusty archives" of Shilts's work, felt especially so during bright January days in 2011 in San Francisco digging through the papers of this prolific writer. Shilts was indeed, as Kridel suggests, a subject "looking over my shoulder, illuminating the corners of the past" through yellowing and wrinkled papers and brittle audio- and videotapes left over from his full yet interrupted life.[1]

# Acknowledgments

With gratitude to my spouse, Randolph E. Scott, for his unending support.

Thank you to all others who assisted me in telling this story, including those who participated in interviews for this work: Linda Alband, Edward Alwood, Dr. Marcus A. Conant, Dr. James W. Curran, Dr. William Darrow, Belva Davis, Michael Denneny, Dr. Don Francis, George Greenfield, David Israels, Cleve Jones, Eric Marcus, Ann Neunschwander, Steve Newman, George Osterkamp, Carol Pogash, Michelangelo Signorile, Dr. Mervin Silverman, Susan Sward, and Rita Williams.

Special thanks to members of the Shilts family, including Gary and Judy Shilts and Reed and Dawn Shilts, for all their assistance and support.

Additional thanks to Robert Winder at the Aurora Public Library, Aurora, Illinois; Dr. James Landers, Dr. Patrick Plaisance, Dr. Joe Champ, Dr. Michael Hogan, and Dr. Greg Luft at Colorado State University; Randy Alfred and the GLBT Historical Society Museum and the GayBack Machine Archive, San Francisco; Marilyn Kincaid and the Reverend Cecil Williams at Glide Memorial Church, San Francisco; Christina Moretta and Tim Wilson at the James C. Hormel LGBTQ Center, San Francisco Public Library; Women's, Gender, & LGBTQ+ Studies at the Library of Congress, Washington, DC; Michael C. Oliveira at ONE Archives, University of Southern California Libraries, Los Angeles; Sally Smith Hughes at the San Francisco AIDS Oral History Project, University of California, San Francisco; Alex Cherian and Robert Chehoski at the San Francisco Bay Area

Television Archive, J. Paul Leonard Library, San Francisco State University; Wes Haley, Alan Mutter, David Perlman, and Susan Sward at the *San Francisco Chronicle*; the papers of Dr. Marcus A. Conant and Dr. Selma Dritz in the University of California Digital Archives; Jennifer S. Argo, Marika Christofides, Dustin J. Hubbart, and Daniel M. Nasset at the University of Illinois Press; Alan Brown, Michael Dotten, Jerry Harris, Drex Heikes, Gail Hoffnagle, Greg Leo, Robert Liberty, Joshua Marquis, and Lauren Peters at the University of Oregon Alumni Association; and Duncan McDonald at the University of Oregon, School of Journalism & Communication. I am grateful to Bill Bridges, Bethany Crum Roush, and Sonya Stinson for editing assistance and to Dr. Donald Abrams, Barry Barbieri, Karl Bridges, Dani Castillo, J. Wesley Cunningham, Jennifer Finlay, Jordan Gorostiza, Dr. James Haney, Dr. Debbie Hill Davis, Mary Beth Ikard, Dr. Alex Ingersoll, Gary Kass, Carrie Lozano, Edward K. Moore, Steve Polston, S. Cory Robinson, C. Scott Sickels, Dr. Gerri Smith, Danielle Stomberg, Jonathan Swain, and Scott Walters for special assistance.

The Journalist of Castro Street

# Introduction

"You're an asshole!"

The yelled epithet had come from somewhere deep in the auditorium, a male voice, but unidentifiable otherwise. The crude remark served its purpose; everyone heard it, including Randy Shilts in, potentially, one of the biggest moments of his professional life.

The shimmering Palais des congrès de Montréal in downtown Montreal was crowded with more than twelve thousand scientists, clinical researchers, and people living with AIDS who had traveled from across the world to attend the Fifth International AIDS Conference and learn more about the deadly and growing worldwide pandemic. Perched on the rostrum on that sunny June day in 1989, Shilts was the closing speaker for the conference because of his best-selling book, *And the Band Played On*. It was an elevated honor for a journalist with no medical or clinical expertise of any kind; instead, Shilts had devoted the lion's share of his professional career thus far to chronicling the AIDS crisis in America.

In the midst of this honor, even at this particular conference, which was more noteworthy for its large mix of rowdy protestors than for any new discoveries on AIDS, Shilts couldn't hide his embarrassment or his anger. The protestors, most of them from the AIDS Coalition to Unleash Power (ACT-UP), disliked Shilts, but they had staked out new ground at this confab, delaying and interrupting various sessions and impeding earlier speeches by Canadian prime minister M. Brian Mulroney and Zambian president Kenneth D. Kaunda.[1]

Moments like this were not uncommon for Shilts—the stark contrast of great honor and respect from some residing alongside great scorn and vitriol from others. His writing as a journalist and author had always seemed to inspire such a reaction, so why should his big moment in the spotlight at the center of the international conversation on the most important public health issue of the century be any different?

Back home at his desk as a national reporter on AIDS for the *San Francisco Chronicle*, he was a respected, sought-after expert on the topic. On the streets of the Castro where he lived, he was just as often cussed and called names, "Randy Shits" being a particular favorite of those who detested him. Interspersed between his appearances on ABC's *Nightline* and CNN's *Larry King Live* were painful, ugly letters to the gay newspapers in San Francisco (and elsewhere) calling him a "Gay Uncle Tom" or a sell-out. Even worse, coming out as a gay man in the early 1970s, when such acts were still quite revolutionary, he was called "a self-hating faggot," accused of turning an unresolved personal rage on the gay men who rejected him.

Neither of those two descriptions completely fits Shilts. He was, after all, a more complex individual than any title such as "expert" or even "asshole" could capture. He inspired a wide range of emotions, from great admiration and affinity to deep disgust and loathing. Earlier in 1989, as he wrapped up what he had dubbed a year spent as an "AIDS celebrity," he offered a revealing first-person essay for *Esquire* magazine, expressing frustration at coming off the author's circuit and returning to his duties as a reporter for the *Chronicle*. "The bitter irony is," he wrote, "my role as an AIDS celebrity just gives me a more elevated promontory from which to watch the world make mistakes in the handling of the AIDS epidemic that I had hoped my work would help to change." Sounding bitter and more than a little defeated, Shilts added, "If an internationally acclaimed best seller [*And the Band Played On*] hadn't done shit to change the world, what good would more newspaper stories do?"[2] Shilts's words provide valuable evidence of his understanding of his role as journalist, author, and writer—as the oft-acknowledged "chronicler of AIDS"—and reveal his perception of the role of a journalist forever changed by this story—*this AIDS story*.

For Shilts, the issue of HIV and AIDS was no longer just another assignment or beat. It was playing out daily in his own life as he raced to cram in as much work as possible against the growing fear of what *might be* in terms of his own mortality. His HIV status, which he kept secret until his symptoms made it impossible to hide and which was the motivating fervor that forced Shilts to pursue the AIDS story for his bosses at the *Chronicle* and his book editors, must have made it obvious to some that it was prompting his rushed way of living. Then again, this was a sober, clear-thinking Shilts who had shed the shackles of booze and, eventually, marijuana, and discovered boundless new energy and drive as he pushed headlong into the daily pursuit of being the "credible journalist" who had become so near and dear to his heart, his very identity.

Some context is valuable. The coverage of HIV and AIDS in the 1980s, spanning a remarkable period that coincided with Shilts's reporting career, evolved immensely over time. During its earliest days, when Shilts and a small handful of others began reporting on the AIDS pandemic, the disease actually had no name because of its many manifestations resulting from the compromised immune systems of its victims. Inappropriately named "the gay cancer" or the somewhat less offensive GRID—Gay-Related Immune Deficiency—it was a disease with a name hastily created in 1982 to describe the clusters of gay men in California and New York City suffering from exotic and communicable diseases such as pneumocystis pneumonia and a rare form of skin cancer known as Kaposi's sarcoma. As time passed and the number of reported cases grew, the disease was renamed Acquired Immune Deficiency Syndrome (AIDS), although the new name was little better than the earlier names, as it emphasized the communicable and global nature of the disease and likely did little to tamp down growing fears of gay men as society's new "Typhoid Mary." Gay men, prostitutes, Haitian immigrants, and hemophiliacs were among the earliest victims of AIDS in America, but only hemophiliacs were granted a pass in the minds of some Americans because of the "innocence" of the mode of transmission for hemophiliacs via contaminated blood supplies.

Shilts was there nearly from the start; his May 3, 1982, inside-page-6 article in the *San Francisco Chronicle* exploring an outbreak of exotic and troubling diseases impacting gay men was among the earliest reporting on AIDS anywhere. Shilts's colleague, *Chronicle* science editor David Perlman, beat Shilts to the punch, publishing his first story on what would become the AIDS pandemic in the *Chronicle* on June 5, 1981. Shilts's leadership on a big story breaking inside the gay community only made sense during the waning years of the 1970s sexual revolution because he was one of the first to tell that story as well (while working for the *Advocate*), often writing about the growing tide of sexually transmitted diseases flowing amid newfound sexual freedom and expression for male homosexuals.

Shilts's reporting on AIDS was ahead of the curve from the start. Journalism researcher Nilanjana R. Bardhan examined AIDS and HIV coverage of five transnational (but solely Western) news services, including the Associated Press, through the 1990s and noted that a shift occurred away from the biomedical nature of reporting on AIDS evident in the 1980s to more emphasis on socioeconomic, public policy, and human rights themes. Story themes regarding AIDS prevention and education remained constant in both eras, Bardhan noted. Along with this change in trend or focus of the AIDS story was a noteworthy decline in the overall volume of stories produced about AIDS, suggesting, as Barnhan noted, that "ideation of AIDS as a moral tale had diminished."[3] Further driving this change in reporting on AIDS had been the stabilization of AIDS rates in most of the developed nations of the world that had the means to support research, prevention, and treatment for people with AIDS. A comprehensive Kaiser Family Foundation survey of more than nine thousand news stories found shifts in AIDS coverage as well, noting that story topics shifted overall from a 1980s emphasis on HIV prevention, education, and awareness to more stories in the 1990s about HIV research and HIV treatment drug and vaccine development efforts. One persistent but consistently small story topic related to social issues connected to HIV and AIDS centered on employment or housing discrimination or on acts of prejudice or violence against people with AIDS.[4] Shilts wrote stories on all these topics.

The implications of a reduction in coverage of AIDS dramatically affected some parts of the world. Thomas W. Netter, former *New York Times* journalist and public spokesman for the World Health Organization, asserted that while the news media does not carry sole responsibility to educate or inform the world about AIDS, "newspapers, magazines, newsletters, television and radio (provided) a vital 'front line' in the global struggle against AIDS."[5] Journalism scholar Sally Lehrman declared that in the years since Shilts and others helped shine the light on AIDS, "AIDS has dropped off the agenda for most journalists," and she noted profound implications of the resulting gaps in coverage, particularly for younger generations and minority cultures who hold on to historical ideas that AIDS affects mostly gay white males and that "new medicines and prevention strategies have contained it." Lehrman pointed to a large *New York Times Magazine* piece titled "The End of AIDS: The Twilight of an Epidemic," published in 1996, as a turning point in media coverage. She noted that a study by Media Tenor International found that in 2000 the evening newscasts on ABC, CBS, and NBC featured just seventy-seven reports on AIDS, or just 0.6 percent of all stories broadcast. The study further found that nearly 60 percent of those stories came as part of coverage of the World AIDS Conference that year in Durban, South Africa.[6] Researchers David Colby and Timothy Cook suggest difficult ramifications for such diminished coverage: "The media identification and definition of public problems work not only on mass audiences. Policy makers are very attentive to news coverage. . . . The media's construction of AIDS thus influences not merely how we as individuals will react, but also how we as a society and as a polity will respond."[7]

The aforementioned Kaiser Foundation study was undertaken at the end of 2001 on the so-called twentieth anniversary of the start of the AIDS pandemic. The study found that the topic of HIV and AIDS had often shifted between being a story about health to one about politics, sexuality, religion, and business. According to the Kaiser study, news coverage of AIDS peaked in 1987 at just over five thousand stories and by 2002 had declined to just one thousand. Interestingly, the Kaiser study noted that news coverage of AIDS peaked six years *before* the first decline in the number of diagnosed HIV and AIDS cases in the United States.

Perhaps not surprisingly, major spikes in news coverage of AIDS occurred as specific news events occurred, including disclosures by celebrities such as Rock Hudson, Earvin "Magic" Johnson, and Arthur Ashe of their HIV status. More stories followed the introduction of AZT (azidothymidine), a protease inhibitor (an enzyme that breaks down proteins and peptides) treatment that is used in combination with a large array of other drug treatments and that has proven effective at slowing or diminishing the ongoing effects of compromised immune systems resulting from HIV. The study also found that issues surrounding the closure of gay bathhouses in San Francisco in 1984 and 1985 (an issue heavily covered by Shilts and the *Chronicle*) trailed only the return of Johnson to NBA basketball and the introduction of protease inhibitor combo drugs in the volume of stories produced in any one year in the twenty-year study.[8]

The Kaiser researchers concluded, "Media coverage of the HIV/AIDS epidemic has, at times, helped shape the policy agenda, while also reflecting current policy discussions, debates and important events. In many cases, the news media have served as an important source of information about the epidemic for the public." In an October 2003 study by the Kaiser Family Foundation, 72 percent of the US public said that most of the information they get about HIV/AIDS comes from the media.[9] Further supporting their claim that reporting about HIV and AIDS may influence public opinion and the creation of policies about the disease, the study's authors noted that their own surveys of Americans about the nation's top health priorities had changed dramatically over the years. In 1987, 68 percent of Americans surveyed by Kaiser identified HIV/AIDS as the nation's top health issue. By 2002 that rate had dropped to 17 percent, placing HIV and AIDS behind other health-related issues such as cancer, access to health care, and rising health-care costs.[10]

5

The consideration of overall AIDS coverage in the media serves to further our understanding of Shilts's reporting about AIDS and its possible impact primarily on American society and its reactions to the deadly AIDS pandemic. Shilts's openly professed desire to influence the timing of some of his AIDS articles to key days of the week or key events is evidence of this. Later in Shilts's career he (coincidentally or on purpose) produced a large number of stories detailing the struggles of discovered or avowed homosexuals in the military trying to hold on to their military rank and/or employment.

It is instructive to consider Shilts in the context of the overall coverage of homosexuality, HIV, and AIDS in his era and via the historically identified roles for journalists, particularly those constructed by early twentieth-century media notables Walter Lippmann and John Dewey. Lippmann suggested that journalists were members of an elite group of intellectually informed and engaged individuals who help the masses navigate the challenges and complexities of democracy. Dewey suggested a more participatory or engaged role for citizens, who benefited from the role journalism played in advancing ideas; however, journalism more likely reflected such attributes than created them. Although Shilts likely would have argued the point in a desire to preserve his oft-claimed position of journalistic objectivity, his life and career when taken as a whole clearly find him occupying a Lippmannesque role of belonging to the social and media elite. Shilts penned the three most seminal books on the life and experience of gay Americans in the last years of the twentieth century. *The Mayor of Castro Street: The Life and Times of Harvey Milk* (1982) was the first mainstream book to take up the life and struggle of one of the nation's first elected gay leaders. *And the Band Played On: Politics, People, and the AIDS Epidemic* (1987) grabbed the intensity of an issue that frightened and defined much of the 1980s. *Conduct Unbecoming: Gays and Lesbians in the U.S. Military from Vietnam to the Persian Gulf* (1993) advanced a political issue that would remain on the nation's agenda for more than a decade. His words went beyond telling the story toward an increased understanding and acceptance of the issues explored, whether it was the desire of Milk or members of the military wishing to pursue careers and lives of professional or personal freedom or the tragic story of the AIDS pandemic that swept the nation and the world. Ultimately, Shilts fully embodied the historic role of a journalist who openly served as both a social and a cultural leader for his times, whether he embraced or acknowledged that role or not.

# CHAPTER 1

# Aurora Dawn

Randy Shilts's hometown of Aurora, Illinois, served as the archetypal backdrop for a popular comedy sketch that attempted to portray the realities of idealized American life in the postwar era. Comedian Mike Myers created the character "Wayne Campbell" and the fictional show *Wayne's World* for NBC's *Saturday Night Live*; it later spawned two successful motion pictures. Myers said he was seeking to re-create the hazy, lazy heavy metal days of the 1970s for kids in towns like Aurora, where nothing special ever happened, as they longed for excitement and searched for ways to express themselves.[1] *Wayne's World*, it seems, succeeded in capturing what it meant to grow up in midwestern American towns such as Aurora during Shilts's adolescence.

Aurora had a problem common in the late 1960s and early 1970s: stagnant population growth and young people leaving town to spread their wings elsewhere. A suburban city hidden in the shadow of Chicago, it proudly claims the title as the second-largest city in Illinois, sprawling across four counties of the northeastern part of the state. The Fox River cuts a sharp dividing line down the center of the city, providing a strong demarcation between east- and west-side neighborhoods and, like many American towns, between those who have and those who have not. Randy Martin Shilts wasn't born in Aurora—he arrived as the third son born to Russell Shilts (whom most people called Bud) and Norma Brugh during a short stint for the young married couple in Davenport, Iowa. While he was still a toddler, Shilts's parents moved to Aurora to make their permanent home. Bud and Norma, both natives of southwestern Michigan, announced their engagement shortly after the Japanese attack on Pearl Harbor and were married in July 13, 1942, when they were both nineteen years old. Bud worked as a welder but had just enlisted for military service for World War II and was soon off to basic training at Fort Campbell, Kentucky. Norma had just graduated high school. The marriage was troubled from the start. "My father told me that they got married just before he went into the service, and when he came back he was ready to pack it up and just forget it and leave her in Michigan," Randy Shilts's oldest brother, Gary Shilts, said. Bud changed his mind and didn't leave Norma. The family followed Bud's job opportunities as they popped up in Michigan, Iowa, and Illinois before settling in Aurora. Bud came back from his military tours a little wiser and a lot more cynical about the realities of life. While in Europe, he had toured the Jewish concentration camp at Dachau in southern Germany after Allied forces liberated it. "He was just overwhelmed," Gary Shilts believes. "He was this rural Michigan kid, and he was unsure of what kind of prisoners these were, these men, women, and children. Someone told him that these were Jewish prisoners, that they were Jews. He was just dumbfounded. . . . It astounded him. He had thought of Jews only as these characters in the Bible, not an actual race of people." His worldview expanded quickly amid the ugly aftermath and ruin of the Nazi regime in Germany.

Back home, by all accounts, Bud Shilts was generally a successful salesman whose dreams of being an architect were frustrated and unfulfilled. He took various sales jobs for lumber companies and later for firms selling manufactured or "prefabricated" homes. For extra cash he would copy architectural designs he obtained and then ask a licensed architect friend to sign them. Bud then quietly sold the plans on the side to friends and others wanting to save some money on construction costs, Gary said.

"We lived in what some sociologists call a 'boardinghouse' family," Gary Shilts said. "Everyone just sort of did their own thing. There wasn't that much interaction among family members," the exception being frequent discussions of politics.

Bud's growing doubts about God and the remnants of a youthful wanderlust cut short by a young marriage and a military tour resulted in his evolving desires colliding with Norma's assigned role as a mother and homemaker. This protected, closed environment allowed Norma to nurse the secrets of alleged sexual abuse she experienced as a young girl, but it still left her feeling trapped. Bud engaged in affairs with women outside his marriage—affairs that weren't always well concealed from Norma. As a result, eldest son Gary believes his mother "had good reason to be drunk all the time. My dad was having a party and she wasn't included.

She was a lost woman. She didn't get a Social Security card until she was required to have one to get a driver's license. She never had a job outside the home. She lived at a time when she had all of the work keeping the house together and raising children basically on her own. Nowadays I think we would consider her life a travesty, we wouldn't treat women like that today." Gary remembers being home on leave from the service during the summer of 1966 and as a twenty-three-year-old witnessing his father's heretofore-secret affair with a woman on the other side of town broken wide open. "Everything came out, and it was really difficult for my mother," Gary recalled. "The significance of all this is the effect it had on my mother that really contributed to her heavy drinking. . . . This wasn't my father's first indiscretion, but it was certainly the most public one."[2]

Norma Shilts was born Norma Jean Brugh near Kalamazoo, Michigan, and met a fellow West Michigander, Bud Shilts, at a high school football game, where he was a cheerleader. "The marriage was a happy one until 1945, and the end of the war, and the two of them (and me) actually had to live with one another," Gary Shilts said.[3] Bud and Norma staged the first of many reconciliations when Bud's indiscretions would seep out of the shadows and into view, Gary recalls, and "in the absence of the pill, over the next 19 years they had five more children" and struggled to keep their fragile home together. "Mom was very intelligent, and she was turned into a housewife, and I don't know how much of that was her plan or whether it was she had a kid, and then another one, and so on," younger brother Reed Shilts said. "I think she felt stuck in some senses, and I am sure there was some frustration combined with having a mountain of mouthy kids."[4]

Bud briefly took night classes at a local community college on the GI Bill and poured himself into his work and "outside" friendships that eventually turned intimate. Meanwhile, Norma Shilts was trying to figure her way as the mother of six active sons and an even more active husband. In the same era, another Illinois woman, Betty Friedan, was offering her thoughts on what women might be feeling about their version of the American Dream. Friedan's 1963 best seller, *The Feminine Mystique,* explored what she described as "the problem that has no name" and gave voice to what many women knew: "A strange stirring, a sense of dissatisfaction, a yearning that women suffered in the middle of the twentieth century in the United States. Each suburban wife struggled with it alone. As she made the beds, shopped for groceries, matched slipcover material, ate peanut butter sandwiches with her children, chauffeured Cub Scouts and Brownies, lay beside her husband at night—she was afraid to ask even of herself the silent question—'Is this all?'"[5]

9

For her part, Norma Shilts's struggle produced perhaps predictable results—at times, she turned to the bottle. This was the 1950s and early 1960s, decades before any widespread depression or anxiety treatment programs were in use. To seek counseling or outside help in Norma's era would also have carried tremendous stigma—and cost, something the Shilts family would and could not undertake.

Norma's everyday challenges were real as the Shilts family grew quickly: Gary was born in May 1943, Russell "Dennis" followed three years later, and Randy was born on August 8, 1951. Three other sons would follow: Reed in 1958, Ronald in 1963, and David in 1968. A twenty-five-year gap exists between the oldest and youngest Shilts boys, seven years between Randy and Reed, providing for a significant generational break in the family. Reed describes a closer-knit family in later years, contrasting with a more distant view Gary observed.

Although earnestly seeking the best for their family, Bud and Norma presided over a sometimes-conflicted family that struggled to keep pace with the ideals of postwar America, challenged by a lack of money and changing social and cultural mores. Tension in the Shilts home had perhaps grown to its zenith in the late 1960s, just as Randy was finishing high school and cultivating dreams of fleeing his parents' house. It was a dream all the Shilts boys engaged, five of the six Shilts boys escaping the thumb of their parents at their first opportunity. Randy's younger brother Ronald left home not too long after graduating high school, engaged in a short flirtation with the US Navy, but mostly left his family back home wondering and worrying about what happened to him. "No one really knows what happened with Ronnie," Reed Shilts said. "He was one of the kids who was messed up, he abused authority, and so everyone thought that going into the service would be good for him. He was on a ship for a while and then was reported AWOL and disappeared."[6]

Years passed with no contact from Ronald until Bud Shilts made the painful decision in 1993 to have his son declared officially dead at the age of thirty under unknown circumstances. Ronald's story was the exception, though, as collectively the Shilts boys were successful in their personal quests to conquer the parts of the world they inhabited.[7]

In 1965 the second oldest son, Russell (whom family members called "Denny" to differentiate him from his father, Russell), escaped to Europe shortly after high school. An accomplished linguist in German, French, Russian, and Polish, he studied mathematics, helped translate American literature into Polish and German, and taught English to Polish students. In January 1980 Dennis wrote to Randy (by now in California) after having heard from across the miles that

Randy had come out to his family. The letter reflected the sometimes snarky but always straightforward nature of the communication between members of the Shilts family. In his letter, Denny edged up to the questions really on his mind, at first asking Randy, "What exactly do you do now? How much [money] do you get and why? What does one learn when studying journalism and how long have you been gay?" He seemed to be unbothered by the revelation about his brother's sexuality, stating, "You may or may not wish to know what I think about your being—uh—whatever the word is this season for homosexual. My prejudice classifies it along with other political, religious and sexual perversions, though not quite as bad as becoming a Baptist or an anti-nuclear energy freak or a Democrat." Dennis told his brother that for him, "a moment's pondering of the actual details of a male homosexual act produces nausea, but that is an esthetic argument and of no further import. . . . Of course this limits our relationship: I can never tell you to 'shove it up your ass' without invoking, perhaps, pleasurable sensations in your above-mentioned orifice, thus nullifying any negative effect intended on my part!"[8]

Turning serious, Denny talked about being envious of Randy's life as a writer in California. He queried Randy about working with publishers and magazine editors and expressed frustration with his own writing. He offered tongue-in-cheek assurance that "none of you have to worry. I can serve as the bad example; every family needs a black sheep." Just as he moved to Wroclaw, Poland, in 1992, Denny sent Randy and the rest of the family a short update on his life, mostly a change of address notice, but he scrawled a note at the bottom for Randy that read, "Ain't heard nuthin' from you for a long time. Saw your name in *Newsweek* a couple of times, though, which, I guess, is sumptin.'"[9] Dennis Shilts died in Wrocław, Poland, in 2010 at age sixty-four.

Randy's younger brother David was born autistic with severe learning disabilities. While autism was the official diagnosis given to David, his brother Gary thinks fetal alcohol syndrome is a more accurate description. "This was the 1970s, and autism disorders were not really well understood then," Reed believes. "Mom and Dad had the typical issues before it was understood what was really happening, but both of them provided for him and fought for his care in the mental health system."[10] Gary Shilts described David as "high functioning" but still not able to care for himself. "At first they called him autistic, but he is not autistic in the classic sense," Gary explained. "He has autistic characteristics, but he is actually fetal alcohol syndrome. I think [my parents] knew this very early on, but they denied it. . . . I remembered that when he was born my mother started her mornings with martinis. She was a solid alcoholic when she was pregnant. Now again, she probably wasn't a classic alcoholic because she didn't have any issues, and she did finally stop, eventually, but she did drink a lot during the time she was pregnant."[11]

Looking back, fetal alcohol syndrome may help explain David's diagnosis, but as he was born during Randy's senior year in high school, the diagnosis did not dispel feelings of guilt and doubt surrounding his arrival. In subsequent years, Randy would ruminate about a secret "joke" he and a female friend had tried to play on Bud and Norma Shilts. Sneaking into his parents' bedroom, Randy used a safety pin to poke holes in a collection of condoms in a dresser drawer. When he later learned that his mother was pregnant with her sixth son, Randy felt guilty, convinced his trick had resulted in the pregnancy. Reed Shilts thinks his older brother Randy carried unnecessary guilt about the birth of David and his disability. "David was high maintenance," Reed said. "He required a lot of attention. When he was very young, it was just like having any baby in the house, but we had to take care of him because Mom was drinking a lot then. There were a lot of situations growing up where David would embarrass us, but he never got any compassion."[12] Eventually, the family decided to move David to a group home setting where his functional skills could develop.

Guilt, it seems, was ever present in Randy's life, learned early on, as it is for most people, at his parents' behest and via Sunday school lessons and sermons at the Wesley United Methodist Church of Aurora. Although the Shilts family were regular attendees of the congregation, religion was not a central part of their life. "When you are a northern Methodist, it is a very generic, non-denominational religion," Randy Shilts told fellow writer Garry Wills for a 1993 profile in *Rolling Stone* magazine. "It never had much impact."[13] Discussing politics of the day was a more important pursuit for Randy—and his father, who likely influenced Randy's youthful interest in Senator Barry Goldwater's 1964 run for the White House. Randy's opposition to the Democrats was also due to his mother's loathing of John F. Kennedy and Lyndon B. Johnson, particularly as the Vietnam War progressed. A Christmas 1962 family photo reveals Randy decked out in his Boy Scout uniform, beaming while holding up a large photo of President John F. Kennedy taped to a dartboard, complete with dart holes in it.

The dartboard display of JFK's image was an unfortunate choice, as months later Kennedy was slain by an assassin's bullets in Dallas, Texas. "We were all upset when Kennedy was killed," Reed Shilts recalled. "One of my earliest memories is watching Kennedy's funeral on TV. I know my mom was very upset. She didn't like Kennedy, but she didn't want to see the president killed, she just wanted him voted out of office."

Norma Shilts was an early opponent of the war in Vietnam. "She was very up to date on politics," Reed said. "She was antiwar way before it was fashionable and was opposed to American boys coming home in body bags from a war in Southeast Asia where she thought we had no skin in the game."[14]

In 1964 Randy was one of the student winners of the "Why I Wish I Could Vote" essay contest, sponsored by the *Aurora Beacon-News*. At thirteen, Randy volunteered for Goldwater campaign efforts in solidly Republican Aurora and Kane County and even founded the local chapter of Young Americans for Freedom (he was eventually elected vice president of the Illinois chapter). Young Americans for Freedom, a conservative youth movement born in 1960, was based on a statement of philosophy promoted by archconservatives William F. Buckley Jr. and M. Stanton Evans to advocate for the social welfare and individual freedom of all Americans.[15] All the Shilts boys could point to their father's interest in the conservative movement—with a heavy dose of libertarian ideals tossed in—as influential in the formation of their worldviews.

At fifteen, Randy won a perfect attendance award for not missing a single day of school during three years at Thomas Jefferson Junior High School. The accomplishment won him the admiration of his teachers, but it was no indication of his commitment to his studies; instead, it indicated his escape from life at home. Randy Shilts's home life concealed a troubling secret beyond his own emerging understanding of his sexuality. When she drank, Randy's mother could become abusive and seemed to direct a good deal of her wrath at the talkative and extroverted Randy. A child rarely tells a family's secrets, and Randy kept his mother's abuse secret until many years later, revealing it in a provocative and public essay.

The public face of the Shilts family was intact, demonstrated even in the *Aurora Beacon-News*, the local newspaper, as Randy's parents smiled widely for a photo commemorating his achievement of Eagle Scout status. Bud Shilts was the leader of Randy's Boy Scout Pack 11, in which Randy earned many badges.[16] Randy's brother Reed recalls, "My dad was involved in our education program and helping us in various functions," but connection to the church and, by extension, God was "more social than spiritual."[17]

In high school, Shilts was an unremarkable student, not the most popular student in the class, but always well liked (enough to win election as vice president of his class). A small cadre of friends included girls who provided an appropriate mask for his emerging sexual attraction to other boys at school. As his young life played out in the shadow of the requirement of all young American men to register for the draft, Shilts's political ideology drifted left.[18]

In his senior year, Shilts tried his hand at journalism and poetry. He offered a poem for *Muses*, the "creative arts magazine" for students, and signed up to write articles for the *Red & Blue*, the student newspaper, penning articles about the student dress code and the ongoing war in Vietnam.[19] In December 1968 he published a timely three-part series on the implications of the military draft, which was in the forefront of the minds of every high school male at the time. The articles were pure opinion, the lead sentence noting, "The draft must be abolished. As I contended in my previous articles, the draft is unconstitutional, collectivist in theory, and very helpful to the concept of irrational wars such as Viet Nam." Shilts seemed more than willing to express opposition to the war but departed from most of his late sixties compatriots by offering rarely found praise for Republican figures on the Right, including President-elect Richard Nixon, Shilts's early hero, Senator Goldwater, and California governor Ronald Reagan, all of whom he highlighted as advocates for an all-volunteer army. He saved his castigation for "most liberals [who] although allegedly supporters of civil rights and equality have generally been avid advocates of the military draft. . . . [I]t is conservatives who have consistently stood against the draft and for a voluntary military."[20] His well-crafted arguments came from his experience on the school's debate team and the National Forensics League, but they didn't keep him from complying with the law and registering for the Selective Service, later gaining a 2-S classification, the student deferment.[21]

High school years were difficult at times, Shilts understanding more and more each day that he was a homosexual in a society that had no tolerance for gays. As he worked silently over in his mind how to come to terms with his emerging sexuality amid bouts of denial, he struggled with oppressive messages from teachers he respected who declared that homosexuals were evil, criminal, or mentally ill. His sexuality would remain a secret throughout his high school years.

Shilts graduated from Aurora West High School on June 5, 1969, the one-year anniversary of the assassination of Senator Robert F. Kennedy. On a "legacy" page in the senior yearbook, one of his classmates wrote, "Randy Shilts: I see a remarkable change in Randy. He changes his name to Barry Goldwater."[22] Randy's brother Gary believes that "high school was a miserable time for Randy. He was not like the other students. He was an outsider. He was a homosexual teenager [in the 1960s] when people didn't even acknowledge that homosexual teenagers existed."[23] His brother Reed looks back and mourns the monumental struggle

Randy was trying to manage with the growing reality that he was a homosexual. "He's trying to struggle with this idea of coming out, and asking himself, 'What is this homosexuality all about? Why is this an issue for me? Why don't I like girls?' I am sure there were thousands of things going through his head in those days that he had no training, or even any comprehension, on how to understand," Reed said.[24]

Although a high school graduate with decent grades, Shilts lacked the money and perhaps some of the drive to go to college. Instead, he settled on enrolling at Aurora College for the 1969–70 school year. The tiny private college, aligned with the Advent Christian Church, was situated less than a block from his family's home at 431 South Calumet Avenue. (Since that time, the college has acquired most of the neighborhood, and all that is left of the Shilts home is a parking lot for a student center.) His transcript shows that his studies were standard fare for a college freshman in a liberal arts college, and he earned As and Bs.[25]

Aurora College was just a way station—an effort to prove he could do college-level work—and reflected no interest in or commitment to Christianity. Shilts had already begun to embrace an Ayn Rand–style atheism. On campus, he organized a small antiwar protest—the first example of such progressive activity at the school. With some college under his belt, Shilts quickly shed Aurora and planned an escape to Oregon with a high school girlfriend—a place that secretly piqued his closeted mind, since his girlfriend had told him she had heard that many bisexuals lived on the West Coast.

Before he left for Oregon, Shilts researched alternative weekly newspapers and encyclopedias about various communal societies formed in Oregon and other northwestern states. "I went to Oregon to be a hippie," Shilts said. At home, he had grown tired of the kitchen table fights over the Vietnam War and civil rights and the tearful personal fights between his parents, and he longed to break free. His decision to leave home for Oregon was one that his parents disliked, especially Norma, who also disliked Randy's girlfriend, Sally Eck, who planned to go west with him. "I remember a lot of people weren't happy about his plans to move west," Reed Shilts said. "I know he and Mom were fighting about it, but I think he was just going to do it, he wasn't going to ask for permission. He was a Shilts kid; he was just going to do it."[26]

Linda Alband was one of the first people Randy met when he arrived in Portland in 1970. A mutual friend recommended him for a vacancy in the 12th Street rooming house where she lived. Alband recalled, "When I first met him he was this closeted guy who really tried to act like 'Mr. Personality.' He could be really obnoxious, especially when he was trying to act straight. He would act like he thought a straight guy should act." Eventually, Alband was in the first group of friends Randy confided in about his sexuality in the weeks and months after his girlfriend dumped him. "Frankly, I think if he hadn't come out, I doubt we would have become friends for more than twenty-five years," Alband said. "He was a much better person; he was so much more comfortable with himself after he came out."[27] Coming out, however, didn't reduce the size of Shilts's ego, Alband said, noting that she and other friends in the rooming house received frequent reminders of his upcoming birthday in the weeks before the actual day—Shilts always referred to his birthday as "Shiltsmas."

Shilts waited until he was well into college and living far from home in Oregon to come out separately to his father and mother during a visit back home. There were many changes back home as well. With another one of Bud's dalliances causing yet another separation for Bud and Norma, Norma moved from Aurora with the three boys still at home (Reed, Ronnie, and David) to a family home at Galesburg, a tiny Michigan town east of Kalamazoo. Family and friends thought Bud stayed behind in Aurora to finish selling the family's home there, but it actually was a part of the couple's latest reconciliation. Bud eventually joined the clan in Galesburg, leaving old "friendships" behind.

Before deciding to come out to his parents, Randy quizzed his older brother Gary about the topic, having surmised that his father and mother may already have known about "that little detail of my personality which I haven't mentioned to them." He reported that his father asked more questions about what he was doing with his life and whether he had a girlfriend.[28] Coming out to his parents grew more important to Shilts. He wrote to his brother Gary:

> If the beans have already been spilled [about being gay], I'd like to know it . . . so that I can stop this silly secrecy and get to the business of knowing the parents and letting them know me. As I've mentioned, I really want to know them—since they are basically nice people—before either myself or they meet an untimely demise. But then, more than anything, I just will not want to be around them when they find out as they may prove to be somewhat irrational and show some of the Midwestern spitfire.[29]

Looking back on his earlier years, when it was a strain to know how much of himself to reveal to his parents, he admitted, "It was always very frightening, telling your parents. Even if you have had conflicts with them, you never want to be alienated from mom and dad. But they were actually very good about it. My

16

dad, when I told him, he just said that he had known I was different since I was 8." Shilts's father, his Boy Scout troop leader, was closer to him than his mother and perhaps heard a rumor or two from youthful indiscretions on scouting camp outs. "I always knew there was something about me that was different," Randy explained. "And I attribute being a well-adjusted homosexual to being an Eagle Scout. You do so much fooling around on camp outs."[30]

Once in Oregon, Shilts enrolled in Portland Community College because of its affordability. The old drag of his mediocre high school career also still haunted him, despite a successful handful of classes completed back at Aurora College. "I had never been that good a high school student because I was just sort of interested in my own thing," Shilts said. "I was reading John Locke when I was 16 but not doing well in a history class, mostly a lot of B's and C's."[31] Linda Alband believes Shilts lacked direction when he first enrolled in community college. "He didn't really know what he wanted to do in college, just that he wanted to go," she said. "He was a work-study student, he had this job managing a parking lot on the campus, but I don't think he really hit on what he wanted to study or even be until he enrolled later at the University of Oregon."[32]

Shilts's next big step—a date he memorialized in a journal as January 15, 1970—had everything to do with the pursuit of "gay liberation," a clearly more personal than political liberation from the shackles of a closeted life. Away from his conservative Illinois home, he began to experience the more accepting (or at least more libertarian) confines of Oregon, a diary entry noting that the attic apartment he took in Portland on Umatilla Street was active. "I was scoring with a blond painter in my attic apartment. . . . I was coming out and my life was truly remarkable, almost saintly."[33] There would be more come-and-go partners but no special boyfriend, mostly a series of brief encounters with men and women during a short-lived declaration of bisexuality. Shilts remained hopeful, even believing his chances of meeting "Mr. Right" might improve with the purchase of contact lenses to replace his historically thick eyeglasses, but long-term relationships remained elusive. Shilts wrote in a journal for several months between 1971 and 1973, 1975 and 1977, and again almost a decade later. There were typical references to topics that haunt most twenty-somethings: loneliness, crushes on heterosexual men he couldn't consummate, concerns about how he behaved after being drunk or high, and worries about money. Frequent entries were little more than coaching words apparently directed to himself to "relax" and "slow down." His journal writing seemed to coincide with the co-counseling he undertook on his own to understand himself and deal with the life changes happening all around him. The concept of co-counseling, popularized in the 1960s and 1970s by theorist Harvey Jackins, likely fit Shilts well. The structure of co-counseling emphasized talking and listening, allowing two participants to switch roles between client and counselor but to work together to resolve the personal or social issues that were affecting their lives.

In his first months and years in Oregon, Shilts experimented with sexual relationships with both women and men but eventually set aside any sexual interest in women once and for all and set out to "gain the respect of the gay people" in his life. He expressed in his journal a clandestine desire to "liberate" one declared-straight male friend whom "I fell in love with at first sight. . . . I was so sure he would change his ways, see the need for liberation, and love me. That's all I've been looking for in the past year, love! I so much dread being alone."[34] A later, undated journal entry shows a growing guilt about "using people for sex" and a desire for deeper connections to the men he was able to get to bed but not able to get into relationships: "My sex life is puttering along and now I see how easy it is to let yourself go without love—just yesterday I sexed with [name deleted] and it was over in 30 minutes and today when I saw him, he ignored me. Was that a hint?"[35] He also made note of the fact that his closest friends were women, with no platonic friendships with gay or straight men lasting very long.[36]

The sexual ambiguity would come and go. The realities of working alongside a highly bigoted man (who, Shilts confided to his diary, was likely a latent homosexual himself) and the experience of an older man exposing his penis to the still-closeted Shilts on a city street would be setbacks. His friend, fond of dropping the word "faggot" into most sentences, was particularly difficult to deal with. "I am tired of having to sit around and hearing people being cut down as 'faggots'! I'm sick of having to hide that part of me—how can I overcome these feelings if I won't even admit it?" Keeping his closet door closed caused Shilts to stifle himself when it came to forming new friendships, afraid that not disclosing his "whole self" to someone would mean it was a friendship "based on a lie."[37]

Shilts's initial understanding of gay liberation matched what most gay men of his era believed it to be: freedom to engage in sex with whomever they wanted, whenever they wanted, and wherever they wanted, shedding any moral or legal restrictions ascribed to sex between two men. It was a natural conclusion to draw for gay men who had come through eras of intense marginalization when the very suspicion (let alone the actual expression) of their homosexuality could result in violence, incarceration, or both. Eventually, however, Shilts began to attach a political understanding to his sexual expression: "I was at Portland Community

College in Oregon, and for me, coming out was very political. I had gay sexual experiences, as we all did, from Boy Scouts on. For me, there came a moment when I had to understand [being openly gay] on a political basis. And it just hit me one day, there's one sentence that explains it all in my mind: 'I am right and society is wrong.'"[38]

From an early point in his coming-out process, Shilts became convinced that the "ultimate goal" was "to have our society accept the fact that homosexuality is equal and on par with heterosexuality, that being gay is no more of a defining characteristic for you as a human being than being left-handed." Even with a growing sense of his own rightness and acceptability as a young man, Shilts still struggled to out himself to others despite deep romantic crushes on other men he knew. Perhaps as a means to delay fully dealing with being gay, Shilts poured himself into the antiwar and women's liberation movements of the 1970s: "I fell into the counter-culture in Portland where I lived and was very hippie, but I still couldn't bring myself to come out. It was this taboo and it was violating this taboo that I couldn't make myself do [even though] I had no links to my home, my family, and I was very independent. I just couldn't bring myself to do it."[39]

His reluctance to come out coincided with a period of progress for gay liberation, coupled with the painful reality that gay men and lesbian women in America had a long way to go to gain understanding, let alone acceptance. It had taken more than two decades to advance gay rights. The very first steps along the path to gay liberation went virtually unnoticed, dating as far back as the 1950 forming of the Mattachine Society in Los Angeles, a pioneering gay rights and cultural organization promoted by neo-Marxian English American immigrant Harry Hay Jr. and some of his friends. Hay's open defiance of social, religious, and cultural arguments against any mainstream role for homosexuals ran counter to more representative messages, such as the one *Life* magazine offered in its June 1964 profile of "the gay world." The article noted that that world was "actually a sad and often sordid world" and referred to homosexuality as "a social disorder [that] society tries to suppress" but that was nonetheless "forcing itself into the public eye because it does present a problem, and parents are especially concerned."[40] Although the 1960s was a decade of progress for minority rights, the March 1967 national broadcast of Mike Wallace's skewed report, "The Homosexuals," as part of the *CBS News Presents* series demonstrated that gay rights had a long, tough road to go. Interspersed among hidden identity interviews with closeted and openly gay men discussing a low, painful life were interviews with psychiatrists, religious figures, and law enforcement officials discussing gays from a problem perspective. There were similarly troubling messages about what being gay meant ringing in Shilts's ears and mind—most notably, the voice of a respected high school sociology teacher who was the very first person to ever mention homosexuality in Shilts's presence at Aurora West High School in 1969. His beloved teacher opined that maybe homosexuals weren't immoral but were just sick. It was a hurtful message that went directly to Shilts's emerging questions about his sexuality as an eighteen-year-old from Illinois.

Amid his newfound freedom as a student at Portland Community College, something finally clicked, and Shilts's heretofore academic mediocrity was replaced by nearly all As and a full embrace of the ubiquitous liberal society surrounding him in perpetually "weird" and accepting Portland. One of Shilts's professors at Portland Community College, Lorraine Prince, would eventually become a personal friend, offering him invitations to visit her and her husband during holiday breaks: "Randy became my friend, and after he transferred to the University of Oregon, and later [when he] moved to San Francisco, he still came to see me, which was always an event. Randy was both a wonderful and terrible house guest; he didn't need 'entertaining,' [he] was invariably amusing and usually introduced us to something cutting edge—music, writing, or (in the old days) some memorable substances! His exuberance and enthusiasm were remarkable."[41]

Classes at Portland Community College were freewheeling, unlike anything Shilts had ever known before. A panel of gay leaders who spoke on campus in a philosophy class intrigued Shilts. He dumped a pending anthropology class assignment and switched his presentation to a tour of what it meant to be gay in the early 1970s. Joining a reassembled panel of "experts" from the Gay Liberation Front of Portland, Shilts used the classroom presentation—on a date he memorized as May 19, 1972—to come out. "I introduced the panel [to the class] and said we were all gay and we're going to talk about what it's like to be gay in America, and all my friends were there, so I told all my friends that day," Shilts later said in an interview.[42] "I swore that I'd never live another day of my life in which people didn't know that I was gay."[43]

# CHAPTER 2

# Eugene Days

After finishing at Portland Community College, Shilts took the expected next step and enrolled in the University of Oregon in the eclectic town of Eugene. In the 1970s the UO campus was a "liberal oasis" in a still mostly rural and conservative state. Tension existed on campus, however. In 1969 the university's football coach backed down from a demand that some of his black players dramatically trim their afro haircuts into a more "acceptable" short buzz. Even graduation exercises were subject to protest: a Black Panther Party interloper interrupted the 1969 spring commencement with an impromptu speech about racial inequities on the Oregon campus and in the nation.[1]

Eugene was a classic American college town with a newfound reputation as a hippie town. Eugene fit Randy Shilts well, particularly given his fondness for smoking pot. Shilts, like many adolescents in his era, prioritized getting high, listening to the music of the Moody Blues, and staring at the three-dimensional album cover for the Rolling Stones' 1967 LP, *Their Satanic Majesties Request*. "I'd get stoned and stare at it and see the little pictures of the Beatles in the corners," Shilts said.[2]

Once on the Oregon campus, he immediately got involved with the gay student group, the Eugene Gay People's Alliance, eventually becoming president of the group. Shilts recalled that the gay student group typically drew a large group of eighty students at the first meeting of a new semester—"everybody came out to see who else was gay on campus"—but then settled into a smaller number of regulars (including Shilts) who engaged Tuesday nights with "rap sessions," guest speakers, and just "integrating, in terms of a positive self-image and understanding [their sexuality]."[3]

Lesbian women dominated the Eugene Gay People's Alliance more than gay men, but Shilts seemed to adjust to the feminist perspective the movement manifested. Early gay rights leaders invited to speak on campus included activist Morris Kight, a cofounder in 1958 of the Committee for Homosexual Freedom (eventually renamed the Gay Liberation Front), and lesbian couple Del Martin and Phyllis Lyon, who founded the historic Daughters of Bilitis Society in San Francisco in 1955. Shilts liked the approach of "rap sessions" led by provocative guest speakers: "I think that's what gay men in the 1980's lost, in terms of really talking about your own personal insecurities. It's sort of how our problems as individuals, being gay and accepting ourselves, how they relate to a broader, political framework within a society in which we were brought up to dislike ourselves and to not have faith and confidence in ourselves. So it was just intensive talking and of course that was in an era when everybody was doing it, consciousness raising." As Shilts and his fellow gay classmates grew bolder, so did the organization's activities. Gay Pride Week soon came along, including the campus's first all-gay dance. Featuring all sixties Motown music as a soundtrack, the dance included three black gay guys wearing wigs and lip-synching the Supremes' hit "Stop! In the Name of Love." For many students, including a small cadre of curious but supportive straight students who showed up, it was an eye-opening event. "It was like a mini-drag show, [even] for people like me whose only experience of being gay was basically in a very political college setting. I'd never seen a drag show," Shilts said. The political nature of being out in these early days was not lost on Shilts, who was already drawn to the messages of individualism contained within Ayn Rand's writings. Shilts described himself as an "objectivist" in this era, and the ideas of individualism strongly connected in his mind as he worked to understand what it meant to be gay. "It all fell into place almost right away," he said, "because it gave me a political context to understand what was going on."[4]

Reawakening his political bug, this time from the Left rather than the Right, Shilts launched a campaign for one of five positions on a student board that determined how to spend about $1 million in "incidental activity fees" paid each year by University of Oregon students. Throughout his campaign, Shilts showed signs of a growing confidence in his own abilities as a gay man and an emerging leader. The *Oregon Daily Emerald*, the student newspaper on the Oregon campus, described Shilts in a candidate profile as a former conservative midwestern kid who moved west and found liberalism. Shilts acknowledged his past youthful flirtation as a charter member of the Young Americans for Freedom in his hometown of Aurora, Illinois, and as a 1964 campaign volunteer for Barry Goldwater. While recognizing the need to shed his conservative past in order to be politically successful in more progressive Oregon, he held on to his admiration of Rand—"I think that still has a lot of influence on me because I'm still a very strong individualist," Shilts said.[5]

For his campaign, Shilts told his fellow students via the profile piece in the student newspaper that despite his conservative pedigree, he had always opposed the Vietnam War. Shilts made note of his interest in literature and poetry, and the student journalist noted that Shilts made it clear in a matter-of-fact manner that "he is a homosexual." Shilts clarified, "I am not an avowed or admitted homosexual because those words connote guilt." The article appeared alongside a photo of Shilts in a wildly patterned shirt, sporting nearly shoulder-length hair and large eyeglasses. Shilts emphasized that his interest in politics was driven less by an interest in serving gay students and more in rooting out what he saw as corruption: "I realized how much dishonesty there was in student government. There was a real need for somebody operating out of his conscience."[6]

The campus newspaper article noted that neither Shilts nor his opponent showed up for an endorsement interview, but Shilts won the paper's nod regardless. *Oregon Daily Emerald* editors noted that "Shilts is an impressive candidate. He is an avowed homosexual, chairman of the Gay People's Alliance and a knowledgeable newcomer to [student] politics. . . . He talks convincingly of bringing some leadership back to student government, and he is more capable than most of providing it."[7] Shilts won the election to the five-member student fee board and was elected its chair after forming a coalition with two other members of the committee, a Latino woman and a black man. Having tasted political victory, Shilts later embarked upon a new candidacy for student body president under the theme "Come Out for Shilts." The student newspaper again featured a "campaign profile" of Shilts and his running mate, Gloria Gonzalez. Shilts said that the centerpiece of his campaign was to retain decision-making power about student policies with students. Shilts said that if a "theme" existed for his campaign, it would be that he was not a politician, and he pledged, "[What] we plan to do is to confront the administration with student issues."[8] Declaring them "a new beginning" for student government, a Shilts-Gonzalez campaign flyer announced they were a political ticket of "a Gay leader and a Chicana leader who have teamed up to offer us a real alternative to old personalities and politicians" and promised that they had "made no deals to get elected, unlike other candidates."[9]

23

Shilts's candidacy for student body president was apparently so noteworthy that the city's daily newspaper, the *Eugene Register-Guard*, noted his candidacy as an openly gay person.[10] Shilts and Gonzalez said their campaign was built around needed budget cuts in the Athletic Department, a freeze in student tuition, development of on-campus recycling programs, rent controls for student housing, tutorial programs for veterans returning from Vietnam, and a childcare center for students with children.[11] Shilts and Gonzalez didn't win. "I lost, but I did very well considering I had only been on campus for five months, so I became very big in student government," Shilts said, noting that he leveraged his position as chair of the University of Oregon's Incidental Fee Committee to direct funds to the Eugene Gay People's Alliance for the first time.[12]

Shilts later said that his early involvement in student politics revealed a certain naïveté that he was longing to shed: "I thought that once people realized that I was running to show that gay people can live openly and they don't have to hide, if I was very assertive about that . . . I figured once people knew that, everybody would come out. It just made perfect sense to do it, that the only reason that people hadn't come out was because it hadn't crossed their minds. I was just so disappointed and very surprised when it didn't work out that way."[13]

Despite his election loss, Shilts was back just weeks later with a large editorial piece in the *Daily Emerald* urging passage of House Bill 2930 by the Oregon legislature, a bill that would prohibit housing and employment discrimination against homosexuals. Oregon was, in contrast to other US states, a rather accepting environment for gay men and lesbian women in Shilts's era. As early as 1974, the city of Portland outlawed discrimination against homosexuals, with the city of Eugene following suit in 1977.[14]

For many years, growing interest in the gay liberation movement became all-encompassing for Shilts. Like a lot of gay men and women just out of the closet, he crashed out, embracing a nearly complete homocentric life. Even papers written for classes at UO took up gay themes, including a poorly received one he saved. Assigned to write a scholarly, senior-level paper, Shilts wrote up a dummy news story for the Associated Press that described him as president of the fictional National Association for the Advancement of Gay People (NAAGP). In the article he took several flights of fantasy about envisioned evenings spent at home with the man of his dreams, enjoying life together in an open fashion. The story took a predictable turn: "Even if I had such a lover, we could not entertain our professional colleagues. We might be fired if they knew we were gay. If we tried to dance at a swank hotel, we would get kicked out. . . . These things would not happen because of any fault on our part. They would happen because the society would consider our relationship sinful, perverted, unnatural, or at best, sick. Why? Because this is the only way most members of our society have been taught to deal with homosexuality." He returned to a theme that would influence much of his professional writing after college: "The prominent task for gay people, therefore, is to teach members of society something different. This is no modest objective." The paper earned an A minus, but his instructor challenged Shilts for his use of a romantic or sexual interlude in his story, reminding him that Shilts himself had earlier complained that gays were frequently sexualized when included in a narrative, if included at all. While the professor saw promise in the work, he declared that there were "disappointing gaps" in the writing and added, "I can think of a half dozen major concepts presented in the [class] readings without even trying that would have had direct application here. At times, this reads more like a happy hour discussion than a quasi-scholarly paper. This makes for interesting reading, but it wasn't the effort I had hoped you would produce at this crucial point."[15] Shilts took criticism seriously and often personally, and he held on to the paper for years after he graduated.

Shilts's Oregon classmates from his era reported that it was a tumultuous time on their campus, as it was on most American college campuses. In the midst of that, they recall a curly mop-top, an opinionated and lively young fellow who was interested in just about everyone and everything. One of his classmates, Mike Dotten, knew Shilts on two levels, through his work in student government and his involvement with the Oregon Outdoor Program. "I found Randy to always be dedicated to his cause—but not overbearing," Dotten said. "He had a great sense of humor and tried to find compromise that would provide incremental, but steady benefits for his cause, whether it was an environmental issue or the Gay People's Alliance." Dotten, who became a lawyer, said Shilts seemed particularly able, even as a college student, to navigate among people who might not have agreed with him. Dotten recalled that the student body president, Greg Leo, was a conservative Republican who went on to become chairman of the Oregon Republican Party. Leo had signaled to student groups that activity budgets were going to be cut dramatically. Shilts responded by submitting a slightly lower budget for the campus homosexual organization. Dotten said, "In the public hearings on the budget, Randy did a remarkable job of advocating for a minority not yet fully accepted, even in Oregon's liberal culture, and presenting the details of his budget while toning down the rhetoric of some of his members who were more strident and confrontational. One could see the outlines of his journalism career developing—careful presentation of the facts, but with an undisguised point of view, presented with humor, integrity and skill."[16] Looking back, Leo credited Shilts with being an important part of his formative years at the University of Oregon: "He is best described by me as a political opponent." Shilts's ire with Leo was over his initial reluctance to finance the gay students' group, including funds for an annual "gay dance." Leo said, "I am not a homophobe, but I did not support the student incidental fees funding dances of any kind, gay or straight. . . . [The money] should not be spent on dances, which should have been funded by voluntary admission fees."[17]

Gail Hoffnagle served on the Incidental Fee Committee with Shilts. She, Shilts, Gloria Gonzalez, Andy Holcomb, and Manuel Hernandez formed the first IFC panel. Hoffnagle recalled that Shilts's leadership as head of the IFC involved many long meetings where public testimony from student groups requesting funds occurred: "He was a very sweet guy, and I liked him a lot. He was very approachable. At the time I would never have predicted his phenomenal success as a writer, but I am proud to have known him." Hoffnagle smiled when she recalled Shilts calling one IFC meeting to a close on a Friday afternoon, announcing without hesitation that "this is a nooky night" and that he wanted to get out of the meeting and get ready to go party.[18]

Leo, who successfully fended off a recall effort supported by Shilts and others, still gave Shilts a lot of credit: "Because of Randy's relentless, pointed and intellectually strong criticism, he actually made our policy stronger, our decisions better, and my political skills sharper. Good adversaries are a bane in the moment and a blessing over time; they press a leader to be better, more competitive, more reasoned, and often more reasonable." That said, Leo still classified Shilts as "annoying," someone who always came prepared with a stack of "razor sharp, pointed questions" for student government leaders. "He was superbly intelligent, extremely well spoken, and horribly irritating at times," Leo said.[19]

Another classmate, Joshua Marquis, who is now a district attorney in a small Oregon community, remembers: "I knew him fairly well, and we had a professional if not occasionally contentious relationship." He recalled that Shilts had pushed for a nondiscrimination clause as an addition to the student newspaper's charter.[20] Drex Heikes, an editor of the student newspaper, also recalled Shilts primarily from his days holding forth in the newsroom of the *Oregon Daily Emerald*. Heikes, like Shilts, pursued a career in journalism after graduating (Heikes eventually won a Pulitzer Prize for a team-reporting project). "He was a mentor and a friend to many people on campus," Heikes said. "It was the 1970s, and the gay movement was in its infancy. Randy had come from a tough situation in Illinois, and he, like many of his gay friends, was trying to find his way. He chose journalism, and the profession is much the better for it."[21]

Robert Liberty interacted with Shilts in his role as a reporter covering student government. "He was thorough and balanced as a reporter for the *Oregon Daily Emerald*," Liberty said, noting that he looks back now with only one regret—that he was not out as an openly gay man in those days. He remembered feeling awkward and guilty when Shilts thanked him for making sure the Gay People's Alliance received funding. "I was in the closet myself, and his kind words made me feel I should have done more," Liberty said, noting that Shilts sometimes endured ridicule from fellow students. A scrawl on a wall in a men's bathroom read, "When you're out of Shilts, you're out of queer," a play on a popular ad campaign by Schlitz Beer at the time that stated, "When you're out of Schlitz, you're out of beer." However, Shilts shared with Liberty that many closeted gay men on campus in those days secretly came to him seeking his advice on how to handle their emerging sexuality and whether to come out.[22]

Jerry Harris, a doctoral graduate student on campus during the same time Randy Shilts was pursuing his baccalaureate degree, connected with him through meetings of the Gay People's Alliance. Shilts had enrolled in a sociology class taught by Harris as a graduate teaching assistant titled Homosexuality: Sociological Perspectives, and Harris recalled him as a fully engaged, excited student.[23]

Shilts said he had "warm feelings" for the University of Oregon because he felt he experienced fair treatment while a student there:

> Back in 1973, when I took my first journalism classes, I was something of a novelty: I had been president of the Eugene Gay Peoples' [*sic*] Alliance. . . . Frankly, I was worried that when I went into the journalism school I might face prejudice, especially because I was open about my intent to write extensively about gay-related issues. Rather than find bias, I only found acceptance and fair treatment. If I got a B on a magazine story about the gay rights movement, it was because I had made a comma-splice error, not because of the content of the writing.[24]

Despite his political success, politics was beginning to lose favor with Shilts. He decided after just a year on campus that "the political process is basically corrupt" and frustrating to his goals. He began to see more limitations than possibilities with the political process. Shilts discussed this period of transition in his life during a 1989 interview with historian and author Eric Marcus. "When I get into something, I like to succeed and I realized, gosh, to succeed in politics you always have to compromise your principles," Shilts said. "You have to be sort of an asshole. You can't live a pure idealistic life, you have to be practical. So I realized I didn't want to be in politics, and nobody trusts politicians. Nobody trusts anybody in politics, so I realized that just wasn't going to work for what I wanted to do, and what was more important was furthering this notion of gay people. I thought journalism fit in very much as a way of doing that." Elaborating on the role journalism could play in furthering his true aspirations, which were related to gay liberation, Shilts said, "I figured all you have to do is get the facts out about gay people . . . and let the facts speak for themselves, which I basically still believe to this day. I was never into advocacy journalism, but basically, I just feel you can put both sides out there and the truth will win out in the end."[25]

In another revealing interview, Shilts detailed his shift: "I could see that society's attitude is wrong, and I was just fine," Shilts said, sounding early themes that love is love, regardless of the actors:

> I saw the limits of what you could do with political activism. I sort of came to the conclusion that most people are prejudiced, not because they are mean people, or evil people, but [because] they lack information. By using information, you could do a lot more to advance understanding than by just being polemic and yelling at people in protest. . . . So I took a journalism class . . . and it was the lightning strike. I found my calling. I basically stopped taking any other courses but journalism. As soon as I got into journalism, I stopped being an activist. I just felt you can't be agitating for something on one hand and still be a journalist. Your job is to tell both sides of the story.[26]

Shilts's remarks are noteworthy. "Activist" was a title Shilts had once accepted and embraced. An editorial written for the campus newspaper in support of a proposed gay rights bill referred to him in a postscript as an activist—"Oregon's first openly gay public official."[27] Activism, however, did not help him defeat society's perspective on homosexuals, which was based in prejudice, a fundamental misunderstanding, and even fear. Moving forward, however, it was clear that he sought to draw a line between his earlier political life and his later journalistic life, but he did so without fully acknowledging the activism that sparked his initial drive toward journalism and perhaps remained with him throughout his life and career. During this transition from activist to journalist, Shilts found guarded "acceptance" among his fellow student journalists who were curious about his shift from campus politico to campus journalist. This take-it-slow, cautious acceptance from his college journalism cohorts would repeat itself years later, as gay rights advocates would be slow to warm to Shilts in his journalism jobs after college, even ones in the gay-owned press. "I had always wanted to work in the mainstream media because that seemed to be the logical place to get information out," he said. Again, in contrast with his desire to be an objective journalist, Shilts revealed his intent to demonstrate his gay activism via so-called mainstream journalism and not just limit himself to the gay press. "It was a wonderful time to be a reporter. The whole gay thing was just exploding. . . . And there was excitement too, seeing a lot of gay people like myself, people who are open and who are committed to showing a new way to be alive, that you didn't have to live in fear and trepidation all the time."[28]

From almost the beginning of his collegiate and later his professional journalism career, Shilts worked hard to buttress his bona fides as a reporter, not an advocate. Shilts employed well-known mainstream journalistic terms and values, including his commitment to the standard of proof for certain claims, and he pointed out the conflicts of interest that can exist among sources. As journalist John Weir noted, "Shilts's attitude of high seriousness suffuses everything he writes. That he may at times be hiding behind his scruples is an accusation leveled at many reporters who righteously advocate objective journalism. . . . Shilts's level of seriousness and professionalism was rare. He was not going to be contained in the era's sometimes flip and hesitant gay journalistic ghetto."[29]

The journalism program at Oregon was in its earliest days when Shilts arrived on campus. One of the professional journalists recruited to teach classes was Duncan McDonald, who went on to occupy a three-decade career at the University of Oregon. There were two students in McDonald's earliest classes as a college professor who would make important names for themselves in journalism: Shilts and a telecommunications major from tiny Ashland, Oregon, Ann Curry, who eventually became a coanchor on NBC's *Today*. McDonald said,

> What I remember about Randy is that he certainly had an interesting aura of excitement around him. He was clearly gregarious. I don't know whether that was forced or not, but at some point, he was so jovial to almost being manic from time to time. As I got to know him a little more over the years, I saw that he could be a very introspective and thoughtful kind of person. He stood out because he was very demonstrative. . . . I know he really wanted to let people know who he was. He was not going to back down from who he was.[30]

McDonald remembered that Shilts demonstrated unusual confidence and security in who he was, including about his sexuality: "I don't think he gave a fat rat's ass about whether anyone thought he was gay or not, or what they thought about it. He lived out there with a lot of bravado, but in his very private and quiet moments, I know he felt wounded and attacked at times, so for that reason, you could easily see how he might overreact as well."[31]

Switching his major from English to journalism briefly delayed Shilts's college graduation date but succeeded overall, as he was named managing editor of the *Daily Emerald* during his senior year. McDonald recalled:

> He clearly had more of a literary flair for his writing than other students. He self-identified and self-selected into fairly specialized reporting very early on. You gotta admire his focus . . . [but] he also had a very big ego. . . . In the class I taught with him, it was a very introductory class; we taught how important the formulaic structure of a news story is, and how we work to say as much as we can in as few words as possible. Randy was trying to be quite literary and quite flowery in his writing. He would get a little opinionated as well.[32]

McDonald said he continually pushed Shilts toward producing more traditional, objective news copy: "I told him, 'You have to find a voice and try to find a quicker way to get to the point. You're not writing for *Texas Monthly* [magazine] now. Pretend you are with [the] Associated Press and write it like that.'"[33]

Shilts racked up several awards and top grades in his journalism classes and began turning his sights on gay topics off campus. During his senior year at Oregon, he saved up enough money to jump on a Greyhound bus for Seattle, where he interviewed closeted gay professionals about their life experiences. That story, along with an earlier one on the fierce competition and elaborate hierarchy of drag show contests in most major cities, won him additional awards, including two from the William Randolph Hearst Foundation in its collegiate writing contests.[34]

Controversy waited in the wings, however, with the revocation of one of the Hearst awards after the judges said they made a calculation error in determining the winners. Shilts's original award was a second-place medallion, $1,000, and a trip to Hearst Castle, near San Francisco. He later learned that his writing only qualified him as a "finalist" and included a much smaller prize of $250. Shilts suspected that the Hearst Foundation was uncomfortable awarding a prize to an openly gay student who had written about gay topics. He believes he also "freaked out" Hearst Foundation officials during a weekend reception they hosted, when Shilts led a handful of his fellow college journalists on a late-night romp to the City Cabaret, a gay bar in the North Beach district of San Francisco. While in San Francisco, the "gay mecca," for the Hearst award activities, Shilts recorded in his diary what he considered rude treatment by the Hearst Foundation staff—one person openly referred to Shilts as "the most obnoxious journalist" in the group. He also remembered sitting through group discussions with his fellow journalism students, who were laughing and ridiculing the idea that one of the students had written about gay topics. They were unaware that the person sitting next to them, Shilts, was that writer.

One of his contemporaries in the Hearst competition in 1975 was a University of Nevada student journalist named Patrick O'Driscoll, later a staff writer for the *Denver Post*. O'Driscoll said that Shilts was the first openly gay person he had ever met or ever realized was gay: "At first, he seemed to fit the homosexual stereotype—a touch effeminate, with frizzed-out locks and flamboyant shirts he seemed to always wear half-buttoned. But, wasn't it the '70s? Everybody dressed flamboyantly. Randy was no different. And that's how he ultimately came across— no different."[35] While the student journalists visited William Randolph Hearst's elaborate mansion, Shilts made a special effort to point out a photograph on a side table of Hearst's granddaughter Patty Hearst, kidnapped just three months earlier on February 4, 1974, by members of the Symbionese Liberation Army. Patty Hearst remained with the SLA until her September 18, 1975, arrest for participation in SLA criminal activities.[36]

Shilts and some of his professors at the University of Oregon engaged in an aggressive but ultimately futile letter-writing campaign to reinstate his coveted Hearst award and the $1,000 prize. McDonald called the Hearst incident "quite scandalous, in my view, not only for the fact that something was withdrawn, but for the discussion of it among the William Randolph Hearst committee, which was generally made up of some very prominent editors and was very, very secretive. It was bullshit. There was no decent explanation ever of why it was removed from him. The only inference you can have is that they said, 'Oh my God, this guy is writing about gay things!'"[37]

Feeling cheated out of the second-place prize and despite his fragile financial state, Shilts agreed to the return of the $1,000 prize to the Hearst Foundation (officials said they planned to cancel the check anyway). John W. Crawford, the dean of the School of Journalism at the University Oregon, said the school's faculty "expressed deep concern about the treatment of [Randy Shilts]" in the Hearst contest and objected to penalizing him for an error on the part of a contest judge.[38] Ira P. Walsh replied on behalf of the Hearst Foundation, using somewhat charged language and noting that the foundation objected to "paying off" Shilts for fear of lessening the value of the awards to the other winners. Again, he acknowledged their embarrassment for the computing error: "We have taken the difficult approach; we have done so because we are convinced it is the right one, and the fair one. . . . Randy Shilts is a bright young man. He is an able student. We believe we would ill serve him by giving him an award he did not merit or win."[39]

There were other more promising moments in Shilts's upstart reporting career. He got an early taste of the kind of impact his reporting could have when a page 1 article he wrote for the *Oregon Daily Emerald* was picked up by the Associated Press and received statewide distribution. Shilts's story detailed how local property tax assessors had engaged in the practice of reporting any incidences of cultivation, propagation, or processing of marijuana noted while conducting their assessments of private property for taxation purposes. Shilts uncovered evidence that the previous Republican county tax assessor had ordered his staff to report such instances to the police; he also reported that the incoming Democratic assessor was going to cease the practice. That the county assessor had acted as an extra set of eyes in the "war on weed" in generally accepting Oregon was big news—and Shilts scored an early reporting success.[40] His bulldog tenacity and willingness to write for nearly every issue of the newspaper found him essentially living in the student newsroom.

Such successes notwithstanding, Shilts was feeling a growing worry about being "so out" about his gay identity, with cautions coming from both his journalism professors and fellow journalism students that perhaps there were benefits to remaining at least partially closeted. He wallowed in the disappointment of having no job prospects as graduation day approached. Seeing other friends who had graduated working as waiters or in other fields outside journalism and writing, "I decided that I'd never make a penny except through my writing," Shilts said. At the same time, he seethed with envy when fellow student journalists won the full-time reporting jobs that were eluding him. He added, "I had this incredible ambition and I was willing to work like fucking crazy through my twenties. . . . My success only came because I was willing to work five times harder than anybody else. What's unfair about it is that people who are just mediocre . . . and don't have that kind of drive can get anywhere because they are straight and don't have to fight prejudice just to make it. You shouldn't have to be extraordinary to make it."[41]

Even a summer internship at a daily newspaper in Oregon or back home in Illinois remained out of his grasp, so during the summer of 1974 Shilts took an hourly wage job as the front desk clerk and "towel boy" at the Majestic Hotel and Club Bath. The Majestic, a gay bathhouse at 303 SW 12th Street in downtown Portland, catered to the closeted and openly gay men of the area. The flatiron building housing the bathhouse in the 1970s and 1980s is now a trendy boutique hotel listed on the National Register of Historic Places. During its day, the Majestic was a historic site for quick pick-ups or for what Shilts referred to as "zipless fucks," borrowing the phrase popularized in Erica Jong's noteworthy 1973 feminist novel, *Fear of Flying*. The bathhouse job had a perk perhaps only a politics and journalism junkie like Shilts could fully appreciate. Scheduled to work days and evenings, he tuned the bathhouse TVs to daily broadcasts of the House Judiciary Committee, which was considering articles of impeachment against President Richard Nixon. Shilts reduced his experiences down to a delightful but unpublished essay about his bathhouse encounters, including job duties that consisted primarily of enforcing strict rules to either charge older, unattractive patrons more for cubicles inside the bathhouse or get rid of drag queens (transvestites) and transsexual men who sought admission.

A "toad chart" hung on the wall inside the bulletproof glass desk where Shilts sat. Unseen by patrons, the chart featured *People* magazine photo cutouts of people such as Soviet premier Leonid Brezhnev and Attorney General John Mitchell. The chart was the bathhouse owner's way "to convey the fact that people who resembled unattractive members of the Nixon Administration were supposed to pay $10 for the privilege of walking around an empty bathhouse in Portland, Oregon," instead of the four dollars or eight dollars charged cuter, younger patrons. "As I began loading towels and spotted sheets into the washer, I regretted that I had not suffered such a summer job back in high school when at least I could have translated my experience into an X-rated term paper on 'How I Spent My Summer Vacation,'" Shilts wrote. "Here I was . . . spending a good portion of my time classifying and lying to potential customers and surveying orgy rooms for people smoking, while in the TV room, the House Judiciary Committee droned on." The bathhouse job was a last resort in order to pay rent that summer—the hoped-for journalism internships had been lost to what Shilts assumed were "more confident journalism students, with far better connections than me."[42]

Shilts's bathhouse job would prove ironic. A decade later, in 1984–85, Shilts was widely viewed as a bathhouse owner's worst enemy. In 1974 he played the role of loyal employee and got an education (and active engagement) in the unbridled nature of sex between gay men who were finally set free to act as they wished behind the privacy of a bathhouse door. "For the uninitiated, a gay bathhouse is not where homosexuals go to get clean," Shilts wrote, apparently anticipating that his article would reach a mostly heterosexual audience. "A patron can go to ostensibly sit in the steam room, but many instead spend their time wandering the hallways past the doors of little cubicles which were barely large enough to contain a mattress. If the patron wants, [he] leaves his [cubicle] door open a crack or so the wandering customers can peer in to see if they should, well, strike up at least a brief, albeit passionate, acquaintanceship."[43]

Larger orgy rooms also existed with mattresses covering the entire floor. Checking the orgy room, ostensibly to make sure no one was smoking and creating a very real fire hazard in a room with a mattress-covered floor, provided Shilts with an overview of "our customers happily engaged in every conceivable permutation of sodomy—just as long as no one was smoking cigarettes." The bathhouse, in Shilts's estimation, was "altogether an institution [that] provides the perfect ambience for that one sexual act after which humanity has so long lusted after—the zipless fuck."[44]

Patrons who abstained from sex but came in, stripped down to a towel, and walked around for hours also gained Shilts's attention. One patron, named "Mr. Businessman" by the rest of the bathhouse staff, never seemed to find a sexual partner and actually was more interested in the congressional hearings on TV than any porn playing in the place. Shilts wrote, "I often found him there, in the TV lounge, as [US Representative] Peter Rodino reigned over hearings that would only prove to Congress what the rest of the nation knew instinctively: that Richard Nixon was a lying son of a bitch who needed to be thrown out of office." Shilts admitted running afoul of Mr. Businessman one afternoon after sharing his views that Nixon was toast—Mr. Businessman, apparently a closeted Republican, was convinced (as was Shilts's father back home in Aurora) that "Nixon is going to come out of this smelling like a rose." Near the end of his summer at the Majestic, Shilts's coworkers stuck a candle in a Twinkie and wished him a happy twenty-third birthday on August 8, 1974. Now fully free of his Republican past, Shilts took it as a personal gift that Nixon took the occasion of Shilts's birthday to announce in shame his resignation of the presidency.[45]

CHAPTER 3

# Living Out

$S$ hilts's sojourns from Oregon and later from California to his parents' new home in Michigan were sometimes disquieting. Following a visit home in the summer of 1974, Randy wrote a diary entry about his mixed feelings of "the desire to go back and see the parents, know them, understand them" and his overriding desire to "quash the feeling for a while" to avoid a follow-up visit. His family could be tough on him—his mother and his brother Gary thought Randy was too vocal in his political opinions for a poor college student without a job and verbally "trimmed his wings" in political discussions that summer (the family was unaware that he had a summer job that year at a gay bathhouse in Portland).[1]

His coming-out process with his brothers was more of an eventuality than the "dramatic" coming-out declaration he had undertaken with his parents. "I don't know if he ever came out to me," Reed said. "When I was young and he was at home, it wasn't an issue. I may not have even been old enough to be aware of 'sexuality.' By the time we were older and Randy became prominent [as an author and journalist], we already knew [he was gay]. I just don't remember anybody sitting down to have 'the talk' about Randy." Both Gary and Reed Shilts recalled, however, that their father was not at all surprised to learn that Randy was gay. "My dad basically said, 'Yeah, I have known Randy was gay since he was six years old,'" Reed said. "My dad told Randy, 'I knew before you did.'"[2]

What was more prominent about Randy over time, Reed remembers, was his political evolution from a Barry Goldwater conservative to a progressive antiwar liberal. Although an evolution, it fit into the Shilts family and its strong commitment to libertarian ideals mixed with a strong questioning of the government. "Personally, I think Randy drifted further left because of Reagan's response to AIDS and came to blame the Republicans more than the entire government, and because everyone around him [in San Francisco] was far left," Reed said. "Maybe the fact that he did not become a [far-left] extremist points out that he had some real backbone."[3]

Randy's visits to the Shilts household in Michigan became less frequent after he settled in the West, usually reduced down to just Christmas or a quick summer visit. It was a conflict, however, he felt deeply—wanting the involvement with his family but longing for the freedom living far from home had given him. His mixed feelings were contained in Shilts's hurt feelings that his parents wrote a letter abruptly announcing that his grandparents had died within a week of one another in June 1971 rather than calling him on the phone. Interestingly, despite his apparent desire to occasionally talk with his parents on the phone, his feelings about his parents could run fickle and contradictory at times. He wrote, "Russell B. Shilts and Norma G. Shilts are but voices I occasionally hear on the phone, I have no concept of what they are and I'm not particularly curious to find out—I only have bitterness and hatred associated with Norma (though I can't remember why) and a detached sympathy for someone named Bud."[4] By the end of June 1971 he had settled on a plan relating to his parents: "I think of the parents—and time is running fast there too—I must establish some sort of contact with them so I will at least know who they are before they die. I have absolutely no conception of what or who they are and if I wait, they'll die and I'll worry about it and it would be something I would regret forever."[5]

Although not close in terms of regular contact, the Shilts boys shared a common trait of being hard workers and young men focused on accomplishing important tasks—typical of children of adult alcoholics. "We all have that streak where we work hard to prove ourselves to somebody," Reed Shilts said. "I'm sure there is something in our collective childhood where we all set high goals and excel[led] to please somebody or something. I'm sure that there are a multitude of psychological assessments about that, but I really never explored them."[6] The oldest Shilts son, Gary, has wondered about the level of accomplishment among the siblings, "but I never felt like we had anything to prove." Gary became a prominent attorney in Illinois and ran for governor of Illinois in 1986 as the nominee of the Libertarian Party, while Reed has enjoyed a well-paid and respected professional life as a physicist and professor.[7]

Duncan McDonald remembered that Shilts, as his college graduation loomed, was determined to try and get a reporting job in San Francisco or another major city as soon as possible: "He had his hopes set pretty high from wanting to go from only some limited collegiate experience to a big daily," although his ambition may not have matched his experience or talent at that point. "I recall how he conducted himself in those days. I can picture a job interview between him and a white male [editor] who is fifty-five years old, and here is this interesting young man who appears far more confident than he had any right to be. You know, those things can really work against you. That was part of Randy's bravado. He was not humble."[8] McDonald affirmed Shilts's suspicion that a level of homophobia in America's newsrooms, even in progressive San Francisco, was not helping him land a job.

Job offers from daily or even weekly newspapers never came through, and so, soon after graduating from the University of Oregon, Shilts moved back to Portland and began accepting freelance writing assignments, convincing himself he could make a go of it as an ad-hoc writer. Shilts wrote to Linda Alband: "I moved to Portland for fame and fortune (and hopefully a fuller romantic life) as a free-lance writer . . . [and] I've decided to settle in Portland for a while." Money remained tight, there was no cash flow, and his "new" used car kept tapping what money did come in. "It will probably be touch and go for some time, but I'm confident that I'll do better in a few months when I get more of a name established. Until then, it's grilled cheese sandwiches, tacos and tuna casseroles."[9]

Some of Shilts's reporting in this era may not have paid well, but it did help form some of the earliest mainstream journalism on the gay life in Oregon, supplanting earlier coverage of gays that focused mostly on arrests of gay men on morals charges. An early freelance article he wrote for the *Willamette Valley Observer* in Eugene, Oregon, was typical. It was a lengthy narrative on the lives of gay men and women in Oregon, but unfortunately it was still packaged under the headline "Secret Identity Troubles Homosexuals" and the inside jump, or continuation, headline listed as "Gay Woes."[10] The tone of Shilts's article mirrored the overall struggle for identity being waged by homosexuals across the nation as "an invisible people" (as historians Dudley Clendinen and Adam Nagourney termed them) who sought a secure place in society—their ability to tell their secret to the world on their own timing was an advantage. At the same time, Clendinen and Nagourney assailed the secret nature of the lives of homosexuals as a disadvantage. They noted that, unlike other minority groups in the nation based on race or gender,

the homosexual population tended to presume, as the culture around them did, that they were flawed, and that the flaw was theirs: a sin they should cast off, a puzzle they should solve. And so, mostly, gay men and lesbians kept their feelings inside, identifying themselves only to each other, if they did so at all. As a population, they existed only in the sense that a secret exists, and is known to exist, without being acknowledged. They did not recognize themselves as a class of people, and the larger culture did not either. . . . They were invisible.[11]

While issues of bias and discrimination are common among all minority groups struggling for acceptance and equality, "the fundamental feeling, the bias which defined this population to begin with is more subtle, more personal than any other. *It is sexual.*" The result was a struggle for homosexuals to construct their own identity and to do so amid a rash of countering messages not only about their worth to society but also about how their presence might constitute an actual threat to humanity. The earliest gay rights leaders, for example, "had to begin with no positive way to see themselves, no precedent on which to stand."[12]

Shilts won his first byline story for a national gay publication in the July 30, 1975, edition of the *Advocate*. His article, "Sodomy Repeal Signed by Washington Governor," reported on efforts by Washington State legislators to make their state among the first to eliminate sodomy and adultery from the state's criminal code—an issue Shilts had advocated for himself just three years earlier as a member of the Gay People's Alliance in Eugene. Shilts noted that some legislators continued to wrestle with "gay myths," some of them citing a fear that the repeal would lead to recruitment of young people into illicit sex by adult homosexuals. For the August 13, 1975, edition of the *Advocate*, Shilts wrote another freelance piece on the push-pull of progressive politics in Oregon titled "Candy Jar Politics: The Oregon Gay Rights Story." He included praise for a local victory in Eugene to prohibit employment discrimination based on sexual orientation put forward by the Eugene Gay People's Alliance. The story broke a major "objectivity rule" for most journalists, who would never report on a subject or movement of which they had been a part. He repeated quotes from an Oregon legislator who said he knew "from personal experience" that homosexuals actively recruit teenagers into their ranks, and then Shilts added in parentheses his own remark after the legislator's quote: "One can envision a large poster of a super-fag ominously pointing his finger, saying, 'I Want You.'"[13] In the October 22, 1975, issue, Shilts was back with "Future of Gay Rights? The Emerging Gay Middle Class," which explored the efforts of middle-class gays to integrate themselves into the political power base of Seattle—a new effort that expended energy toward expanding rights rather than energy toward ensuring the cover of the closet. He noted the active role gays had played in turning back a mayoral recall effort—and noted that the mayor had visited "half of the city's gay bars and discussed the relative merits of cock rings with the owner of a leather shop."[14]

In the May 19, 1976, edition, *Advocate* publisher David B. Goodstein announced Shilts's appointment as a full-time reporter. The move to full-time staff member signaled a shift in Shilts's reporting for the *Advocate*, moving beyond "regional" or "profile" stories to ones more focused on analysis. Included was a report on the emerging gay enclave of the Castro District in San Francisco, which turned into a thoughtful examination of whether the area represented newfound political power and strength for gays or was evidence that gays had been successfully shuffled off to their own segregated ghetto, as other marginalized communities had experienced.[15]

Shilts's new full-time tenure at the *Advocate* was not without problems. Frequent tension rose between Shilts and Goodstein, the *Advocate*'s savior or its Judas, depending on whom you asked. The Shilts-Goodstein relationship would eventually break into open defiance on the part of Shilts and warfare on the part of both men. Goodstein, of another generation and nineteen years older than the upstart and often brash Shilts, had acquired the *Advocate* seemingly more from a motivation to expand a hobby that just might make him money someday than from any desire to advance gay liberation. Goodstein, a graduate of Cornell University and Columbia University, was a lawyer and Wall Street financial expert who after coming out as gay lost his job. Goodstein eventually moved to California and acquired the struggling *Advocate* in 1975.[16] By then the *Advocate* was loosely holding on to its claim as the first truly national gay publication. Founded in September 1967 by three closeted gay men, Dick Michaels, Bill Rand, and Sam Watson, and originally named the *Los Angeles Advocate*, it was published primarily in response to the stepped-up harassment of gay nightclubs and bars by the Los Angeles Police Department. Within a year, the publication's circulation had grown to fifty-five hundred copies, its first iterations produced with typewritten columns. Never able to survive on subscriptions alone, the *Advocate* (having shed the prefix "Los Angeles" from its masthead) fell into reliance upon advertising from pornographers, gay bathhouses, matchmaking and dating services, cigarette companies, and alcohol distillers and distributors to stay afloat. A bimonthly, tabloid-size publication by the mid-1970s, it used newsprint rather than glossy magazine paper stock, and its circulation grew to more than forty thousand nationwide.[17] Goodstein brought his "make money" approach to the publication, and it flourished, moving away from a singular focus on news and including more lifestyle-oriented stories covering literature, art, travel, celebrities, and other topics. Eventually, it was published just once a month. Goodstein fired the *Advocate*'s installed staff and hired just-out-of-college nobodies such as Shilts as regular contributors at bargain-basement prices.[18]

With the promise of full-time work for the *Advocate*, Shilts moved from Oregon to San Francisco. Clendinen and Nagourney reported that Shilts showed up for work "with long, bushy hair and a mustache" and took the first steps away from his apparent "divided loyalties while in Oregon between being a serious journalist and a gay activist." Ultimately, "it was clear to the people at *The Advocate* meeting Shilts for the first time, that his driving interest was not really gay liberation, but in proving his [journalism] professors wrong and making it as a mainstream journalist." Clendinen and Nagourney noted, "Shilts's first stories were written with the kind of distinctive voice that most journalists don't display until well into their careers."[19]

Ironically, soon after Shilts moved to San Francisco to join the *Advocate* full-time, Goodstein moved the magazine's editorial offices to San Mateo, California, closer to his home, as an open and tangible declaration of his desire to decouple the publication from the gay epicenters of San Francisco and Los Angeles. Shilts settled quickly into what he called "the Sodom of the West"—San Francisco—in the heart of the swinging and decidedly gay 1970s. Writing to his brother Gary, he declared, "I'm now a Californian (gulp) in the semi-romanticized city of Zebra killings, the Golden Gate Bridge, and, not the least, Patty Hearst. I'm still not fully recovered from leaving the mountains of Oregon behind for this decidedly urban setting . . . and leaving behind all my friends in Oregon isn't easy and I've been feeling the big city blues." He continued: "The whole scene here sort of freaks me out. I can't believe it—every house has a locked grill before you get to a door which has two sturdy locks. . . . San Francisco, however, is the most beautiful of the big cities. It does have a unique charm about it with the very neat architecture, interesting parks and the tremendous diversity."[20]

Eventually promoted by his editors to wire correspondent and national correspondent, Shilts covered a wide array of news stories about gay life, scraping by on the paltry salary Goodstein and Co. would pay. Shilts said he could count on $600 to $1,000 a month from Goodstein, and although it did not fulfill his desire to work in the mainstream media, "I was covering stuff that I liked and it was a good training ground."[21] Shilts also enjoyed the fact that the *Advocate* used almost as much copy as he could produce, but he felt constrained in sending home clippings to show his parents that he had landed as a journalist. "I was writing for this publication that had all these dirty classified ads in it, and I couldn't send home to my parents a publication that had ads with 'Gay man wants somebody to piss on.' It was so embarrassing," Shilts said. What stood out in Shilts's memory—and in the memories of those who worked with him—was his never-ending ambition to write yet another story. "It was never a question of whether I was going to make it, because I knew I was," he said. "I just worked around the clock and every day of the week, always writing something."[22]

In the summer of 1976 Shilts won a prime assignment to cover the Democratic National Convention in New York City for the *Advocate*. Shilts's coverage took a slice-of-life look at the convention and its day-to-day experiences, particularly through the eyes of four openly gay delegates credentialed for the event. He also covered an activist group of some ten thousand gay Democrats left outside Madison Square Garden to protest the absence of any mention of gay rights or related issues in the Democratic Party's platform. Shilts's story lamented the poor location for the "gay caucus" of four Democratic delegates to meet—their assigned meeting location was stuffed away in an obscure hallway, deep in the convention center, far away from the other state and interest caucuses occurring elsewhere. His story also called out Democratic National Committee officials for their oblivious attitude to the existence of a gay caucus by the DNC. One party official brushed off Shilts's inquiries about this being the first Democratic convention to ever recognize a gay caucus, noting, "Anybody can meet and call themselves a caucus of the Democratic Party. It's no big deal."[23] Shilts noted that the Democrats of 1976 were highly contrasted with the raucous—and losing— groups that gathered in 1968 and 1972 amid crushing Republican victories. As Shilts put it, the Democratic Spirit of '76 was focused on a no-hassles, no-fights drive to nominate former Georgia governor Jimmy Carter for president, and the delegates doing so "are as middle-of-the-road as Perry Como."[24] Mainstream coverage of gay participation at the 1976 Democratic confab was limited to a *New York Times* article on how the DNC planned to promote safety amid progay and antiabortion protests aimed at its delegates.[25]

The compare/contrast approach employed by Shilts—showing the "conventionality" of the four openly gay DNC delegates contrasted with the loud, sometimes even flamboyant demonstrators outside the arena—was a classic example of the objective style he attempted to employ. The one gay candidate Shilts could find, a candidate for a statewide office in an undisclosed state who remained in the closet, would only participate in the story if he could use a pseudonym and keep his identity secret. Shilts posed the obvious question: Do you plan to come out? to which the closeted candidate replied incredulously, "Are you kidding!"

Shilts concluded his reporting on his first national political convention with this statement: "If the gay convergence on the Big Apple did anything other than raise serious questions about the future of the gay movement, it wasn't overly obvious in the muggy heat and the sweltering air of the 1976 Democratic convention."[26]

Political news with gay implications remained a focus area, with Shilts's writing showing a good understanding of the legislative process at the state and federal levels, carefully dissecting how moderate Republicans in one state avoided calling much attention to their bipartisan support with Democrats of sodomy repeal bills. Shilts noted that the "decidedly low key approach" worked in Oregon and Washington, the latter state taking up the effort by splitting up the proposed reforms to the criminal code "into six separate pieces of legislation dealing with categories of reform such as property crimes, personal crimes, and the most controversial section, victimless crimes. The victimless crimes bill struck down sodomy and adultery statutes, as well as revising prostitution laws so that patrons and hookers would be equally punished."[27]

Shilts's reporting about the sodomy law repeals in some states also included losses—such as in Arizona, where efforts failed and sodomy laws remained on the books until 2001. (Sodomy laws were finally repealed by the US Supreme Court in all states via the *Lawrence v. Texas* ruling in 2003.) His reporting reflected his understanding that the gay rights fight in this era was happening at the state and legislative levels (as opposed to the larger federal and court-based battles that would follow). As part of his growing tableau of stories, the *Advocate* assigned Shilts to its Dispatch page, described as a roundup of gay news from around the nation. His story selections included legislative updates about gay rights battles across the nation and the emerging Miami / Dade County gay rights fight, dubbed by gay leaders "the Orange Armageddon."

Another *Advocate* story explored the closeted life of "gay professionals," with Shilts describing, "They hold some of the most respectable positions in society. They serve on civic committees, manage businesses, hold public office, and teach Sunday school. Yet overnight any one of them could be a social outcast. Fear gnaws at them daily. They must always conceal a secret that could cost them their jobs, their homes, and for some, their families." Shilts's analysis reflects his growing understanding that many gay men and women (including himself) medicated themselves with alcohol and drugs in order to cope with being the constant "other" in a heterocentric American society. Shilts directly addressed the bigotry, and he did so by revealing some of his own fear of being cast as part of a "lunatic fringe of hairstylists and bathroom dwellers" and noting, "Discrimination

perpetuates a vicious circle in our society. As long as it persists, most gay professionals will be afraid to come out of hiding. And as long as most gay professionals stay covert, the deeply embedded myths about gay people will not change."[28]
Other stories followed about gay parenting, gay vacations, the fight by an open
lesbian to keep her teaching job, foster homes for gay children, gay athletes, on-
campus gay groups at America's colleges, a trend of gays joining the Unification
Church and the Scientologists, others becoming Buddhists, and gay book reviews.

"Pitch letters" from Shilts to his editors in this era provide a good insight into
Shilts's ability and drive to "sell" his stories to his editors. In a memo to *Advocate*
editors Robert McQueen and Sasha Gregory-Lewis dated January 16, 1976, Shilts
told his editors, "Here's the gay alcoholism opus. It is by far the longest piece I've
ever written with its 51 pages. . . . If nothing else, this project has been tremendously helpful in terms of experience and I'm sure that such future investigations
will reflect that experience." Shilts added gratuitously,

> I'm worried the lead may be too long. It does, however, contain an average
> night-on-the-town for the run-of-the-mill bar goer (and I say this from plenty of
> personal experience)—and it is chocked [*sic*] full of symptoms of alcoholism.
> . . . I do, however, feel that this style is justified. The humorous style provides
> a relief of tension from what otherwise is a very grim article. . . . [W]ith good
> layout, I'm convinced that this story can reap a lot of good effects on [*sic*] our
> alcoholism-ridden subculture. I personally stand behind everything in the story
> and do not feel that I am exaggerating the problem for the sake of good copy.
> We should, however, be prepared for a lot of letters. As Smith [a source cited
> in Shilts's alcoholism story] noted, the denial is pervasive.[29]

By 1977 Shilts was twenty-six years old but still wrote the requisite "gay youth"
story for the *Advocate* with a sense of heart and recognition of the pain that surrounded the coming-out process for many. His take in the June 1, 1977, edition of
the magazine under the title "Gay Youth: The Lonely Young" opened with the fact
that he was offering "a story about violence, ostracism, alienation—and sometimes even suicide" but that "it's a story that needs to be told because increasing
numbers of gay people are coming to grips with their homosexuality at younger
ages. Their stories are often unpleasant."[30] Shilts's story started with first-person
accounts of a lesbian girl who was ostracized at her high school and who was
longing for graduation day to arrive so she could flee; a gay San Francisco boy
turned out of his home after announcing his sexuality who eventually turned
to prostitution to survive; and a third boy who eventually killed himself rather

than face the scorn his family and friends offered. The regular clinical and social experts were present and quoted in the story—though Shilts offered a far more sympathetic viewpoint than the *Life* magazine or *CBS News* stories a decade earlier. Resources did exist—rap groups, telephone hotlines, and youth drop-in centers were developing. Issues remained, including the rarely reported reality of the reticence of older gays, particularly men, to involve themselves in any way with younger gays for fear of raising accusations of child molesting. Shilts's story also carefully distinguished between the opportunities and experiences of gay youth in large cities in the nation, where most, if not all, of the available support programs existed, out of the reach of those youth growing up in more rural or suburban areas, as Shilts had. For some of the latter group, Shilts reported, the closet remained the safest and best alternative, even in the increasingly progressive 1970s.

A December 1977 feature article took up the sensitive issue of domestic violence in heterosexual families, ignoring the reality that such violence also existed within the confines of some troubled gay relationships. The story also ignored, not surprisingly, revelations about any of the domestic violence Shilts would later confess had punctuated his young life back in Illinois.

Sensitive topics such as domestic violence among gay couples, issues that many gay leaders wanted tamped down amid the ongoing fight for equal rights, drew Shilts in. His journalistic instincts told him that despite the cautions and outright challenges of others, writing about the gay life meant covering it all. "Covering it all" delivered to Shilts some of his earliest reporting on gay-related health issues that would come to define most of his subsequent writing, particularly, his eventual leadership in reporting on AIDS. Many have cast Shilts as a "pioneer" of the AIDS story, but stories about the health risks associated with gay sex were not new territory for him. The only discernible difference between new and old stories about gay-related health issues was that Shilts's stories later in his reporting career on the pages of the *San Francisco Chronicle* were far less detailed and graphic than those he had been able to publish in the *Advocate*. Shilts did some of his first reporting on topics related to gay sex in this time frame, one titled simply "VD" in April 1976 and another called "The Hazards of Sex" in December 1976. The *Advocate* dubbed Shilts's effort "a special report on the potential dangers of a variety of sexual practices" and included a sidebar on the kinky and alternate sexual interests of some gays. The reports Shilts wrote were part of an ongoing commitment to investigative reporting on gay topics that the *Advocate*'s aggressive publisher, Goodstein, supported. Author and media historian Rodger Streitmatter noted that Shilts's reports on gay STDs were "crucial" in laying the groundwork for understanding the coming AIDS epidemic.[31] In his report on VD, Shilts's research uncovered that federal funding of $33 million was targeted each year to combat and prevent sexually transmitted diseases, but only $160,000 of it was specifically for outreach to gay communities. Shilts reported that infection rates for gonorrhea and syphilis among gay men were cause for immediate concern.[32]

For the January 12, 1977, issue of the *Advocate*, Shilts returned again to gay sex and health issues but this time decided to explore "the decade's best-kept medical secret: Hepatitis doesn't come from needles." For additional drama, Shilts offered the hepatitis report as a first person-account about his own previous diagnosis of Hepatitis B, an increasingly common liver infection among gay men and others that is primarily spread through exchange of semen and other bodily fluids from an infected person to a noninfected person. "I had fallen victim to the newest venereal disease—hepatitis," he declared. Sounding alarms that would punctuate his writing for many years, he noted, "My experience is hardly unique as viral hepatitis is emerging as one of the most significant health problems among gay men," referring to it as being in "epidemic proportions" in some gay enclaves in US cities.[33]

He couldn't have known it at the time, but during this period Shilts was touching on a key thesis around which he would construct his award-winning book *And the Band Played On* a decade later. Other major themes of his later reporting would also emerge as Shilts wrote, "Hepatitis is no longer a disease restricted to the social fringes of alcoholics, derelicts and drug addicts—if it ever was" and that medical health officials were beginning to coalesce around the idea that it was sexually transmitted, as the virus is present in saliva, semen, urine, fecal matter, and vaginal secretions, as well as blood. "The promiscuity factor in the gay community heightens the problems of sexual transmission among the gay male population," Shilts wrote (promiscuity was a controversial theme among his gay readers that he would never abandon), adding that "the more people with whom one sleeps, the greater the chances of picking up any number of diseases."[34] His were some of the very first words written in opposition to the free-for-all sexual expression that personified the earliest days of the gay liberation movement, which had focused at times, it seems, almost exclusively on sexual freedom, with little or no time spent on issues of economic, political, cultural, and social advancement for the LGBT community. Joe Brewer, a gay psychologist, explained the sexual aspect of gay liberation in an interview with Shilts: "Stripped of humanity, sex sought ever rising levels of physical stimulation in increasingly esoteric practices." Fellow psychologist Gary Walsh viewed gay sexual promiscuity in a more positive vein, noting that it represented "a means to exorcise guilt . . . ingrained in all gay men by a heterosexual society."[35] Nancy Walker, an early community volunteer for Boston's *Gay Community News* (one of the earliest national gay newspapers and published between 1973 and 1992) offered a sentiment that eventually took hold: "Some of them wanted to be able to fuck in the parks. Well, that's wonderful, but if they did, I wouldn't take my children down there. How far is sexual freedom supposed to go? Are you allowed to have intercourse on the street corner because you feel like doing it? How does that make you different from a dog? . . . We have to have a little bit of self-control, a little discipline. I'm sorry, but I'm not interested in sexual freedom. I'm interested in being able to live."[36]

Irrespective of the argument about the limits of sexual freedom as part of a gay liberation movement, little notice of gay sex or gay health by media outside the gay community existed. The *Village Voice's* Arthur Bell noted that most mainstream media simply refused to acknowledge sexuality at all among gay people unless it was in the context of criminality or limiting public sex.[37] "Because of the diverse levels of severity with which this disease strikes, hepatitis itself is a public health worker's nightmare," Shilts wrote. He warned that those who had "light" cases of hep "are most likely to become chronic carriers of the disease since their body's immunological systems do not mount a major attack on the viruses." Noting the reluctance of some public health officials to cooperate with gay social workers, Shilts's text extended ideas about gay men changing their sexual practices, noting that oral-anal contact was a primary mode of transmission: "Nothing short of chastity will offer sure-fire prophylactic protection—which is a major part of the problem." Shilts acknowledged that it's difficult to tell people not to have sex, and "until science comes through with vaccines or cures, the only things gay people can do are either to be chaste or to be vulnerable to this ambiguous disease," Shilts concluded.[38]

Ignorance of gay sex also persisted, as Shilts learned via his reporting about two early VD cases in New York City after both men contracted infections at a bathhouse. Rather than exploring their sexual activity, public health officials ordered the bathhouse pool drained and a review of food-handling procedures for bathhouse employees. Shilts reported, "Many gay health workers, however, are mystified about what can be done to thwart this growing problem. . . . Little can be done to prevent the disease short of total abstinence from anal sex." Shilts was aware that his article was appearing in a gay publication and that he would be allowed more graphic treatment of the subject. He quoted one unnamed doctor as saying, "The more meticulous the personal hygiene, the less chance of getting

[STDs] there is. But that's not very good, because if you're going to stick your tongue in somebody's anus, no amount of hygiene will help."[39]

Shilts's willingness to take on such issues (including the task of having to convince his editors to engage such topics) revealed his growing sense of the role he believed a journalist could play in leading society in positive directions. From these early days of his journalism career, Shilts knowingly (or unwittingly) embraced the societal leadership role as a journalist.

On the first-year anniversary of his full-time status at the *Advocate*, Shilts formally lobbied his boss, editor Robert McQueen, for a pay increase. In a December 14, 1977, letter, Shilts said he was hoping to "contribute a little statistical data" to assist McQueen in determining that a raise was in order. He noted that his stories had been front-page features thirteen times during his entire tenure with the *Advocate* but that "this is just the tip of the ice berg of my work since so much of my time has been devoted to such unglamorous, but important, staff writing.... All this might sound like idle and somewhat irrelevant boasting, and indeed, I must confess that I am proud of this prolific output, unmatched by any *Advocate* employee save, perhaps, the senior editor." Pushing his point amid a recognition by his bosses that he had an enormous ego, Shilts proclaimed that his rising "national reputation" for reporting surely was worth an addition to the "grossly inadequate" weekly net pay he was receiving, sans any health care benefits. Shilts ended his pitch with a couple of minor usage errors (reflecting that it may have been written after a few libations): "If I were a rambunctious type, I would say that such a paycheck is almost an insult—almost more trouble than its [*sic*] worth. Thankfully, however, I'm much to [*sic*] charming to be so rambunctious and, knowing that your charm exceeds mine many times fold, I'm sure we can see our way toward an appropriate increase this week."[40] It's unclear if Shilts ever got his raise, but the chutzpah he demonstrated in advocating for it reveals that his ambitious nature permeated nearly every aspect of his life.

Shilts's ambition extended to his personal life as well, as earlier in 1977, while on assignment in Tulsa, Oklahoma, he met one of his true loves, Daniel Yoder. "I saw his smile across the crowded Queen of Hearts disco and I knew I had to have him," Shilts wrote. "We were in bed that night and I told him we were meant to be together.... [A] nice weekend in snowy Tulsa with him."[41] Yoder later moved to San Francisco to live with Shilts in a long-term relationship that eventually dissolved into just a friendship. "Dan was this small-town Midwestern boy who moved to San Francisco to explore what it meant to be gay," Linda Alband recalls. "Dan was not very adventurous sexually, and so I think both he and Randy were a little bit frustrated with each other and ended up being friends and roommates and just sort of going their own ways romantically."[42] By the end of 1977, however, Shilts seemed pessimistic about the future for him and Yoder, noting candidly that the opportunity for a permanent love had "slipped through my fingers again. Our shitty sex life made it pretty obvious we wouldn't be married forever, but we got along very well."[43] In June 1978 the couple formalized their "divorce" but remained living together in a Liberty Street apartment in San Francisco for more than a year afterward. In Shilts's personal diary, he often expressed love for Yoder and referred to him lovingly in one passage: "Daniel is sitting here in the living room. Today is the first anniversary of our 'divorce.' I still love him so, but clearly I like our relationship as it is. But then, I could not imagine living without him."[44]

Yoder, who suffered from congenital hearing loss, often worried Shilts. "I don't think he is aware of how bad his hearing is," Shilts wrote. "He must have learned everything he knows from books since he had a hard time hearing teachers. He's so smart—that much explained why he never did better in school. He simply misses so much, so often asks about something I spent time explaining to him days before."[45] Yoder was devoted to Shilts even amid the eventually sexually open nature of their relationship. Ultimately, Shilts and Yoder remained close for many years, sharing a strong bond and friendship, despite the sexual distance between them. When Yoder died at the age of forty-three on August 22, 1995, his cremated remains were buried on a plot Shilts purchased in Redwood Memorial Gardens in Guerneville, California. Yoder's small headstone read, "No one could have a better friend."[46]

At work, the editors of the *Advocate* asked Shilts to write profiles of prominent openly gay figures. Some of those stories set a pattern for future stories written by Shilts. His thoughtful profile of openly gay journalist and author Arthur Bell for a story published in March 1977 noted that Bell had a problem: "He's a reporter who likes to report. So when backroom bars became the rage of the New York gay scene, he descended into their libidinous depths and told his readers what the backrooms are all about. All this creates a problem because Bell is openly gay ... [causing] gay politicos to turn red and become very unreasonable when they talk about Bell because of the problem of writing about gay life—warts and all. And a lot of gay people simply would rather not have those warts talked about." Shilts reported that Bell's weekly column in the *Village Voice* inspired regular letters to the editor: "Straight people think he is too pro-gay; gay people think he isn't pro-gay enough."[47]

Shilts would later refer back to his story about Bell and what it taught him about avoiding becoming an advocate via his journalism, as Bell had attempted to do. Shilts professed that it never had been much of a problem: "I don't think anybody is really objective, and I can't claim to be objective, but I think you can be fair and tell both sides of the story, no matter who you are or what you are writing about." Divulging the inherent lack of objectivity, Shilts said, "I feel strongly that gay people should be accepted, but I always felt it would be wrong to manipulate information or slant your stories in order to manipulate people. If you just stick to the facts, you are doing the right thing. I never wanted to march. You give up some prerogatives about being an activist when you become a journalist, because it is like public officials—you don't want to create the appearance of impropriety."[48]

Shilts seemed to be clinging to a naive notion of truth and facts to support his ideas of objectivity. It appeared, at times, that Shilts struggled to hold on to ideas about journalistic objectivity and integrity that he formed early in his career as a young Oregon college student. His belief in the authority and power of journalism had proven a powerful force for change in his life, and it altogether fit with his growing role as societal or cultural leader helping to interpret the world to others via his words.

During this period, Shilts's editors at the *Advocate* granted him a plum assignment in the spring of 1978 to report on the fast-growing "Save Our Children" campaign, the first organized effort to repeal gay rights ordinances, started in Miami / Dade County, Florida, in 1977. Born as a reaction to the emerging gay rights movement, "Save Our Children" sought to turn back early victories gays had won in Miami and elsewhere that prohibited discrimination against them in areas of employment, housing, and public accommodation. Evangelical Christians and conservative Republicans proved a powerful combination, enlisting the smiling facade of former beauty queen–cum–gospel and pop singer Anita Bryant as their spokesperson. Bryant's highly politicized 1977 memoir, *The Anita Bryant Story: The Survival of Our Nation's Families and the Threat of Militant Homosexuality,* had won many converts. Bryant and her eventual collaborators, including the Reverend Jerry Falwell, collected significantly more than the ten thousand signatures needed to revoke Miami's antidiscrimination law (known as Dade County Ordinance 77.4) and in doing so invoked the familiar tropes that nondiscrimination laws protecting the rights of homosexuals were tantamount to granting "special privileges" or extraordinary rights to homosexuals. For added measure, they hammered hard on the idea that gays were a threat to the health and safety of children, positing that since homosexuals could not reproduce, they had to recruit among children via outright sexual molestation or conditioning of acceptance of their lifestyle.[49] Bryant's take—that homosexuals were a "militant threat" to the heterosexual norm—was a masterstroke toward winning support from nonfundamentalist Christians and others. By casting heterosexuals (and their children) as potential "victims" of a growing gay liberation movement, support to repeal Dade County's antidiscrimination law increased significantly.[50]

Shilts traveled to Eugene, Oregon; Miami, Florida; Wichita, Kansas; and St. Paul, Minnesota; to report about efforts in each of those cities to repeal previously enacted gay rights ordinances. Describing himself as "in the center of all the fear and loathing the Bible could muster," Shilts found humor in antigay rhetoric that spanned verses from the biblical book of Leviticus to quotes from the *National Enquirer*. People in towns like Wichita, Shilts wrote, understand that the Bible and the *National Enquirer* are the best-selling book and newspaper, respectively, in the nation. "People believe them," Shilts said. "And they weren't about to buy some big-city line about granting equal rights to the very corrupted souls that had Sodom and Gomorrah buried under a holocaust of fire and brimstone." Shilts wanted his readers to understand that Far Right and anti gay conservatives were serious people, a lot like the people he had known in his youth: "The born-again Christian movement represents one of the most significant cultural trends of the decade. . . . They may be funny to look at—they wear tacky polyester suits and make tacky polyester comments—but there are about 50 million of them. . . . These religious fundamentalists believe the world rapidly is going to hell in a handbasket . . . and the advance of gay rights merely represents the final straw." He added that despite the fact that Wichita, Kansas, seemed as unlikely a place to pass a gay ordinance as any, the effort had "activated heretofore latent political energy" of serious proportions.[51]

The repeal efforts eventually succeeded almost everywhere, pushed forward with the help of Bryant and other national figures. Farther north in the Minnesota capital city of St. Paul, the proponents of repealing the city's little-noticed four-year-old gay rights ordinance were terribly underestimated. Gays in St. Paul and adjacent Minneapolis were used to a much more open lifestyle in the more progressive northern city, but the result was the same. The ordinance faced repeal by a wide margin in April 1978 voting, with equally strong votes to repeal gay rights ordinances a month later in both Wichita and Eugene. The only city where the repeal effort failed was Seattle, Washington. Gay leaders who had enlisted the help of political progressives and civil rights leaders to make gains on the local level soon began to understand the power and strength of the antigay movement embodied in the "Save Our Children" movement.[52]

Not all of Shilts's political reporting in this era was so serious. Shilts had made national headlines with exclusive political coverage for a freelance report he sold to the *Washington Post* on the prison wedding of Willie Carter Spann, the bisexual nephew of President Jimmy Carter. New York's *Christopher Street* magazine liked the article so much that it contracted Shilts for a longer piece, a profile of Spann's behind-bars life (he was serving time in California on burglary and drug charges). The story, titled "The President's Nephew," featured Spann proclaiming to Shilts, "I'm not that unusual. You've seen me before. I'm any hustler you've seen standing on a corner. I'm any junky you've seen on the street. I'm anybody you've sat next to in a gay bar. I'm any prisoner you've ever known."[53] The colorful documentary quote he had drawn from his source reflected the growing talent Shilts was displaying for aptly and interestingly capturing both the personality and the style of his story subjects.

# Finding a Voice

Shilts was such a prolific writer that it is not altogether surprising to find that his writing style continued to grow in confidence and that his ability to provide meaningful analysis of the issues he covered improved. Evidence of this is found in a letter Shilts wrote to the editor of the *New York Native* that demonstrates that he had moved beyond general reporting and had become a growing authority on the topics he covered. Writing about San Francisco mayor Dianne Feinstein's attempt to win a second full term as mayor (having become mayor upon the assassination of George Moscone in 1978 and elected to her first term in 1979), Shilts focused on Feinstein's often-inconsistent relationship with the city's gay community. He gauged that while Feinstein had won praise from gay leaders for appointing many of their number to city boards, commissions, and other key positions in her administration, true allegiance from gays eluded her. Feinstein's relationship with gay voters was damaged as early as December 1982, when she vetoed a bill passed by the Board of Supervisors that would have legalized gay marriage in the city. In her veto message, she said the draft of the bill was not specific about how gay marriage would go forward amid no state or federal laws permitting such unions. As Shilts wrote, "The real issue, everyone knew, was whether homosexual relationships would be granted the same legitimacy as heterosexual relationships. . . . [The bill's] intent was to frame into law a gay tenet of the gay liberation movement—that homosexuality is a lifestyle as equal to and on par with heterosexuality"—something Mayor Feinstein wasn't ready to acknowledge. He wrote that "for all the acceptance gays had gained, homosexuality was still not accepted as equal in the city they called Mecca. A prevailing morality that viewed homosexuals as promiscuous hedonists incapable of deep, sustaining relationships ensured that it would be impossible to legitimize whatever relationships they could forge."[1] Shilts enjoyed retelling the story of how Feinstein allegedly had shown disgust and fear when asking one gay leader in a private conversation what a "glory hole" was and a waffling level of support for gays when she told the decidedly placid *Ladies' Home Journal* magazine that "the right of an individual to live as he or she chooses can become offensive. The gay community is going to have to face this." As Shilts wrote, "Feinstein's major liability, in short, is that she's widely perceived as a prude. This problem never dogged [her predecessor] the lusty Mayor George Moscone." Remaining doubts among gay leaders who continued to question her commitment to their cause hurt Feinstein's feelings: "Around the country, Feinstein is viewed as the mayor who coddles gays; in San Francisco, they gather beneath her balcony to swear revenge." Shilts concluded, "Without any doubt, Mayor Feinstein's 14-year record on gay issues surpasses that of just about any other major politician in the United States. But in a city where gay rights is a fait accompli, she inflames passions in part because she has so clearly understood the notion of gay civil rights, yet has stubbornly resisted the broader concept of gay liberation."[2]

Shilts's growing confidence was showing back in the newsroom at the *Advocate* as well. Initially he and most others had gone along with David B. Goodstein's heavy-handed approach to the news that would appear on the pages of his publication. As gay historians have noted, Goodstein aspired to be a national leader of the gay political movement, but he remained a contentious figure who won as many enemies as friends. Shilts revealed to his friends and some gay leaders that Goodstein had no patience with those who disagreed with him and understood the power that came with owning the nation's largest and only national gay newsmagazine. As part of wielding that power, Goodstein declared that the *Advocate* would not print the names of people whom he regarded as "enemies of the movement."

Goodstein appeared quite open about his "love-hate" views on the gay community, summarily telling one interviewer that the "gay ghetto" of San Francisco could be encapsulated into easy-to-identify categories: gay men over the age of thirty who had lived in the city at least a decade, were employed professionally, generally were closeted, and were concerned for the arts; "Castro clones," who were openly gay as an act of rebellion against their small-town roots and hung out "like teenagers, drinking too much, taking too many drugs, fucking day and night, and infecting each other with diseases"; and finally, "political radicals," who, like Jewish ghetto dwellers in the East, patronized Castro businesses and rarely ventured outside the city for any reason. As *Washington Post* journalist and author John-Manuel Andriote noted, "Even if Goodstein's observations were accurate, they smacked of economic elitism. And criticism of the rampant promiscuity in the gay ghetto was ironic coming from the publisher of a newspaper supported largely by advertising paid for by bathhouses and other sexual services."[3]

Shilts felt directly the heavy hand of Goodstein over his work, and sources and other gay activists treated him with the same disdain that seemed to grow for Goodstein with each passing year. Shilts quoted Goodstein as declaring, "I can't stand Harvey Milk" in a newsroom tantrum at the *Advocate* as "his face blushed, his arms waving about his roly-poly figure" and his loud voice "resounding through the partitions of the nation's largest gay paper." Shilts said that Goodstein's "penchant for mixing journalism with his idiosyncratic theories of gay activism had earned him the nickname, 'Citizen Goodstein.'" Goodstein detested the rise of Harvey Milk, a man he considered a know-nothing camera shop owner and part of the militant gay activists, whom Goodstein termed the "offbeat liberation fairies" who trolled the Castro.[4]

One of the gay men who regularly "trolled" the Castro was a young gay activist named Cleve Jones, an early precinct volunteer who worked for Milk's political campaigns and who later conceived of the NAMES Project AIDS Memorial Quilt. Jones, fresh from his former life back in Arizona, recalled meeting Shilts in 1976 on a street corner of the Castro, "which is where I held court," Jones said. "I mean, I was an activist from the minute I got here and spent most of my time, my office was the sidewalk on Castro Street. I'm sure that is where I met him." Only three years younger than Shilts and a fellow gay refugee to San Francisco, Jones recalled that the two hit it off famously from the start and enjoyed many long conversations about the gay liberation movement beginning during the period when Shilts worked for the *Advocate*. "We became fast friends and collaborators to some extent, on a few things we were both trying to make happen," Jones reveals, indicating that Shilts held on to some of his advocacy ideas about gay rights even as he moved deeper into his journalism career.[5] Jones remembers frequent trips to the bars on weekends with Shilts, though hanging out at gay bars didn't hold as much draw for Shilts as did staying home and getting high. Shilts confided to a cousin in a letter in 1976 that "despite the proliferation of gay bars, I've developed a tremendous hate for gay bars. Consequently, I don't go." He noted, "I feel like retreating from it all" and complained that "gay bars put one in a tremendously cheap position, having to stand around like a tramp waiting for someone to pick you up."[6]

As a gay reporter covering a gay beat, Jones believed "Randy was in a very difficult position, and as I think about it, it is so rare now to see a headline that says 'first gay person' to do anything. But back then, those who were out in front and visible took a huge amount of flak from everyone, and it was hard."[7] Jones said that among those who could be critical of Shilts's work (but always behind his back) was Harvey Milk. Until Shilts began researching Milk's biography, he was unaware that Milk was not that fond of him. In his personal papers, Shilts saved a thank-you card from Milk with a handwritten note that said, "Randy, thanks for your warm note when it was needed. Harvey."[8] Jones explained, however, that Milk could grow angry about some of the things Shilts wrote about: "You know, Randy was bending over backwards. He was the first out gay guy working in mainstream media, so he had to constantly, I think in his mind, prove his independence and impartiality. And so one never knew what Randy's story was going to be like, if one were going to be looking at it from the perspective of its potential impact on the [gay rights] movement and the cause." Jones also believed that Shilts's initial "social awkwardness" may have made the more gregarious and confident Milk uncomfortable at times. "But I liked him. Randy was a good friend of mine," Jones said. "We got along very well I think partly because we were both very young, very visible, but also because we had that connection, and our lives were somewhat similar."[9]

Shilts's commitment to journalistic integrity could not only make gay sources such as Jones and Milk uncertain what to expect from him but also put him at odds with *Advocate* impresario Goodstein. Shilts recalled one ultimately unsuccessful but direct attempt by Goodstein to manipulate the strong-willed Shilts to his view of journalism. Goodstein ordered Shilts to write up a special exposé about activist Morris Kight, who was rumored to be a heavy drinker, and to do so with a six-pack of beer in hand for Kight to "loosen him up" for the interview. Shilts never fulfilled the assignment.[10] Shilts determined that the information Goodstein provided was not reliable, nor did it warrant a story—it smelled like a hatchet job. Although doing an initial interview (sans the beer), Shilts slow-walked, producing a story on Kight until Goodstein's attentions turned elsewhere. In his personal diaries, Shilts said he hated defending the *Advocate* to the gay community and its more leftist political leadership. "God I hate *The Advocate*," he wrote during a forty-two-day trek across the country mining for story ideas and contacts.[11] One of the *Advocate* sources Shilts was loath to engage was Tom Reeves, a Boston-area professor who helped create the controversial National Man-Boy Love Association and wrote for the Boston-based *Fag Rag* newspaper, which was published from 1971 until the early 1980s. Shilts found Reeves "bizarre" and in a voice that would reflect his growing impatience with the more fringe elements of the gay liberation movement declared that Reeves and "radicals are just disgusting."[12]

Surviving his direct defiance in not "doing a number" on Kight as Goodstein wanted, Shilts would not endure the final straw. Goodstein had begun to immerse himself and everyone around him in what he called "The *Advocate* Experience," based on the Erhard Seminars Training (EST) sessions championed by self-help guru Werner Erhard. Goodstein required his staff to attend a weekend-long session in order to engage in "self-actualization" and "self-realization" workshops designed to promote personal acceptance and awareness by gay people of themselves that they then could presumably transfer into changing society's level of acceptance of homosexuality. Ordered to attend a weekend of "The Advocate Experience" and to begin writing about it for the *Advocate*, Shilts attended briefly, was disruptive by quietly ridiculing the presentations from the back of the room, and promptly quit the *Advocate* (along with other notables such as Sasha Gregory-Lewis and Urvashi Vaid).[13] He took to the pages of rival publications to ridicule Goodstein and his "Advocate Experience" efforts. A few years removed from his *Advocate* tenure, Shilts said, "Goodstein had a narrow view of news. As long as I came up with blockbuster stories that translated into big headlines and splashy art . . . everything was okay. But when I pitched a story that might threaten ad revenue or that didn't lend itself to sensational treatment, his eyes glossed [*sic*] over. For me, journalism had to be more than that."[14]

Goodstein sold the *Advocate* shortly before he died in 1985 but not before its circulation surpassed fifty thousand nationwide, topping out at a circulation of about one hundred thousand in 2005.[15] In subsequent years, with Goodstein a distant memory, Shilts's byline returned to the publication as a guest writer. Goodstein's influence over Shilts's perception among gay leaders, however, remained intact for many years. Because Goodstein had closely aligned himself with the more conservative Alice B. Toklas Democratic Club (rival to the more progressive and sometimes even militant Harvey Milk Democratic Club, founded after Milk's assassination in 1978) in San Francisco politics, many assumed Shilts shared Goodstein's more slow-going approach to gay liberation. While the Toklas Democrats' adherence to machine and Democratic Party politics was more rigid than that of the upstart Milk Democrats, Shilts seemed to align (at least privately) with Milk, again placing him at odds with Goodstein.[16]

It's unclear whether Shilts understood that his tenure with the *Advocate* might be approaching the end when it did, but the freedom of his assignments there allowed him to pick up another journalism gig as an on-air reporter for KQED-TV in San Francisco. George Osterkamp, former news director for KQED and later a producer for the CBS primetime news program, *48 Hours*, recalls that an ambitious Shilts was determined to get a freelance job for *Newsroom*, KQED's hour-long nightly news program. The show ran on the Bay Area public television station from 1975 to 1980, funded by a grant from the Ford Foundation. Paying only seventy-five dollars a story, Shilts was successful in getting more than 95 percent of his stories on the air and always seemed to have a quiver of story ideas at hand, Osterkamp said. Hiring Shilts to cover primarily the expanding gay community in San Francisco was unusual and gained KQED headlines across the nation via an Associated Press story that called attention to the so-called novelty of hiring an openly gay reporter. The story generated dozens of stories nationwide and came from prompting by Shilts himself to convince KQED's tiny public relations staff to send out a news release. "I'd like to say that we were braver than we were, but with a freelance position, I was not obligating the station to a long-term situation," Osterkamp said.[17] For his part, the twenty-five-year-old Shilts told the *Bay Area Reporter* (a gay newspaper founded in San Francisco in 1971 that is still in publication) that his hiring was "not really a breakthrough" because

> a great many gay men and women already work in the media, in print and on the air. It's just that most of them are in the closet! Most media people don't talk about us unless it's in a "queer" joke. It's rather funny to go through this experience; they [the media] give the impression that they had to go outside of the existing group of already employed journalists to find someone to say that they are gay and "come out" for the media.... Gay politics, their social and economic activities should be covered with the same professionalism as the activities of the Board of Supervisors and the straight community.[18]

The Associated Press version of the "gay reporter is hired" story made special note that Shilts was comfortable going into gay bars and other gay establishments for his story on alcoholism in the gay community and quoted Shilts as saying that "being openly gay has slowed me down career-wise, but it hasn't stopped me." Shilts said, "What I do is basic beat reporting. My beat is the gay community. I may not get as far in journalism as I would like, but I'm much more relaxed personally," emphasizing that the news media frequently report news about homosexuals incorrectly. "The stories are usually distorted to emphasize the bizarre or radical," he said, emphasizing his belief in his ability to be objective in covering gay stories or any others.[19]

While the *Bay Area Reporter* provided an article and photo of Shilts announcing his new position at KQED, the paper's editors also took up the issue of "the place of the gay press" and noted, "To witness the major San Francisco newspapers pandering to the gay public, for their attention and their wallets, is to watch an amusing scramble. *The Chronicle, The Berkeley Barb, The Bay Guardian,* and even *The San Francisco Examiner*, are currently engaged in a courtship without an identifiable suitor. . . . The shift could well be ominous." The *Bay Area Reporter's* managing editor, Paul F. Lorch, noted that whether the newfound interest in gay topics by the mainstream press meant the death of the gay press was unknown, stating, "Whatever happens, we don't cotton to the notion of straight journalists 'straightening' out gay news to make it palatable to folks out in the avenues or the rednecks in Brisbane. . . . We have no argument with others speaking and writing about us, but not *for* us. Not until those feature writers, journalists and editors emerge as upfront, visible gay people" (which would seemingly portend well for Shilts's new role). Lorch acknowledged that much of the gay press remained an amateur endeavor subsidized by unseemly sources but added, "Nevertheless, in the jungle and jamble of print, a mass of information is being disseminated, hundreds of voices are telling their thing. Never before in gay history has there been such an experiment, exposure or exchange."[20]

Osterkamp told the AP that hiring a gay reporter "was such an obvious thing, we should have done it two years ago. We were the first in the area but I predict other stations will follow" (they didn't). He added, "We are dealing with a significant portion of the San Francisco Bay area that is too large to ignore. Randy is bright and functions as a journalist, not an advocate."[21]

Shilts experienced firsthand the challenging navigation all minority reporters face, as media scholar K. A. Nishikawa and colleagues noted: "Minority journalists do not completely conform to mainstream [journalistic] norms and attempt to walk a fine line between being a minority journalist and acting as a professional journalist." They acknowledged that some "journalists struggle with advocacy, some are surreptitious about advocacy, and a few are proud of their roles as advocates." Still others may engage a form of "stealth advocacy" via "subtle strategies" that may influence coverage based on their very presence in a newsroom and by pointing out or suggesting stories or story angles that may illuminate additional cultural differences or nuances.[22] The challenges suggested by Nishikawa and colleagues seemingly confronted Shilts from the start of his journalistic career and remained forever in his path.

Media scholar Edward Alwood devoted an entire text to examining the role of gay and lesbian reporters in so-called straight news settings at America's newspapers and TV stations. Alwood believes Shilts enjoyed an appropriate, perhaps even extraordinary, rise within journalistic ranks via his post-*Advocate* freelance jobs for both KQED-TV and later KTVU-TV.[23]

One of Shilts's first stories for KQED was a February 15, 1977, campaign profile of a then-little-known camera store owner, Harvey Milk, who was seeking election from District 5 to the San Francisco Board of Supervisors. Shilts followed that up with coverage of Milk's inauguration as a supervisor on January 9, 1978, and his walk from the Castro to San Francisco City Hall followed by a couple hundred supporters. Shilts was in tow asking questions. His personal recollection of the historic inauguration day for Milk was subdued and more focused on Shilts's own personal hurried schedule:

> What a day. Up at 7:30 to shower, shave and then rush to KQED newsroom to type the scripts of today's two stories. The scripts are minutes from being done when it's time to go to Castro Street to start filming the story about the city's first gay supervisor walking to be sworn in on San Francisco City Hall steps. Sure enough, there are 100 [people] there to walk with him—great TV news. I interview Harvey as we walk toward the San Francisco [City Hall] Rotunda— Harvey talked about a letter from Altoona, Pennsylvania. Harvey's always good for a quote. The symbolism of our interview is almost poetic—the nation's first gay San Francisco supervisor talking with the city's (and the nation's as far as the KQED PR department can figure) only openly gay TV reporter.[24]

Milk's reference to a letter (which Milk actually referred to in subsequent speeches as a phone call) from a gay youth from Altoona would become part of the legend of the man—he noted the youth's quiet, scared voice on the phone thanking him for running for office. "You've got to elect gay people," Milk would later say, "for that child [in Altoona] and for the thousands and thousands of gays like that child know that there is hope. There is hope for a better world, hope for a better tomorrow. . . . I know that you cannot live on hope alone, but without it, life is not worth living. And you, and you, and you—you gotta give 'em hope."[25]

The array of stories Shilts brought to the *Newsroom* agenda covered a broad cross section of issues at the forefront of the emerging gay rights struggle: employment rights for teachers, political activity and lobbying for gays, differences between more militant and conservative gay leaders, child custody cases, police brutality issues, and gay political issues throughout the Bay Area, including emerging gay issues in adjoining San Jose and Santa Clara Counties. A July

5, 1977, report was typical as Shilts zeroed in on physical assaults against gays in both the Castro and Mission Districts of San Francisco. Shilts ended his report with a stand-up on Castro Street, declaring, "Gay people are simply afraid to walk the streets at night. Beatings are an everyday occurrence in the Castro neighborhood."[26] Physical violence against San Francisco gays was at the center of some of Shilts's most important early reporting, especially stories he wrote for both the *Advocate* and KQED about the violent June 21, 1977, murder of thirty-three-year-old Robert Hillsborough, which prompted massive demonstrations by the gay community, demanding action from city officials. Hillsborough, a gay man, was stabbed to death by what witnesses reported was a group of Latino youth who attacked Hillsborough and his friend because they appeared to be gay. The arrest of four young men occurred, with nineteen-year-old John Cordova identified by the police as the ringleader. He reportedly shouted "Faggot! Faggot!" as the stabbing took place.[27] Cordova was "outed" as being a closeted gay man by Shilts and other reporters who covered his subsequent murder trial. In January 1978 Shilts received word that Cordova's attorney was telling others that Shilts's reporting about his client's alleged latent homosexuality represented an "abomination" for the convicted killer. Shilts may have been worried, because he wrote in a diary entry, "That info makes me gulp" and added, "Four years from now—when out of prison—will Cordova come to gun down the gay reporter who first revealed his long-denied homosexuality?" He followed worries about his own safety with an open discussion of whether it was appropriate to out people—a topic he would have to revisit often in his reporting career. Joking that if he didn't get a big new job, he would accept that "as advice from the cosmos that I shouldn't announce another's homosexuality. Yet, it's my duty to give the public the total scope of reality and not to hide things. Some people, notably Latinos, are so freaked out about being gay that they would kill to prove they are not gay to the world—and to themselves."[28]

Osterkamp recalled that Shilts's outspoken and active personality was well suited to the KQED newsroom: "He was such a charming man, essentially he could disarm most anybody, even thirty-five years ago when there weren't many openly gay people active in the media. . . . For the most part, Randy's charm overcame any sort of resistance there might have been." Shilts's tenacity was often on display, Osterkamp said, including his ability to work around roadblocks he encountered when preparing his stories. Sources within the San Francisco Police Department, for example, were not always cooperative with a gay reporter, but "I think when he ran into someone difficult, he would just go around them to someone else," Osterkamp said. Although he heard on occasion rumors that Shilts may have been struggling with a source for information, Shilts never came asking for help. "I think that would have been a sign of defeat for Randy to do so," Osterkamp said.[29]

Shilts's role at KQED did not come without a learning curve—the print-trained reporter knew nothing about shooting and editing film (in the final days of film before the station switched over to Beta videotapes), but he learned quickly, Osterkamp said. Highly defined roles between reporters and filmographers/videographers meant that his input had to be limited to suggested shots, not actual shooting or editing film or tape. "His basic challenge was to do an on-air presentation, and I would say that at KQED, in those days, we were quite ecumenical in what we would accept as airworthy," Osterkamp recalls about Shilts's first on-air efforts. "Randy was certainly not the worst, but I think he might have had trouble in a commercial TV station trying to satisfy the on-air requirements."[30] Osterkamp's take on Shilts's talent for TV seemed to align with his own personal view on the issue—Shilts wrote in his personal journal that he sensed that his future in TV news (specifically at KQED) was not bright. "Things have been going poorly," he wrote, noting that a promise of a full-time position failed to materialize and recording that Osterkamp often found fault with his reporting and on-camera performance. Writing about his boss, Osterkamp, Shilts said, "He started holding up my stories, losing his temper irrationally and then said I would have to either (a) take voice lessons and improve, or (b) leave KQED *Newsroom*, or (c) be a reporter-producer (a wholly unacceptable alternative). It came on me like a ton of bricks." Coping with the criticism and his own rising fears, Shilts drank more, smoked more pot, and eventually took to his bed to escape the realities around him. Efforts by friends to get him a regular opinion column for the *San Francisco Chronicle* failed. His freelance relationship with the *New West*, a weekly alternative newspaper, began to sag as well, an editor there telling him that they wanted a nongay writer to pull together a large story on the growing impact of the gay vote in San Francisco. "I'm getting badly screwed over again, Goddammit I'm getting screwed over on all sides right now and it's making me sick," Shilts wrote in his journal. "The questions I asked myself [before] about are not any more answered than they were then. Things could go better for me than before or just keep the mediocre same."[31]

Days rolled into weeks as Shilts couldn't bring himself to go back to KQED after a confrontational meeting with Osterkamp, noting, "Jesus, I haven't even been honest enough with myself about how my relationship with KQED is rapidly disintegrating. My whole façade and dreams, of being a TV reporter, are falling apart, going away. It was so humiliating to be given the ultimatum [by Osterkamp] that I just can't force myself to go back into that office to look that George Oster-kamp asshole in the eye."[32]

One of his friends and fellow journalists, David Israels, judged that Shilts became a more polished journalist after his time at KQED. "Television was not his métier," however, in Israels's observation. "I always thought that his television reports were not as clear as his writing became in print," Israels said. "When he was doing television he was younger and less experienced. It was a good place to learn, and I mean it was local television after all. There was that difference that I noted. He was always fast; he was an incredibly fast writer. He could handle complex stories quite well."[33]

Giving Shilts feedback on his stories was a mixed bag—on some days he was eager and willing to accept editing suggestions or other comments on his stories, and on other days he took personal offense at or was insulted by feedback. Regard-less, Shilts never lacked an authoritative posture in his stories, Osterkamp said, which quickly won him a continuing role as a panelist to discuss stories on the *Newsroom* set with anchor Belva Davis. The on-air analysis role afforded to Shilts via the *Newsroom* format affirmed Shilts's growing consideration as a "journalist as expert," a concept well suited to the consideration of Shilts's career. Although he had always demonstrated an authoritative, even expert tone in his reporting, moving to journalist as expert was an easy transition. In his first major reporting roles for the *Advocate* and later for KQED-TV, Shilts experienced unusual oppor-tunities for a reporter of his length of experience. The *Advocate*, always a publica-tion run on a shoestring when compared to any other publication that purported to be a national news magazine, needed writers like Shilts to offer commentary, analysis, and interpretation. The issues covered by the *Advocate*, after all, were rarely simple news stories but were often controversial by their very nature.

At KQED the format of the *Newsroom* show (later renamed *Evening Edition*) naturally cast its reporters and anchors, such as Shilts, in the role of expert. As his colleague Belva Davis explained, the format of the show allowed Shilts and other reporters to come on-set to either set up or backfill stories prepared for the telecast. Eventually, Shilts appeared as a panelist on the show, his presence being the centerpiece of one of the most unusual moments in the show's history, Davis believes. As Proposition 6 moved forward in California in 1978, Shilts occupied an on-set chair along with Davis and state senator John Briggs, the ambitious Republican behind the effort to ban openly gay and lesbian individuals from being classroom teachers in California's public schools. In the heated exchanges that followed, Davis recalled that Briggs said that gays were showing up almost everywhere, alluding to Shilts. While outing Shilts and subsequently trying to tip his role on the show from journalistic expert to gay representative, Briggs created more than a few moments of awkwardness. Davis, who still gets angry about the confrontational approach Briggs chose to take with Shilts live on the air, recalled that Shilts did not "bite" on the remark Briggs made, and the discussion moved forward, with Shilts holding on to his role as journalistic expert. Davis stated, "He [Shilts] was outed as a gay reporter on one of the live shows that we did with Senator Briggs. We had never brought up [on the show] the fact that he was gay or that he was there to just do gay stories."[34] Davis said the live exchange between Senator Briggs and Shilts was nerve-wracking, as Briggs began "scorning [Shilts's] questions by declaring he expected as much from 'a homosexual like you.' We fumbled our way through the rest of the newscast without addressing the subject again, but the minute we were off the air, Randy, who talked in rapid-fire spurts, uncorked a barrage against Briggs. Most of the rest of us didn't know quite what was appropriate to say."[35]

Osterkamp said he couldn't recall a time when Shilts was overtly political or opinionated in his stories or appearances on the live show, even amid the heat of the "Briggs Initiative" (officially known as Proposition 6). His October 9, 1978, report for KQED-TV was typical. While stating that Prop 6 "stands as the most controversial issue facing voters" in the November election, he stepped back to ask about the effort, "Is it an assertion of parents' rights, or the beginning of a homosexual witch hunt?" Shilts had a gift for setting up the two poles and narrowing the argument down to its simplest terms. Senator Briggs was a central figure in Shilts's reporting; he noted that for sixteen months Briggs had "maintained that the mere presence of openly gay teachers in schools may provide role models who can lead children into adopting a homosexual lifestyle."[36] Briggs rode the wave of growing political influence that fundamentalist Christians from California and across the country were creating in funding the campaign for the Briggs Initiative.

While giving Briggs ample room to explain how his new law would work, Shilts also raised important questions about the definition of the term "homosexual conduct." As written, Proposition 6 offered a broad interpretation of the term to include "advocating, soliciting, imposing, encouraging, or promoting" homosexuality, whether the person was gay or straight. Opponents of the effort had gained important support, including Governor Jerry Brown, former governor Ronald Reagan, and even President Jimmy Carter, but the fight was uphill from the start. The "No on 6" forces emphasized the unenforceable nature of Briggs's proposal, its potential shift of limited state and local resources away from other education and law enforcement priorities, and the perceived unconstitutionality of the proposal. "For nearly a decade, gays have organized politically to gain acceptance of homosexuality as a viable lifestyle," Shilts wrote, "one that is equal to heterosexuality. Nothing has underscored their success more than the fact that gay civil rights has emerged as an important national issue in the last year. But it is also true that in virtually every public vote, advocates of gay rights have been decisively beaten."[37]

California voters took a different path, as Proposition 6 was defeated on Election Day, November 7, 1978, by a surprisingly wide margin of 3,969,120 to 2,823,293 (or 58 to 42 percent) statewide.[38] Upon its defeat, Shilts reported on KQED about the Castro District celebration led by the city's newly elected, openly gay supervisor, Harvey Milk. The city streets filled with an estimated eight thousand dancing and excited gays who kept the party going for hours. Noting that a victory against the antigay forces led by Briggs seemed unimaginable just six months ago, Shilts reported that the defeat of Prop 6 created "a night of turn around, a night of celebration for a cause that has taken so many beatings. It was the first election gays had won." Shilts, photographed at the "No on 6" campaign headquarters standing next to a beaming Milk, reported that Milk "struck a conciliatory note" but couldn't resist adding that the victory may have been as much a repudiation of Senator Briggs as anything else.[39] Briggs, it was widely believed, had come out a loser following a series of debates across the state with Milk during which the glib gay pol had clearly bested his opponent on style, if not substance.

Milk was drunk with happiness at the outcome, telling the *Chronicle*'s Jerry Carroll that the vote was a call to all closeted homosexuals to come out "so everyone knows who the gay people are. We owe it to the straights." The results firmly in hand, politicos of all stripes jumped in, supporting, even in limited ways, the victory Milk had won. Mayor George Moscone, who had publicly opposed the gay teachers ban, declared, "This is not a victory over a lightweight like John Briggs. It is a victory over the despair that has fallen on gay people. It's a victory of intellect over emotion."[40]

"For all the celebration," Shilts cautioned, "most seemed aware that last night was more [a] pause than an end to the controversy over gay rights. The election battles over, the last few months are likely just an opening phase in the drama of our society's coming to grips with this new and unfamiliar issue of homosexuality."[41] In retrospect, Shilts's words seem prophetic—at least the aspect of the coming drama in the movement.

Reporting assignments at KQED had placed Shilts alongside Milk, Moscone, and a variety of other progressives, but they also meant he had to interact with conservative Republican leaders who were reticent to embrace the city's gay population. Perhaps no other source collaboration cultivated by Shilts mystified—and angered—gay activists more than his gentlemanly interactions with Briggs, an arch conservative Republican from Orange County who had visions of one day being governor of California. After serving a decade in California's lower house, Briggs won election to the state senate in 1976 and promptly set about making a statewide name for himself. Briggs traveled to Miami, Florida, in 1977 to closely follow and engage the "Save Our Children" campaign of Anita Bryant and others to overturn that city's antidiscrimination policy concerning gays. It was there that Shilts met Briggs during forays into south Florida to cover the Bryant campaign as it gained national attention. The two men hit it off, enjoying lively conversations about the "Save Our Children" campaign and political issues in general. In the infancy of their friendship, it was clear Briggs had not caught on that Shilts was gay, learning that only later, and as a result Briggs had come to like and perhaps even respect Shilts.

Back in California, Briggs had ideas of his own regarding how to address the still-cradled gay rights movement: he settled on a ban on openly homosexual men and women from teaching in the state's public schools. Briggs originally timed the creation of what became known as Proposition 6 to coincide with the June 1978 Republican primary, believing it would help drive up support for Briggs and his fellow Republicans, but he failed to get enough signatures to qualify until the November 1978 election.[42]

Shilts quickly gained Briggs's trust as a reporter interested in writing about his efforts, and in private moments between Shilts and Briggs, Shilts came to believe that Briggs was not particularly put off by gay people but understood them and their issues to be good political fodder for his ambitions to be governor of California. The senator's commitment to the antigay initiative was a mile wide and an inch thick: "Briggs never tried to hide that the initiative was, at least in part, a means to a different end: higher office. In the course of the campaign there was no better witness to the depth of Briggs's commitment to the anti-gay cause, or lack thereof, than Randy Shilts," Dudley Clendinen and Adam Nagourney concluded.[43] The trust Shilts inspired in Briggs and gay leaders on education-related issues reflected Shilts's depth of understanding of the issues involved. He had written about the termination of gay teachers before, including a 1971 article detailing the firing of Peggy Burton, a lesbian high school biology teacher in Salem, Oregon. Burton subsequently engaged in a multiyear battle to regain her job that went to the US Supreme Court in November 1975, with the high court declining to review an appeals court ruling that upheld her termination.

One of the projects Shilts undertook was a further review of the statewide battle over Proposition 6 and his conviction that Briggs simply didn't believe his own antigay rhetoric. Perhaps calling upon the familiarity of his decidedly Republican roots in his native Aurora, Illinois, the ambitious young reporter befriended the ambitious politician so much that he shared with *San Francisco Chronicle* columnist Herb Caen an amazing exchange between the two men. Following a speech to what was supposed to be a friendly audience in San Jose, California, Briggs whispered to Shilts, "You know, there were homosexuals in there." Shilts naturally asked the senator how he knew such a thing, and Briggs offered, "You can tell by looking at them." Caen promptly reported on the fact that Briggs needed to look more closely at those covering his campaign in order to know who *all* the gays were, and Shilts's open secret finally reached Briggs. Later, when other reporters asked Senator Briggs if he personally knew any homosexuals, the only examples he could cite were Shilts and Harvey Milk. Of Briggs, Shilts said, "I simply knew a different John Briggs—a privately charming fellow who changes dramatically in public debates. . . . Increasingly, I suspected that John Briggs does not really believe what he says about gays. His easy acceptance of a gay reporter was no less surprising than my acceptance of him. Just as Briggs never seemed at all personally threatened by working closely with me, I never felt personally threatened by his rhetoric. Instinctively, for reasons I would not understand until later in the campaign, I never took his protestation against homosexuality seriously."[44] An almost apologetic Shilts wrote that Briggs had acted "coldly oblivious to the tragic side-effects his campaign wrought on California gays," but he added that he believed Briggs had "acted more out of ignorance than viciousness."[45] The "chumminess" Shilts had developed with Briggs while reporting on him for KQED-TV didn't prevent Shilts from trying to sell his story in print (titled "The Private vs. the Public Senator John V. Briggs"), a story that questioned Briggs's true commitment to banning gays in the classroom. Shilts reported, "Moreover, this odd-couple friendship has given me a chance to see the private John Briggs, a man who cuts a strikingly different profile from the public crusader."[46]

Shilts held on to a photograph of himself and Senator Briggs talking to one another outside Briggs's legislative office. The undated photo carries an autograph from Briggs that says, "Randy, Sorry, I would love to, but . . ." (referring to the fact that the two men stood just inches away from one another in the photograph). The friendship between the two men embodied a philosophy Shilts wrote that Briggs espoused: "If you give me the finger, I'll give you the finger. If you're fair to me, I'll be fair to you." In his assessment, Shilts said that public discourse prompted by the Proposition 6 effort had actually brought out the worst aspects of the senator's personality and cast him as an easily hated caricature for gay activists. Shilts got as close as anyone to a public figure—close enough, still, to determine that the private Briggs could be a "disarmingly charming fellow" with "a likeable personality."[47]

The respect and even affection between the two men was reciprocal. One of Shilts's former classmates from the University of Oregon, Bill Bucy, wrote Shilts a letter in 1978 after having participated in an editorial board meeting with Senator Briggs as part of his work at the *Sacramento Bee*. Bucy shared with Shilts, "I write to tell you what an admirer you have in John Briggs. During an interview yesterday, Briggs, off the record of course, spent at least five minutes praising your work and your objectivity in covering Proposition 6. In fact, he called you 'the straightest reporter of any sexual persuasion' he has met." Bucy told Shilts that, given Briggs's apparently negative views on both reporters and homosexuals, the comments from the senator were "high praise indeed" and are "an indication of your professionalism reaching a new level."[48]

Clendinen and Nagourney believe Shilts's friendliness with Briggs "gave birth to a permanent mistrust of Randy Shilts among many gay activists." That distrust showed up quickly via a hand-drawn cartoon pasted up on mailboxes, utility poles, and poster boards throughout the Castro District in late 1978 under the headline "The Human Side of Hitler." The cartoons featured an Adolf Hitler version of Briggs talking with Shilts (identified as "Shits") and the "Shits" character saying, "Oh yes, I got along famously. . . . He's actually quite charming when he's off stage. When he's on-stage, we smile pleasantly at each other whenever he calls for the annihilation of gays and Jews." Another blow came in the last panel of the cartoon, with the "Shits" character declaring, "Look at it this way, I'm an up-and-coming aggressive journalist who happens to be gay. If I don't suck up to the straight bigots in the straight media, what kind of career am I going to have?"[49] Shilts understood the criticism he faced from not only placing himself inside the Briggs story but also humanizing a character whom opponents of Proposition 6 sought to demonize. "Some gays came to consider my close, well-publicized relationship with the senator to be nothing short of traitorous," Shilts wrote, but without acknowledging that some of that publicity had been of the self-generated variety.[50]

If Shilts's public association with Senator Briggs had cost him credibility in some quarters, Briggs would repeat the experience. In 2011 a long-since retired

John Briggs and his wife, Carmen, had settled into a retirement community near Henderson, Nevada. As Briggs attempted to obtain a nonpartisan position on the community's neighborhood association board of directors, his past came back. An opponent of Briggs for a board seat reminded his fellow Nevada retirees that Briggs had led a strong "antihomosexual campaign" in California in 1978. Briggs acknowledged, "With the passage of over 30 years, America has changed, including me," he said. "I am astounded and saddened by an obvious smear by reciting events of the 1970–80's era, so as to leave the reader with the false impression that I am an 'intolerant person' who should be shunned today." Claiming that he was a friend of the late Harvey Milk, Briggs noted that they did not socialize together, but after their "vigorous debates" on Proposition 6 they had "laughed, talked and became friends" and that Briggs "mourned with others when his all too short life was ended by a madman." Briggs did claim a personal friendship with Randy Shilts and proclaimed, "My friend, Randy Shilts . . . almost single-handedly changed America's attitude, along with mine, toward gays and AIDS," and he told the story of how he came to autograph a photo of the two of them "walking suspiciously close" to one another.[51]

While Shilts's professional relationship with the conservative Briggs seemed to flourish, another prominent and liberal political figure reported a challenging and irritating series of interactions with the aggressive Shilts. In 1982 novelist Gore Vidal launched an ultimately unsuccessful campaign for the Democratic nomination for US Senate in California against California governor Jerry Brown (a seat eventually won by Republican Pete Wilson). As his campaign got underway, Vidal recalled meeting Shilts, then the only openly gay reporter in the state, who was writing a story on the Senate campaign for the *San Francisco Chronicle*. Vidal said Shilts repeatedly confronted him over the fact that he was not running as an openly gay candidate, although Vidal's sexual orientation was no secret. Vidal did not view his sexual orientation as a topic that was anyone's business—even voters'. Each time Vidal resisted Shilts's suggestion that he make a public statement about his sexuality Vidal said "he took it a little more badly, and then he took it upon himself to punish me with some unnecessarily, pointedly nasty reportage. I made it my own brief to make sure that Randy understood that his behavior and critique were neither fair, nor professional. Several noisy confrontations occurred between Randy and me to little effect, and his *Chronicle* stories continued to damage the campaign and help, I felt, secure the nomination for Jerry Brown."[52]

In the aftermath of the rare gay victory and the turning back of Proposition 6 in November 1978 came an unexpected move. Two days after the vote, one of the most outspoken foes to the growing influence of homosexual voters in San Francisco and statewide, clean-cut thirty-two-year-old supervisor Dan White, announced he was resigning from the San Francisco Board of Supervisors less than a year into his first term. White told reporters that he could no longer support his family on the $9,600 annual salary for a supervisor, especially since he had to resign as a city firefighter before taking his seat on the board. Adding pressure to White's life was a fast-food venue at the Pier 39 tourist attraction that demanded a major time commitment from White and his wife, Mary Ann. "What is happening is that neither my family is being taken care of as they should be, nor are my constituents," White said. "The people of San Francisco need full-time legislators, and the supervisors should have a full-time salary." *Chronicle* reporter Marshall Kilduff reported what many suspected was the real reason behind White's departure: "disappointment when his colleagues on the board voted against him or did not appear to work as hard."[53] Behind the scenes, White had begun to boil after losing a fight to keep a juvenile delinquent services center out of his district (with a vote by Milk tipping the issue out of White's favor) and experiencing a growing sense of isolation and betrayal. During their first few months on the board, ironically, Milk had sought out a friendly relationship with White. They frequently met over coffee, and Milk was the only board member White invited to his son's christening at a local Catholic church.

Mayor Moscone, however, was the one who held the power to appoint White's replacement. He said he had consulted with White about a replacement to fill out the three years remaining in his term, but White said he had made no specific recommendations for a replacement. That would change, however, after many of the city's conservative leaders, including police and firefighter union officials, cornered White and talked him into going back to Moscone just a week later to seek reappointment to the seat he had just forfeited.

While conservative forces backing White desperately wanted him to remain on the Board of Supervisors, White said his change of heart was motivated by the sincere level of support he had received from constituents. White denied that his turnabout created cool political relations with Moscone and other liberals (including Milk). Moscone, described as "cheery and friendly" when asked about White's reversal, told reporters he supported White's return to the board. "As far as I am concerned, Dan White is the supervisor from District 8," Moscone said. "A man has a right to change his mind."[54] However, it was also conceivable that Moscone changed his mind after as he found a more liberal replacement for White who would solidify and satisfy the city's prevailing political winds from the Left.

Moscone was a handsome, jovial, tall man who had embraced the city's gay community. In a 1977 interview with Shilts for KQED, he discussed the merits of soliciting gay voters in the city: "Gay support is a campaign asset in any campaign. People look for it and people try to exhibit a platform of fairness so they can attract a level of support from the gay community. It is my hope that we would get at least the lion's share, or a fair share [of gay support]."[55] Moscone repeated his support for the city's gays and expressed disgust at the repeal of a gay rights ordinance by voters in Miami, Florida: "If this city were to do what Dade County purports to do, which is to discriminate against people because they are gay, then I don't think it would be an issue here. I think demonstrations [here in San Francisco] would be both anticipated, and in my view, appropriate."[56]

Moscone's support of progressive forces in the city apparently ran deep, as supervisor Carol Ruth Stiver and the mayor's friend, California state assemblyman Willie Brown (eventually elected mayor in his own right in 1996), joined Milk in urging the mayor to skip over White for the vacant board seat.

Amid the political maneuvering at City Hall, on November 18, 1978, came the shocking news from Guyana that more than nine hundred members of the San Francisco–based Peoples Temple commune had participated in a mass suicide. News also came of the accompanying murder of US congressman Leo J. Ryan of California and four others, who were on a fact-finding visit to Jonestown, Guyana. On the same day that the startling reports continued to pour in from South America, Moscone and White met privately, with Moscone reportedly telling White that he needed to demonstrate a high level of support from constituents in his district as part of any effort to reinstate him. By November 20 Moscone's office was floating the idea publicly that the mayor was considering candidates other than White. Two black neighborhood leaders in White's district confronted him with angry voices, withdrawing their support for his reappointment and claiming that he never sought or took any of their counsel or advice about community issues.

Other obstacles arose when *Chronicle* reporter Maitland Zane, citing unnamed City Hall sources (most likely including Milk and Stiver), reported that White "had emerged as a hardline conservative with a pro-development, pro-downtown voting record, as well as an antipathy to the city's large gay community. He was the only supervisor to oppose the closing of Polk Street on Halloween."[57] A few days later, Milk went public with his support of keeping White off the board, saying he supported community activist Helen Fama for the post: "She's not a militant feminist, but she's a strong advocate for the women's position." He told the mayor that "if he decided not to reappoint White, he should definitely pick a woman like Helen Fama." The only existing board member publicly supporting White's reappointment was the president of the Board of Supervisors, Dianne Feinstein, while Moscone hinted to reporters that he continued to receive negative reports about the manner in which White had served during his brief stint on the board.[58]

Matters would take a shocking turn on November 27, 1978, when White hailed a political aide to give him a ride to City Hall, where he climbed in a basement window (to avoid the metal detectors at the building's main entrances) and proceeded to the mayor's office without an appointment. White, angered by a phone call from a reporter the night before informing him that Moscone was not going to reappoint him to the board (the mayor had not been courteous enough to tell White directly), was granted private access to the mayor. Moments later Moscone lay dead on the floor of his inner office, suffering from four gunshot wounds to the chest, arm, and head. White shot Moscone after he told White face-to-face that his term on the board was over. White then quickly reloaded his handgun, exited the mayor's suite, and went down the hall to the cubicle offices for city supervisors. There he found Milk and asked him to join him in White's now-vacant office. He repeated his act of murder, mercilessly unloading his weapon five times into Milk's body, including two execution-style wounds to the back of Milk's head. It was a big and heartbreaking story, and Shilts was part of the team coverage KQED-TV afforded the incredible events, including the arrest and confession of White for the murders. Although he had known Milk professionally and somewhat personally for many years, Shilts was stoic in his on-air presentations about the assassinations, but he accurately reflected the shock and disgust the entire city—not just the gay community—felt at such a violent turn of events.

CHAPTER 5

# The Life and Times

George Osterkamp, Shilts's former TV boss, believes he greatly under-estimated the challenges and pressures that Shilts faced as a gay reporter: "I think he faced more controversy than I was ever aware of at the time. He had to go back and deal with people in the gay community, many of whom had very strong opinions about how the movement should go, and they saw Randy as either an opportunity or an obstacle to where they thought the movement should go. I think that Randy had to walk a path that was strewn with more landmines than I ever realized."[1]

One of Shilts's fellow freelancers at KQED was Rita Williams, who went on to enjoy nearly four decades of work in local television news in the Bay Area, retiring from KTVU-TV in 2012. Williams, Shilts, and Phil Bronstein were the three free-lance reporters contributing to KQED's evening newscast. The set-up involved all three reporters pitching their story ideas to the show's producers and hoping for a green light to proceed. Williams believes Shilts's high energy and earnest interest in his stories translated well on television, particularly to a detail-hungry audience of PBS viewers. Williams said the competition required to get a story on the air was well suited to Shilts's competitive nature. She described the *Newsroom* telecast as

> an idea where all the reporters would come back into the studio with their stories at the end of the day, and we would have an hour-long time slot with no commercials, and then we would quiz each other on the air about our stories. It could be really brutal because we had some really big stalwarts in journalism in California as guests [on the studio panel] who would ask tough questions

about your story. You couldn't just report what everybody said; we had to put more into it than that. You couldn't just do a hack job like so many TV reporters try to do today; you really had to know your stuff and do sort of a minithesis every night on the air.[2]

The "competition" between Williams and Shilts was a friendly one, the two aspiring reporters quickly becoming friends both at and outside work. She acknowledged that Shilts would share story ideas with her if he already had a story that was going to air that particular day or week and he was too busy to get to another one. "I was new to the Bay Area, and I didn't have as many sources at that time as Randy did," Williams said.[3] She also credits Shilts with helping her get over her naive attitudes by taking her to a gay bathhouse to see what it was all about and by pulling back the curtain on one of Harvey Milk's most famous political schemes: Milk "accidentally" stepped in dog feces in Buena Vista Park at the news conference where he announced a new city ordinance requiring citizens to clean up after their dogs. A Milk aide had clandestinely placed the dog waste in the park prior to Milk's news conference. "Hardly anyone disagrees that you gotta do something to get the dog stuff up off the ground and the sidewalks," Shilts said. "Milk was doing something that was not involved with a gay issue but being a gay person and being out there showing that gay people, gosh, we're just like everybody else and that we're interested in more than the twenty minutes a day we might spend in having sex. . . . That was when [Milk] emerged as really *the* gay leader." Milk had emerged as a powerful and effective leader of the gay movement, and Shilts clearly understood the drama of Milk's life and demise. "It was like a play," he said, "all building up to that tragic ending. The whole last year and a half of [Harvey's] life [in 1977–78] is like a play, especially getting into the last six months where you build up the tension to the final act, and then you have your tragic resolution."[4]

As an author and later again as a reporter, finding enough to write about was no problem for Shilts, particularly in the incredible year of 1978, which saw some of the nation's biggest stories unfold in San Francisco. Covering the mass suicide led by Jim Jones and his Peoples Temple followers was not on Shilts's beat. It didn't stop him from trying, however, to sell a freelance story on the topic. He drafted an ultimately unpublished analysis of how the media had covered Jones and his followers in the lead-up to the incredible events in Guyana. His story had an acknowledged problem: except for two reporters, no active members of the San Francisco press corps wanted to talk on the record about Shilts's thesis that the "lazy and easily intimidated media" in the city were quick to ignore early warning signs from Jones and his followers (some of whom had fled the cult) or to take on the city's liberal political establishment, which "had nothing to gain—and much to lose—by giving the People's [sic] Temple a thorough going over."[5]

Regardless of the big stories breaking in San Francisco, all journalism imposes a feast-or-famine lifestyle on its denizens. The up-and-down nature of Shilts's career often showed up in his diary, which was sometimes filled with thoughtful and detailed examinations of what was happening in his life, followed by huge gaps. Shilts's scrawled entries fill the journal pages with wide, fluid strokes of the pen in prolific bursts in the early and mid-1970s, after he graduated college, and again briefly in 1984 and 1986, when he began to confront and overcome his addiction to alcohol and marijuana. In a "looking-back" entry Shilts wrote, it's clear he had read back through all the preceding entries: "Jesus, what a trip to read all these entries. It seems all I ever thought about was career and sex. Here I've got all these entries on 1976–77 and I never talk about Harvey Milk or all that idealism—just whether I'll be a success or not." Later entries switch to a more positive vein: "Now that I have achieved so much of that success, I have a hard time recalling the times when I was so driven. Was that really me? Sure it was. Then I wanted a job. Now I wait for a Pulitzer Prize. Then I wanted sex, now I wait for a life-long relationship."[6]

Shilts's work for KQED ended in 1980 with the demise of the Ford Foundation grant the station had tapped to fund the program. Shilts struggled not only with his inability to find work and his newfound reliance on the pittance paid by California's unemployment insurance but also with a renewed affection for heavy drinking and daily marijuana use. The fear surrounding the loss of his job at KQED was aggravated by the fact that Shilts had previously ended his relationship with the *Advocate*—and had done so in a way that left him no option to return. "I was just so angry" at not being able to get a job, Shilts said. "Unfair is the word that always came up, and I just got drunk all the time. I just drank a lot."[7] In the midst of his drunk and drugged response to a collapsing journalism career, Shilts had to face up to an angry cadre of gay leaders who were aligned with Goodstein and the *Advocate* and were smarting from Shilts's scathing critique of "The Advocate Experience" touted by the magazine's publisher and published in a rival publication, the *New West*. Shilts was deep in a funk, writing, "It's all going nowhere. Would it be any different if I were heterosexual? I'll never know. Maybe it has a lot to do with the terms on which I barter with the world. Being open is a terribly non-conformist status. . . . I have been a non-conformist all my life and probably always will be. To a point. Yet, I want worldly success. Recognition is probably a better word. I need that recognition as a basic part of fulfilling my insatiable ego."[8]

Some clarity was coming into view. Shilts began to examine the recent past, which found him with a foot in both the print and broadcast worlds of journalism, seemingly caught between the lure of TV and the "instantaneous fame" it offered him within the gay community and the entire Bay Area and his desire to be a serious writer. "My entire gestalt has been taking me in another direction—into working hard to be a good writer," he wrote. "It's rewarding to see me improve, but the external rewards are slower in coming. So what—even a cover story in *New West* is gone in two weeks and the people will want something else—on and on—[you're] only as good as your last two week story."[9] Whether he realized it or not, Shilts had tapped into a direction for his life and career that would reap tremendous rewards—all those he had dreamed about in the past from his days longing to leave Aurora.

Success would not come easy—editors of the *San Francisco Chronicle* had rejected an earlier idea to give Shilts an opinion column on the newspaper's editorial page, and a columnist position at the rival *San Francisco Examiner* also failed to materialize (despite Harvey Milk lobbying the paper's editors for the new position). *Rolling Stone* accepted and then rejected Shilts's lengthy review of the Village People and their popularity in the gay community. In his personal life, "The Advocate Experience" article in *New West* had raised a lot of eyebrows and tempers, and several gay leaders directly addressed their anger to Shilts. "Many people are angry at me," Shilts wrote in his journal during this time, adding,

> I seem to have gotten a lot of their feedback, people who hate me. I can't stand it when people dislike me—they make me feel like they're right and I'm wrong. At the same time, however, they were acting like a bunch of fools at that [*Advocate*] seminar. I shouldn't give a shit. It's not like they ever liked me or respected me before. I need to get my confidence up. They are a bunch of fools and I shouldn't let them get me down. I do need to do work on my obnoxiousness, however. . . . I have been too big for my britches, sounding off my big mouth too much, out of some vague insecurity I'm not even sure about. . . . I have to be more delicate with people from now on.[10]

Despite the onset of heavy drinking in 1980–81, Shilts said he remained hopeful he would find work. He continued to apply for both TV and newspaper jobs, though he wanted a newspaper job most. Edward Alwood reported that Shilts believed that since "gays had become headline news" via the 1978 Briggs Initiative and similar ballot initiatives elsewhere in the nation—not to mention the unspeakable violence that had cut down Milk and George Moscone—that a job for an ambitious gay reporter was surely in the wings. Dozens of query letters to newspaper editors and TV news directors in San Francisco, then Los Angeles, then New York, and then even Washington, DC, media resulted in nothing. Shilts lamented to Alwood, "Nobody believed I was qualified to cover anything except gay stuff. Of course, it was assumed that since I was a homosexual, that's the only thing I know how to cover. At the same time they didn't believe I was qualified to cover gay stuff either, because of course I would be shamelessly biased."[11]

Shilts told Alwood that a news director at one TV station told him she couldn't hire a gay person because ratings would fall—audiences didn't want to see gay people on TV. An April 1980 rejection letter from KRON-TV (at that time the NBC affiliate in San Francisco) was typical: "Dear Randy: Thanks for sending the letter and tapes. I'm sorry to report that I just don't have a job for you. I am, therefore, returning the tapes."[12] Since the TV well apparently had run dry, Shilts went back to what he knew best: freelancing for both the *Village Voice* and *California Magazine*. Eventually, the Oakland CBS affiliate, KTVU, hired Shilts to do freelance reporting on the gay community, but his work at KTVU ended within weeks after he did an interview with a local publication, *Boulevards Magazine*, which named him one of its Top 10 most eligible gay bachelors in the Bay Area. "The news director [at KTVU] saw that and freaked out and told my best friend at the station that the interview was a disaster for my career," Shilts said. "The news director felt it was one thing to be gay, but you shouldn't talk about what you wanted in an ideal boyfriend."[13] His short stint at KTVU did get him some critical notice: he won a local Emmy Award nomination for his story about children of Holocaust survivors.

As the weeks and months dragged on and full-time job opportunities remained elusive, Shilts cobbled together state unemployment checks and widely dispersed freelance assignments to keep his head above water. One of those freelance stories was a long essay on the assassination of Milk and Moscone at the close of 1978. It was so well done that some of Milk's supporters and friends in New York held on to it and used it as the basis for the idea of a biography of Milk and his extraordinary life. Michael Denneny and his friend Charles L. Ortleb sat around a West Village coffee shop in New York City in those days, struggling to process the realities of 1978, which had seen antigay political forces gain power in the same year that had seen the nation's first openly gay elected official cut down by an assassin's bullets. "Given the temper of the times, we feared that it was the beginning of a backlash that could wipe out the gay movement, much as had happened in Germany in the 1930s," Denneny said. "We thought getting Harvey's story into a book would at least preserve the memory. Randy was a natural candidate—probably the only guy we knew on the West Coast who was in a position to undertake such a book."[14]

Denneny, along with Sasha Alyson, who founded Alyson Publications in 1980 as the nation's first book publisher committed to gay and lesbian topics, was a bit of a rarity in publishing circles; he was openly gay and advocated for getting more gay voices and more gay stories into print. He had met Shilts for the first time in 1976 when they both were guests at a dinner along with two other men who would become major figures in the gay liberation movement: Cleve Jones and Armistead Maupin. A graduate of the University of Chicago and exposed to its prestigious Committee on Social Thought, Denneny had some specific ideas about what books could and should do for the gay liberation movement. African American, Latino American, and female writers were already making progress, but gay voices in print remained rare—publishers were often convinced that no audience existed for gay writers beyond basic erotica. Originally an editor at Macmillan, where he said he was frequently advised to be "less out" about his sexuality, Denneny was a part-time editor for *Christopher Street* magazine, one of the first gay publications in New York City. Denneny saw a specific purpose for publishing gay books: gay people "saw ourselves through straight eyes. I never worried about educating straight people. All of us were self-hating. We needed to reformulate gay imaginations, re-imagine sex, and relationships. The way you do that is with books."[15]

In approaching Shilts about the Milk bio, Denneny recalls, "Randy was poor and had to have a job to keep living, so we worked out a deal whereby we would pay an advance of $4,000 to $5,000 and have Randy write up a thirty-thousand-word essay on Harvey. I could use that essay as a proposal to try and get a book contract, which is, in fact, what happened." Denneny said that Shilts's treatment of Milk's story was "very impressive," and *Christopher Street* magazine published it in March 1979. Translating the Milk essay into a book, however, was "an uphill fight," Denneny said. Denneny personally handled the presentation and "pitch" of the Milk biography to the editorial boards at St. Martin's Press, where he worked at the time, and found a lackluster response. Most of the concern about a Milk biography centered on the idea that he was too local or too regional of a character to inspire any interest outside of California and that topics about gay politicians would lack widespread appeal among readers. Denneny persisted: "In those days we used to have sales conferences twice a year where you go to an auditorium and the whole sales force would gather, with all the editors, and this would be two or three hundred people. You would present the new list of books and describe each one. Every other editor absolutely refused to present the Milk book, so I ended up presenting it at the sales meeting."[16]

After lengthy arguments and a little strong-arming by Denneny and some of his bosses, the idea of a Milk biography received the green light. The approval came with a paltry $12,000 advance payment for Shilts—barely enough to cover his travel and other expenses in the long months of research and writing ahead. Denneny said, "I think it sold somewhere between nine and twelve thousand copies in cloth, and we put Randy out on a sort of abbreviated book tour," including readings before gay liberation organizations, one or two of which, surprisingly, had never heard of Milk, despite their active role in the still-developing gay rights movement and his New York roots.[17]

In prepping the Milk bio, Shilts laid claim to his overall analysis as having been "profoundly shaped by my five years of reporting in San Francisco as both a television correspondant [sic] and a freelance writer. During that time, I knew Harvey Milk and covered the panoply of other figures in this book." Because Shilts had extraordinary access to Milk's papers, belongings, and a long list of friends and supporters who had uplifted him for years, the foreshadowing Milk provided of his own pending death was captured brilliantly by Shilts. "Harvey had always told them it would end this way, with bullets in the brain," Shilts wrote, "but only when they see the black rubber body bag, covered with a crisp, pleated sheet, being rolled to the waiting ambulance does Harvey's prophecy become the palpable reality that makes for bad dreams and bold headlines." In fact, Milk tape-recorded himself discussing the idea of his assassination. Eerily, on the tape Milk declared, "If a bullet should enter my brain, let that bullet destroy every closet door."[18]

Equally dramatic was the tremendous outpouring of grief that followed Milk's death, with Shilts estimating as many as forty thousand marchers walking silently from the Castro to City Hall: "In three-piece suits, black leather jackets, blue jeans, and neatly pressed dresses, they gather under the cloudy autumn sky to remember the gangly ward politician with the funny name, the thick black hair, the corny jokes and the New York accent." Shilts analyzed the reality of the attention paid to Milk by this group: "The emphasis surprises few in the largely homosexual crowd. The mayor had given them leadership, but Harvey Milk—the nation's first openly gay city official—had given them a dream."[19]

In search of meaning for the inexplicable violence that had taken Milk just as he had reached the mountaintop, Shilts wrote: "In death, Harvey Milk's dream started casting a shadow far larger than anything he could have fashioned in life; such is the nature of mortals and martyrs, dreams and their shadows. Castro Street had become Harvey's hometown and he had worked to make it a hometown for tens of thousands of homosexuals from around the world. 'The mayor of Castro Street,' that was Harvey's unofficial title. And now the mayor of San Francisco and the mayor of Castro Street lie dead. What is left is the dream and its lengthening shadow."[20] Although Shilts began Milk's story where it had ended, in a pool of blood on the floor of a City Hall office, Shilts spent considerable time setting up the context in which Milk was an early leader for homosexuals. The historic perspective became even more important in subsequent years. Rewritten history or papered-over memories often missed the fact that to be "out of the closet" in the era and manner of Milk was nothing short of an extraordinary and revolutionary act. In a tale that mirrored that of Shilts himself, he wrote about Milk understanding very early the difference that dwelled deep within his heart and mind. It may not have had a name, but as time passed, Milk, like many others, began to understand what it meant to be homosexual. Shilts noted, "Some noticed something different" about Milk even as a boy. "Not peculiar or odd, just different. Harvey Milk would strain, sweat and wrestle to keep the difference a secret only a few could know. On the rare occasions when the cover did slip, he would realize the size of the stakes. They were high enough to keep him sweating and straining for many years, like so many others."[21]

Shilts retold the story of a frightening experience in Milk's young life as he began to discover other men who carried his same secret. A "rousting" or "round-up" of gay men from a popular meeting spot in New York City's Central Park snagged Milk one sunny Sunday afternoon in 1947. Luckily, the cops on the beat just warned the young men about hanging out together and necking under the sun in the meadows and undergrowth of the park. "Anger had no place among homosexuals of those years, only fear," Shilts wrote. "Not only fear of the police, but fear of himself and of his secrets being revealed by an afternoon's routine police action. Harvey was lucky. . . . [The] police often didn't bother to lock up their quarry. Just put a little fear of God in them."[22] Shilts also captured one truism for a young homosexual like Milk in New York City in that era: "Harvey was one of the lucky ones of his generation. At least he had lovers, knew other gay men, and could pursue sex and romance. These alternatives were available only to gays who lived in a handful of major American cities. Most homosexuals simply lived without. But even the lucky ones like Harvey paid the price of vigilance for their liberty. The constant fear of the loose phrase, the wrong pronoun, the chance moment, the misspoken word that might give it all away."[23] Eventually shedding an interesting professional mix of schoolteacher, stockbroker, and Broadway producer in New York for the pursuits of a small businessman in San Francisco, Milk arrived in the city in 1972, before its label as the gay mecca. Like New York and other major cities in the United States, San Francisco had its unspoken and quietly operating "underworld" gay society—a society that existed alongside a drug culture and a flourishing prostitution commerce—but the closet door was about to blow open. Initially a hippie and part of the growing counterculture (partly because San Francisco was a place where a closeted gay man could exist in relative safety and invisibility), Milk was like many who spun off the antiwar and counterculture movement in order to explore other avenues of civil rights injustice such as women's rights and eventually gay rights. By the mid-1970s San Francisco was well on its way to becoming the hoped-for gay mecca, and Milk was front and center in all the action through his shoestring business operation, Castro Camera. Shilts wrote about an "explosion" in the gay rights movement in the months and years following the 1969 raid of the Stonewall Inn in New York City, an event noted for the fact that homosexuals used to being pushed around by graft-driven cops finally fought back:

> The gay movement experienced an explosion unprecedented since the first days of gay liberation fronts following the Stonewall riots. Gays who had come to San Francisco just to disco amid the hot pectorals of humpy men became politicized and fell into new organizations with names like Save Our Human Rights and Coalition for Human Rights. No longer was the gay movement the realm of offbeat liberation fairies.... [It became] a necessary response to a clear and present danger. These young gays might have taken their locker-room beatings at home, because they knew they could always go to San Francisco one day, but once in San Francisco, there was no place else to turn.[24]

Shilts's words make clear that he was probably writing as much about Milk and San Francisco as he was about himself.

The early gay era in San Francisco had a clearly sexual element, Shilts noted: "Promiscuity was practically an article of faith among the new gays of Castro Street, stemming from both the free-love hippie days and the adoption of aggressive male images." Gay men like Milk and his growing cadre of friends understood that "something vital was indeed growing in the Castro. Something clearly was happening. In 1975 and 1976, however, it was just hard to tell what that something was. All that was clear was that wave after wave of gay men were descending on Castro Street.... They were people from all backgrounds who had come to Castro Street to be gay, and they had a lot to sort out."[25]

Milk had to sort out how to keep his struggling Castro Camera store at 575 Castro Street open amid a growing list of bureaucratic rules from City Hall. A local teacher and customer asking to borrow a slide projector for a classroom presentation because school funds were so scarce that the school didn't own a projector inspired Milk's political aspirations. The teacher's dilemma in having to beg a local business for basic supplies irked Milk both as a former schoolteacher himself and as a citizen of the city. Soon after, he jumped into local politics, moving beyond his preliminary efforts, which included forming a Castro Street business and community association. At first, Milk found a welcome from the city's liberal Democrats, who wanted to mine the growing gay community for campaign cash and votes. They weren't necessarily interested, however, in nominating gay men or lesbian women as candidates for public office. Shilts noted that Milk had other ideas: "'It's not enough to have friends represent us, no matter how good friends they might be,' he told a statewide caucus of gay Democrats. 'If we remain invisible, we will be in limbo, people with no brothers, no sisters, no parents, no positions of respectability. The anger and frustration some of us feel because we are misunderstood—friends cannot feel that anger and frustration. They can sense it in us, but they cannot feel it. . . . It's time we have many legislators who are gay, proud of that and do not remain in the closet.'"[26]

Although his 1977 election to a newly formed district seat on the San Francisco Board of Supervisors is what most people remember, Shilts noted that Milk had one earlier political success by being named by Mayor Moscone to the city's Board of Permit Appeals a year earlier. Shilts wrote about the symbolism of Milk's appointment, which came with the addition of a black woman and a Filipino man to a board that held powerful sway over the development and direction of the city.[27]

Shilts accurately analyzed that Milk had a lot to learn about politics. Milk could be "hyperactive," Shilts wrote, and "instead of boyish . . . [some saw] a spoiled child, demanding nearly superhuman efforts from his employees, friends, and campaign workers. He ran off at the mouth with long trains of hyperbole. His temper flared easily—especially at his lover Scott [Smith]—and he seemed inordinately preoccupied with minutiae." Milk was also a man of many dimensions, Shilts posited. "If Harvey Milk shouted too loudly at Scott and his closest friends, he could also purr softly into the ear of any reporter who happened by—and usually come out of it with some good press," he wrote. "Milk demanded too much of those around him, but his demands of others paled in comparison to what he demanded of himself."[28]

Denneny led the publicity efforts at St. Martin's Press to drum up interest in the book about Milk, including issuing positive advance reviews. In a March 1982 interview about the book with the *Los Angeles Times,* Shilts breathlessly took in the attention the book offered him. The *Times* offered, "Shilts has written and is promoting . . . one of the first avowedly gay nonfiction books to be accepted—embraced even—by the mainstream press and public."[29] But from there the *Times* story moved decidedly on the story of Shilts himself rather than on his work about Milk's life, detailing Shilts's coming-out journey, his commitment to being an openly gay reporter, and his long struggle for acceptance—and employment—in journalism. "From the outside, it looks like a solid rise," Shilts said of his résumé. "But do you know how much I've been through? Do you have any idea?" Shilts settled into the rarefied role as journalist and author by noting that many others had said they wanted to write a biography of either Milk or Moscone, but only he had actually done so. Shilts's bravado was on full display as he told the *Times* reporter, "A straight journalist could have written this book, yes, but only if they had overcome their own biases about writing what is essentially a gay book. In a way, it's 'Randy Shilts's Greatest Hits.' I mean, I was there, I covered it." He said he accepted the casual title afforded him as "the gay reporter" but was quick to sound a defense he would return to often: "I am not a propagandist. My existence is a political stand."[30]

For its take on the book, *Publishers Weekly* wrote, "In brash street prose, the passions and purposes of Harvey Milk are celebrated throughout these pages. . . . [N]ot a moment of the drama and suspense of the shooting, the tension of the trial or the shock of the murderer's near-acquittal is sacrificed. . . . [Shilts] succeeds in bringing [Milk] to life, loping, shabby, romantic, and driven by the foreboding of his own violent death." The *Library Journal* offered, "Journalist Shilts's spare prose weaves a compelling story that transcends biography to serve as a metaphor for the history of this country's gay movement." Kirkus Reviews said Shilts's work was "first rate" and had appropriately balanced the story of Milk's private and public lives—the result being "honest and illuminating without being lurid" and presenting the hero of the story, Harvey Milk, "as a character that can transcend gay audiences and appeal to all readers."[31]

Author James Kinsella thought Shilts was particularly well suited to write the Milk story. Shilts had told Milk's story before in the pages of the *Advocate*, and Kinsella concluded that Shilts had "woven together . . . a highly readable account of the life and times of Harvey Milk. Far from glorifying the man, which became a popular pastime after his death, Shilts's book described him as a political animal in the center of social upheaval. The work was received enthusiastically nationwide."[32]

One particularly blistering negative review, however, published in the morning edition of the *Fort Worth Star-Telegram,* barely contained the reviewer's contempt for the very subject of homosexuals. "Nothing exceeds like success," reviewer Michael H. Price wrote. Shilts's book, which documented the "gay upheaval . . . and activism with which Harvey Milk propelled his community into the middle-class mainstream," was told by a narrator, Shilts, "who does not know when to shut up." Price laughed at Shilts's claim that the story reads only as a gay journalist could tell it and said the result "was less a work of historical scholarship than a celebration of the gay movement from an inside-out perspective." The review was brutal but represented the reviewer's apparent loathing of anything gay. Calling the book a "hodgepodge of valid information and overwrought emotionalism, top heavy with trivia and self-indulgence," the reviewer stated that it existed simply as an affirmation that "gay is OK" (apparently an affirmation Price objected to), missing the point that Milk's life was about advancing the lives of gay people and not one of seeking special privileges.[33]

Shilts dedicated the book to his parents, Bud and Norma Shilts, and praised Harvey Milk's ex-lover Scott Smith for sharing volumes of information about Milk's life. Shilts also mentioned his St. Martin's editor, Michael Denneny; his friends Dan Yoder, Steve Newman, Ann Neuenschwander, and Tom Lang; and his brother Gary Shilts.

After the book was published and during its short publicity tour, Shilts told Randy Alfred, host of KSAN Radio's *The Gay Life* (a weekly radio news program), that he took ten months to write Milk's story after conducting 140 separate interviews and went broke in the process. He prepared for *The Mayor of Castro Street* (as he would again later for *And the Band Played On*) by reading as many of James Michener's books as he could get his hands on. Shilts admired Michener's style in *Hawaii,* the 1959 best seller that artfully demonstrated Michener's episodic, narrative style, which mixes history and anthropology with fictional devices, including internal thoughts and reconstructed dialogue between central figures.[34] "I read *Hawaii* by James Michener, and that gave me the concept of doing books where you take people and have them represent sort of different forces in history and different social groups," Shilts said.[35] It was a style that won both praise and scorn, the latter of which raised questions about how Shilts could actually know what particular actors in his story were thinking or saying at any specific moment in time when he had not been an eyewitness or an "earwitness"—a vast departure from what many journalists would normally be comfortable doing. Nevertheless, Shilts believed that his "reporter's-eye view" of Milk's life and death and the resulting actions in San Francisco and beyond made for a fascinating story, appropriately told "through a reporter's point of view, which aren't bad eyes, which isn't a bad way to look at this story."[36] In his introduction to the work, Shilts asserted,

83

"Because I'm an acknowledged gay journalist, I've also had access to interviews and anecdotes which generally elude other reporters" (read: straight reporters).[37]

Shilts's unapologetic amity for Milk shows through, even with unflattering references to Milk and his private life on full display and even though the Milk story ends on a tragic, violent note. A further example is found in Shilts's praise of Milk as a natural legendary figure for gay people but also as an extremely naive political operative. "When you look at what [Harvey] did, he registered voters, he walked and canvassed precincts, he built his economic clout," Shilts said. "Well, that's as old-fashioned American as you can get and he didn't expect to be gunned down by a colleague whom he should be debating." Shilts included in his research of Milk's life the fact that the groundbreaking San Francisco pol always sought to keep reporters as part of a friendly relationship. Shilts said, "I always thought that Harvey loved me, but in doing the research for the book, I found out that he sort of thought of me as this very obnoxious, unpredictable guy. But I always thought that Harvey liked me a lot, but it was just that he was following his number one rule: always be nice to reporters."[38]

Shilts made a special effort to acknowledge that lesbians were not a central part of the Milk story ("Harvey did not have much contact with lesbians either socially or politically"), foreshadowing a criticism of both Milk and eventually Shilts himself that gay women were noticeably absent from his words. Shilts seemed to understand clearly at this early stage of his career that criticism comes with praise—that when you publish your words for others to read, the good comes with the bad. He noted that *The Mayor of Castro Street* "will not please ideologues [sic] looking for a political tract. Conversely, some might complain that it is sympathetic to the gay point of view, because no traces of moral outrage against homosexuality are to be found on these pages." He said, "I suspect others might fret that this book is indiscrete in its discussion of private topics not normally raised in the journalistic forum." Again, his 1982 words preview the coming criticism that would bombard Shilts with his second book. "I can only answer that I tried to tell the truth and, if not objective, [to] at least be fair; history is not served when reporters prize trepidation and propriety over the robust journalistic duty to tell the whole story."[39]

Foreshadowing was a key element of Shilts's account of Milk's life, using the often-cited audiotape that Milk recorded for posterity in the event of his death by assassination. Shilts also found the parallels in Milk's life mirrored in the gay liberation movement. "Milk was tired of waiting on 'liberal friends' to make political advancement possible," Shilts wrote. "Harvey had a very simple prescription. Gay candidates for public offices were the best tool for advancing the gay movement, he reasoned." Milk's demand to participate in and not just support the progressive agenda left "entrenched gay leaders" angry and alienated. No longer would the gay movement gain its power simply by trusting friendly liberals: "Milk insisted that his campaign could train a new corps of activists. 'A committed novice from the streets was worth a dozen old-timers,' Milk said."[40]

The story, however, could not be limited to just Milk's part of it. Shilts took time to set up the history of the gay liberation movement in San Francisco and the sometimes sad, self-destructive, and even deadly experience of early gays in the city. Coincidentally, Shilts pinpoints 1975 (the year *he* moved permanently to San Francisco and not the earlier date, when Milk arrived) as the turning point for the city and the gay community.

The Castro District faced some of its most harrowing days during the "White Night" riots, which erupted in San Francisco on May 21, 1979, following the conviction of former San Francisco supervisor Dan White on lesser included charges in the assassinations of Milk and Moscone. Assigned to cover the riots, which were driven by more than twenty thousand gay and lesbian protestors, who marched from the Castro to the San Francisco City Hall in protest, Shilts tackled a tough assignment reporting the details of the riot. He later acted as a news analyst, reviewing the actions of the San Francisco Police Department, the gay community, and Mayor Dianne Feinstein on the KQED set as the "gay expert." This period in Shilts's career, retold later on the pages of the Milk biography, revealed an important time when Shilts had to address the sometimes-thin line between objective journalist and entrenched member of the gay community. Shilts had been there amid the angry response to White's near acquittal and talked personally with patrons of the Elephant Walk Bar, a popular gay bar at the corner of 18th and Castro Streets, who withstood a barrage from angry police acting in retaliation. The bar, famous for being the original locale for drag disco superstar Sylvester and the Weather Girls, was ground zero for violence following the White trial. Witness reports indicated that a band of rogue San Francisco police officers, angry about the earlier fracas at City Hall, descended upon the Elephant Walk Bar, smashing bottles and glasses to the floor, pushing patrons into the street, and busting the heads of those who resisted. The next morning Shilts talked to bar patrons and a bartender, each of them describing a surprising and unprovoked attack by the police. Unedited KQED tape digitized for a northern California television news archive at San Francisco State University recorded Shilts asking one man, "Can you describe what happened in twenty-five words or less?" and asking others, "Do you think this represents an anger that goes beyond the particulars of what happened [in the White case] in court yesterday?" Shilts revealed his struggle with objectivity by asking several people a variation on the question, "Some people say this will hurt *us* politically, that there will be a backlash against *us*. What do you think?" His insertion of the word "us" into his questions revealed that while he was reporting on the events of the gay community, he simply could not completely remove himself from occupying those events on some personal level. His perhaps growing animus toward his fellow gays was also apparently present, with Shilts asking one man, "Are there any leaders in the gay community right now?" Shilts concluded that the violent pushback from a heretofore mostly cooperative gay community meant that "a lot more than glass was shattered last night in the Castro. A lot of myths about the gay community also got shattered."[41]

The violent riot at San Francisco's City Hall made headlines across the nation and resulted in injuries to dozens of people. Doors and windows to City Hall were smashed, and ten San Francisco police cars sustained damage. After the dust settled from the White Night riots, Shilts proudly voiced an "I told you so moment," saying, "I remember being at the City Hall the day after the riot, and I was at the press conference with [Mayor] Dianne Feinstein. Everybody was saying how surprised they were that it happened. Well, I was saying, 'Hey, I'm just a dumb reporter, and I could tell you I knew there was going to be a riot. Why didn't you guys know it?'"[42]

Shilts struggled always, as did many gays, to maintain any sense of objectivity when discussing the arrest and prosecution of White for the murders of Milk and Moscone, openly suggesting in his stories and his commentary on them that a conspiracy was in play to help White escape full responsibility for his violent acts. While praising the San Francisco Police Department's professionalism overall, Shilts said, "None of that professionalism is involved in the Dan White confession." Going further in a radio interview with Randy Alfred on KSAN, Shilts took special note of the fact that the homicide detectives who interviewed White after he turned himself in for the two murders avoided key questions that would have been useful in building a case for murder against their former police colleague. Shilts told Alfred and his audience: "And then you go from there to a prosecutor who went out of his way not to introduce any kind of information [regarding intent]. . . . You had to work at ignoring the kinds of things that were ignored by the prosecution. It was not, it could not have solely been done out of ignorance. Maybe I'm saying too much already, but there is something really, really wrong in [the Dan White case], and this city will not be cleansed of that trial and all that it represented until it gets a real thorough examination."[43] Fellow gay journalist David Israels of the *Bay Area Guardian* recalls that Shilts dealt with the stories of the Milk and Moscone murders and the subsequent White Night riots as breaking news. Israels, who still today calls White "an outright murderer," said,

> Randy [Shilts] was far more interested in what the meaning or repercussions of the verdict was in the wake of the assassinations and trial. On those issues I think he was a reporter. He could act professionally, and he was fair and balanced, as most reporters [are] who claim that they are objective. But there really is no such thing as objectivity. . . . The very act of reporting creates an effect on the thing you are reporting about; there are some things you put in and some things that you leave out. You have to construct a story, a narrative. You are expected to be fair and to be balanced. I think that's certainly how Randy presented himself, and he was very insistent on that.[44]

Israels said that Shilts talked to him on occasion about the pressure he felt from gay leaders to write articles that were more favorable, or at least more helpful, to gay civil rights causes. Israels thinks, at least partially, that Shilts enjoyed "stirring things up" with people on either side of an issue: "Randy sometimes took delight in doing things that were annoying to those who wanted to be politically correct." He thinks Shilts knew that "sometimes he could report more critically on the community than people wanted him to, and the criticisms came, and he enjoyed some of those because they seem to testify to his, for want of a better term, his objectivity or professionalism."[45]

White's lenient sentence, seven years for the conviction of voluntary manslaughter rather than the original charge of murder for the slayings of Milk and Moscone, meant he could be back in the community after a short prison sentence of just over five years. In January 1984 Shilts was cast in an interesting role both as a reporter for the *San Francisco Chronicle* covering the implications of White's pending release and as a source for other reporters writing about what White's release might mean to the gay community. Shilts wrote a lengthy story on White's pending release that was picked up and carried in newspapers across California and the country. In it he quoted a variety of sources, including Mayor Feinstein, California governor George Deukmejian, San Francisco city supervisors, and Milk's friend Bill Kraus, a former Milk aide.[46]

Shilts reported that "Off White" signs had popped up in the Castro District once news broke that White was to be released on parole to his home in San Francisco and concluded that "as brutal as the crime was, most San Franciscans agree that it would have passed into the city's memory if it had not been for White's trial," emphasizing that "a parade of psychiatrists told the largely white, working class Catholic jury" that White acted out of a diminished capacity and the infamous "Twinkie" defense, in which White's attorneys made the claim that their client's judgment was impaired by restless days of eating Twinkies and other junk food prior to the shootings. Shilts didn't hold back on the prosecution of the case, referring to their case as "bumbling." In a traditional show of balance, Shilts reported that White still had supporters in his "working-class native San Franciscans" neighborhood. They continued to affirm White's earlier assessment that the city was being overrun by what White had termed were "social incorrigibles and deviates."[47]

For its pick-up of the Shilts story about White's pending prison release, United Press International reduced its quotable sources down to Shilts, referred to as "a widely-known writer on San Francisco's homosexuals." UPI turned Shilts's news account of posters with the words "Off White" appearing in the Castro District into first-person eyewitness reports from Shilts (rather than his story sources) and quoted him: "I think there are isolated individuals who are angry enough and crazy enough to hunt him down and kill him. There are people out there who want him dead."[48] California prison officials eventually agreed that White's release should be to Los Angeles rather than San Francisco. He served one year of his probation there before returning to San Francisco, where his life continued to spiral downward. White committed suicide in the garage of his family's home via carbon monoxide poisoning on October 21, 1985.

Shilts understood that the Milk-Moscone-White story had been high drama, matching almost anything commonly found in fiction. "People sometimes say to me, 'Have you ever thought about writing fiction?' and I always say, 'I could not be as imaginative as the world is. What you get, you couldn't make up.'" Shilts believed, though, that part of getting the story in such imaginative and amazing detail was analogous to being a good reporter: "Always asking extra questions—always, because there are two ways you can be a journalist. You can ask enough to get enough information for a story, or try to do more than enough because it is always the little connections that come out in side comments."[49]

That die-hard commitment to drawing out detail would serve Shilts well as he moved on to the largest—and most complex—story of his career, the coming AIDS pandemic.

# CHAPTER 6

# Becoming the AIDS Scribe

The 1980s opened with Randy Shilts in search of full-time employment and struggling with nagging personal issues related to his alcohol and marijuana use. Hope was on the horizon, however, with an opportunity to take an even bigger step up in journalism. Shilts, often hailed as one of the nation's first openly gay reporters for a major daily newspaper, was not the first choice on the list. As the editors at the *San Francisco Chronicle* began to understand that they could no longer ignore—or deny—that gay people were a major political, economic, and social force in the community, the stoic *Chronicle* took a bold step and sought out an openly gay reporter to cover gay-related stories in the city. The *Chronicle* already had an unofficial "gay beat" via the work of city-side reporter Ron Moscowitz, a writer who moved over to journalism in 1967 after working as an aide to California governor Edmund G. "Pat" Brown, who had been retired from Sacramento by Ronald Reagan. Moscowitz had begun quietly covering gay news as early as 1977 and wrote a noteworthy series of articles in 1979 about a policy of the US Immigration and Naturalization Service that prohibited openly gay tourists from entering the country. By 1980 *Chronicle* editor Jerry Burns wanted a more permanent arrangement and approached Moscowitz about the job. A recent heart attack and pending early retirement took Moscowitz out of the running, however, and Burns put out the word that he was interested in hiring from outside.

The unemployed Shilts got wind of Burns's interest, promptly called the editor, and landed the job. As a result, his title as "the first openly gay reporter on a major daily newspaper" actually needs an asterisk. Burns counted on Shilts's ability as a reporter but not on the iconic figure he would become. Burns said, "Little did I know I was creating this media star when I hired Randy. I knew he was, in the first place, an outstanding reporter. In the second place, I knew he was one who deeply cared about the community and all the parts that go into it. I also knew he was ambitious and had stars in his eyes, and boy, has that turned out to be true!"[1] Shilts made the transition to work as a journalist at a major US daily newspaper rather seamlessly, it seems. His arrival at the *Chronicle* did not produce headlines or stories as had his hiring a few years earlier at KQED, but his addition to the news staff didn't come without some questions. Editor Alan Mutter recalled that some questions of objectivity persisted for some, but he and other editors were consistent in their statements to the newspaper's editorial staff (and to readers) that they saw no conflict of interest in having a gay man report on gay issues, including AIDS, a disease epidemic primarily impacting gay men. Mutter said, "The bottom line is professionalism."[2]

During his first days at the *Chronicle*, Shilts said that he kept a small notebook in his pocket in which he planned to record the slights, indifference, or open intolerance he expected he might have to face among his journalistic peers. He never wrote anything down, he said. "Everybody went out of their way to be nice and supportive of me, and there had been somebody else in the newsroom before me who was gay, so the editors and reporters were friendly," Shilts said. Originally assigned to cover general assignment stories, including some stories from the gay community, as a new reporter Shilts took whatever an editor sent his way. "That was fine with me, because I didn't want to cover just gay stuff, even though that was part of what I wanted to do," he said.[3]

Shilts eventually moved from general assignment reporter, to assistant city editor, to national correspondent. Embracing his role as assistant city editor allowed him to continue work on his idea for a second book (what would become 1987's *And the Band Played On*). It wasn't an unprecedented idea—*Chronicle* reporter Paul Avery had taken time off to write books about the Patty Hearst–SLA kidnapping scandal and the Zodiac serial killer, while Tim Reiterman at the rival *San Francisco Examiner* had used his reporting on the Reverend Jim Jones and the Peoples Temple to produce an authoritative book on that deadly cult. Shilts said, "The *Chronicle* was a very gentlemanly place, and people went out of the way to be very supportive," and his fellow journalists seemed to make a special effort to show that "they weren't going to be biased, which surprised me," given the paper's consistently Republican inclinations on its editorial and opinion pages.[4] Shilts may not have felt any trepidation from his colleagues, but some existed, according to fellow *Chronicle* reporter Susan Sward: "The men in the City Room were nervous" about Shilts's arrival. "Randy wore wildly flowered ties, he had suspenders, and initially, you could just feel a nervousness when many people in the City Room dealt with him," Sward said.[5] She also revealed that Shilts's enthusiasm about his stories could create problems: "You weren't supposed to be excited about things. If you came up to the [city] desk all in a lather about something you were covering, they would look at you like you had some kind of problem. Randy violated that rule and he didn't care what people said to him about it, he was going to care."[6]

Any nervousness or reservations about Shilts's approach in the newsroom didn't last long, however, as Sward believed his wide-open personality quickly won over any doubters: "He had an infectious personality. . . . He could laugh at himself. He [also] had an enormous ego. . . . [He] was an enormously engaging person, and at the same time, he was a tremendous journalist. Bit by bit, those who were nervous about him came to admire his talent." Sward recalled that it was nearly impossible not to notice Shilts in the otherwise buttoned-down newsroom. "The curly mop-top of blond-brown hair, the boyish grin, the happy laugh," she recalled. "He had ego, a lot of it, and he made no effort to hide it. In fact, he would throw back his head and laugh with great gusto when someone called him on his latest exhibition of self-love."[7]

Wes Haley, who worked for twenty years as a newsroom manager and staff assistant for the *Chronicle*, said the first call that would come to his desk almost every weekday morning was from Shilts—just after 4:00 a.m. "I was never sure if he was just going to bed, or just getting up," Haley said, but Shilts's daily calls to check in on "what was going on" were like clockwork. Haley took it upon himself to help keep Shilts organized. "Randy was a slob, but he liked things neat, if that makes any sense," Haley said, admitting that he frequently organized papers piled on Shilts's desk as a way of helping. "Randy liked anything that was about Randy," Haley said. "That's the thing, Randy loved Randy. If people were paying attention to him and someone was cleaning up his desk, that pleased him just fine."[8]

The story that would define Shilts's legacy as a journalist and author came in via overheard conversations and discussions throughout the gay community during his very first days in the *Chronicle* newsroom. Rumors about a "gay cancer" or serious illness affecting the gay community quickly reached Shilts, who was always tapped into the latest news in the gay community. Dr. Marcus Conant, a local dermatologist, was among the local health professionals sounding early alarms of a problem as he began to treat more gay men showing symptoms of a rare skin cancer, Kaposi's sarcoma. Conant first made contact with Shilts in August

1981, sharing clinical information about Kaposi's sarcoma. Shilts filed a story on the subject (later picked up by the Associated Press) but cautioned Conant that he was not sure if his editors at the *Chronicle* would do a local story on it: "I've held back from doing a local angle on [KS]—which would see much more prescient play in favor of doing a story when it will be constructive when you have your plan ready." Shilts said he wanted to avoid writing a story that would cause worried readers to bombard the health department "with questions that can't be answered." He advised, "*The Chronicle* wants me to keep generally on top of gay community issues" and invited Conant to share story ideas with him.[9]

David Perlman, the *Chronicle*'s science reporter, followed up and was truly in the foreground of coverage of this new health threat. He actually beat Shilts to the story by writing as early as June 1981 on a troubling report in the federal government's *Morbidity and Mortality Weekly Report* about an alarming increase in diagnosed cases of a rare form of pneumonia caused by a parasite known as *Pneumocystis carinii*. The report indicated that this sometimes-fatal version of pneumonia was showing up among gay men in San Francisco and other major cities, especially Los Angeles and New York. The report from the Centers for Disease Control and Prevention indicated, "The fact that these patients were all homosexuals suggests a connection between some aspect of a homosexual lifestyle or disease acquired through sexual contact."[10] The same page of the *Chronicle* that day carried the happy news that the 155 men of the San Francisco Gay Men's Chorus were about to embark on their first national tour—a group eventually decimated by the ravages of what was to become the AIDS epidemic.

Perlman said Shilts indicated an interest in reporting on the emerging story during his first days on the job: "I think he was interested almost as soon as he got here because he already knew that many of his friends in the Castro were coming down with very strange and very rare forms of pneumonia, and what even he himself and his friends would refer to at the time as 'the gay cancer.'" Perlman noted that while he may have been the first to write about what became known as AIDS in June 1981, Shilts "was the first reporter that I know of who could see that this was not simply going to be a gay disease. . . . He made it noticed here on the *Chronicle* and in the news, and you can remember how hard he fought to get his stories on page one."[11] Perlman, a fatherly newsroom figure with an open personality, often took new reporters, including Shilts, under his wing and offered helpful feedback. The two men came to an informal but lasting agreement that Perlman would cover most of the scientific and clinical issues surrounding the still-unnamed AIDS story, and Shilts would cover the social and political aspects of the issue.

Shilts's first consideration of the issue came in a story about gay men's health for a May 13, 1982, story, "The Strange Deadly Diseases That Strike Gay Men." Using "diseases" as plural represented the perhaps broader focus of the report, which would soon give way to more specialized reports that looked beyond the "strange diseases" showing up in gay men to the underlying cause of *why* they had become susceptible to diseases previously thought eradicated, or at least rare. As usual, Shilts's reporting was gripping, telling the story of a forty-five-year-old San Francisco man identified in the story only as "Jerry" who was slowly being over-taken by purple spots and lesions on his skin, later diagnosed as Kaposi's sarcoma, a rare form of skin cancer previously affecting mostly elderly Greek men. In the first four months of 1982 alone, 335 men (almost all openly gay) across the United States had been diagnosed with Kaposi's sarcoma, and 136 of them had died—a death rate far exceeding the earlier public health alarms arising from the advent of Legionnaires' disease and toxic shock syndrome. The cases of KS among gay men were so common that doctors had begun referring to it colloquially as "gay cancer."

Shilts reported, "Jerry is a victim of one of a series of baffling diseases hitting primarily gay men with increasing frequency across the country." This Shilts story was one of the first ever in the mainstream press to carry the moniker assigned by scientists to the health problems as GRID, or Gay-Related Immune Deficiency, diseases. "Scientists have had as much trouble isolating a cause for the outbreak as finding a cure," Shilts reported. "Put simply, researchers attribute the GRID diseases to a massive breakdown in the victims' immune system," leaving the oth-erwise healthy young men unable to fight off natural exposure to cancerous cells, pneumonia parasites, or other invading infections and organisms. Jerry's story was not uncommon—Shilts reported that sixty-five Bay Area men experienced GRID-related problems, and nineteen had died. The story included information about the Shanti Project, a community-based support group for gay men suffering from GRID diseases, and the heartbreaking story of one gay man who became ill and had "lapsed into a semi-coma, as his relatives tried to strike his lover's name from the [hospital] guest list and forbid him from seeing the dying man."[12]

The depth and detail of Shilts's reporting would again demonstrate the value of his personal connections across the city's gay community and with an early gay ally, Dr. Selma Dritz at the county health department. Dritz, who would become famous for her chalkboard-drawn "maps" tracking the earliest cases of GRID (which would eventually become known as AIDS), was intensely "worked" by Shilts for information for his stories. Paul Monahan O'Malley, at the time a communicable disease investigator for the San Francisco City Clinic and later a clinical manager for communicable diseases with the San Francisco Department of Public Health, noted, "There was some concern as to how Randy Shilts knew some of the information he wrote. He was someone who lived here in the [gay] community, and he wasn't like an outsider coming in here; he was very savvy at what he did. I don't think Selma [Dritz] may have realized that he was able to ask questions and put two and two together sometimes, because he was so familiar with what was going on in the community."[13]

Personal papers retained by Dritz (who died in 2008) indicate clearly that a social, friendly, and personal relationship had developed between her and Shilts, including gushing thank-you notes from Shilts sent to Dritz, along with personal invitations to Shilts's annual birthday bash (still known as Shiltsmas). In a note to Dritz dated May 13, 1983, Shilts wrote:

> After talking today, it struck me that you probably don't get enough pats on the back to daily cope with one of the most depressing, morose and relentless plagues of our time. Those of us who are gay get a boost from our peers, but you're stuck in the category of a professional—not part of the community, in the San Francisco tribal sense—I have no doubt, however, that your dedication to accurate information has already saved some lives (when reporters falter). I'm not the only reporter—or gay person—who is struck with total admiration of your work.[14]

Shilts wrote a second note to Dritz three years later as he began work on his book *And the Band Played On*. He said his work had impressed upon him "how much of human history relies on a few people who are willing to do the unrewarding work that needs to get done. You were doing that work for years, even before AIDS, and the fact that you were in the health department tremendously aided the nation in understanding the disease because of the unique relationship you have established between gay doctors and your office. . . . Every day, somebody should say 'thank you' to you."[15]

Despite his "chummy" relationship with Dr. Dritz, Shilts's early articles also gave voice to his oft-repeated concern that public health and government response to the problem moved slowly because gay men were the most impacted group in society. Shilts quoted Congressman Henry Waxman, a California Democrat, as declaring that "there is no doubt in my mind that if the same disease had appeared among Americans of Norwegian descent, or among tennis players, rather than among gay males, the response of both the government and the medical community would have been different."[16]

O'Malley helped conduct the very first studies of sexually transmitted diseases among gay men. Focused primarily on the growing rate of infection for Hepatitis B among gay men in the mid-to-late 1970s, O'Malley used his background as an STD counselor for the US Air Force during the Vietnam War to his advantage. O'Malley said he witnessed firsthand the close relationship Shilts developed with Dritz, suggesting that Shilts gained unfair (and perhaps inappropriate) access to health department records and investigations into the spread of STDs in the city. "Shilts interviewed a lot of [the] people [investigated by Dritz's team] himself, and the concern was always, 'How did he get confirmation on some of this information?'" O'Malley said.[17]

On March 23, 1983, Shilts caused a major stir when he wrote an exclusive story about a confidential public health report he had obtained through means he would not disclose. The report estimated that 1 of every 350 single men in San Francisco would likely contract an infection known as HIV by the end of the year. The report, purportedly leaked to Shilts by his friend Bill Kraus, a congressional aide to US representative Phillip Burton (and later to his wife, Sala Burton, who succeeded Burton after his death), was startling in its frankness about the already emerging reality of how the mysterious disease would ultimately decimate the San Francisco gay male community.[18] Researcher James Kinsella noted, "Not included in [Shilts's] bleak summary was the number of people who had been infected with the virus, but were not showing any signs of the illness. No one knew that total, which was the population most likely to be passing on the disease." Kinsella raised the specter that in writing these stories, Shilts couldn't help but think back on his own life and begin to realize that his odds of having come in contact with the disease were frighteningly high.[19]

Gay leaders lambasted Shilts's report as misleading and as dangerous ammunition for those who advocated quarantines for gay men and for those who just placed the blame on gay men for the emerging health crisis, Kinsella noting that response to Shilts was "quick and harsh." Of particular concern to gay leaders were details raised in the report about gay sexual practices that, for many, centered on the city's wide-open gay bathhouses, where multiple partners could be engaged in a wide array of sexual conduct. Gay men, previously suppressed in their sexual expression, had viewed the city's tolerant attitude toward gay sex as emancipating and feared that bathhouse closures or restrictions would be a troubling step backward. Shilts wasn't backing down, however; in May 1983 he wrote an analysis piece that discussed the phenomenon of some gay men just giving up, resigned to the inevitability of AIDS infection, and thus doing what they wanted to do sexually and socially for as long as they could. Such reporting by Shilts, Kinsella noted, "further goad[ed] the gay community which was sensitive about its privacy. Some feared publicizing the minority of gays who continued to play the game of high-risk sex with many partners might just be what homophobes could use to quarantine gays or bring back other primitive measures left behind in a not-so-distant past. Some gays also believed that publicity about AIDS could taint them and reduce their political power in San Francisco."[20] One of Shilts's editors during this period, Keith Power, a former assistant editor at the *Chronicle*, offers that in retrospect, "it is difficult to reconstruct those early days of the AIDS plague . . . to hear the hysteria and see the anger and fear of the unknown in people's faces. The fact that it is difficult is Randy Shilts's bequest to San Francisco. He made us understand." Power admitted that Shilts's journalistic pedigree prior to arriving in the *Chronicle* newsroom provided him "faint qualifications, many of us believed, to be hired to write for our newspaper." Quickly, Power said, Shilts's enthusiasm, energy, and courage captivated him. "We did not anticipate the sheer productivity of this young man," Power recalled, although there were some who would groan during daily editorial meetings: "Not another AIDS story!"[21]

Power attributes to Shilts a "campaign" via his reporting for the *Chronicle* to shut down the city's bathhouses and his ongoing commitment to call attention to the need for gays to move their liberation movement beyond "reckless" sexual affairs and drug-enhanced lifestyles. Many resisted Shilts's call for a change to the hard-fought personal freedoms of gays, Power noted, indicating he detected that a "shadow" hung over Shilts in the latter years they worked together as the AIDS story grew.

Over time, Shilts began to turn his reporting interest almost full time to the emerging story of AIDS, much to the dislike of several gay leaders in the community. Shilts said that many of them viewed AIDS as a massive public relations problem, one that was even secondary to ongoing civil rights struggles to overturn housing and employment discrimination or even persisting sodomy laws in many states that made homosexual sex a criminal act. Shilts said that gay leaders were ill-equipped to "let go of civil rights rhetoric in favor of public health rhetoric" and were slow to recognize that the seriousness of AIDS was overtaking the gay rights or gay liberation "movements." Asked outright by some gay leaders to stop writing about GRID (and later AIDS), Shilts said, "I told them I don't get paid to *not* write news stories. To me it was so obvious the news value was there. It just made me so mad. Who were these elders of Zion who were going to decide what gay people had a right to know or not? You see, if I had been serving what was then perceived as the political interest of the gay community, I would not have written about AIDS."[22]

When Shilts finally followed up with Conant, the doctor recalls his first interactions with the young reporter as being abrupt and efficient. Initially, Shilts focused on GRID's most obvious manifestation, the embarrassing and unsightly purple and black skin lesions that were showing up among gay men: Kaposi's sarcoma. As an openly gay dermatologist, Conant was a natural choice for gay men to seek out for help, and his practice treating KS patients grew quickly. Tensions about the treatment in mainstream medical clinics of patients who had some unknown form of a communicable disease grew as well. Pressures prompted Conant and others to form a foundation to help pay for KS care for uninsured patients and to fund research; they also started work on reviving a local public hospital where patients officially diagnosed with GRID (later AIDS) could receive treatment without the scorn and fear permeating other medical facilities, such as those at the University of California, UCLA, and Stanford University. Shilts's inquiries to Dr. Conant became more frequent and more serious as Shilts reported on efforts to get a specialized clinic and ward started to treat patients with GRID-type maladies. "Over time, we became quite close and I would call him, or he would call me, depending on what was going on, and I was a frequent source for him," Conant said. Conant said Shilts was very committed to having medical and scientific facts correct, so "he would let me hold forth and then he would send me copies of what he was going to write, just before he published it. He was very gracious about that. I cannot recall ever having to make even one suggestion about a change in something that he wrote. He was a damn good reporter.... I never had any problems with him at all regarding the accuracy of his writing." Conant clarifies, however, that Shilts was not simply acting as a conduit for information. "He could be very challenging at times," Conant said. "He wanted, and I appreciate it, more than an opinion. He wanted, if not evidence, at least a strong argument for any position you offered."[23]

Whether he knew it or not, Shilts's reporting had impact. His reporting flowed from a workman-like commitment to checking in with sources on a regular basis, and it began to attract attention. Dr. Arthur J. Ammann, a pediatric AIDS immunologist who attempted to draw down some of the first state-level funds ever appropriated for AIDS research, felt that attention. Ammann had submitted an application for his work at the University of California but was growing frustrated by the slow response. During one of Shilts's routine check-in calls to see what was new, Ammann briefly mentioned his concern, prompting a new Shilts story:

"UC Researcher Accuses University of Withholding Funding for AIDS Research."
Ammann felt the sting of his closeness to Shilts—his bosses were unhappy, and
"everyone who put in an application was awarded money except me."[24]

It's clear that in the earliest days of the pandemic, Shilts viewed the AIDS
story as a deep well for important and impactful news stories. One of the more
controversial stories Shilts undertook raised eyebrows both locally and across
the nation because of the questions it raised about the actual transmission of the
virus causing AIDS. In March 1985 Shilts reported on the story of Mary Agnes
Bauer, a seventy-year-old San Bruno, California, grandmother, who had died of
AIDS-related causes in September 1984. Bulldogging his way into finding out
Mrs. Bauer's name and never pausing before printing it, Shilts reported that Mrs.
Bauer had fallen ill after receiving contaminated blood transfusions during heart
bypass surgery in 1979. More alarming, however, were claims by Mrs. Bauer's
seventy-two-year-old husband, Donald, that he had now contracted AIDS from
his wife through saliva from kissing her. Shilts wrote, "If Bauer is suffering from
AIDS, he would be the first known patient to have contracted the virus through
saliva." It was a big claim and one that health officials locally and with the CDC
immediately questioned. None of that slowed down Shilts, who even reported
a conversation he engaged in with the Bauers' family physician, who publicly
confirmed that the elderly couple no longer were sexually active; therefore, saliva
was the only known means of transmission between them. "This is a very affec-
tionate family," the doctor told Shilts. "Mr. and Mrs. Bauer kissed each other on
the mouth all the time. They were very supportive of each other."[25]

For its pick-up of the story for the national wire, the Associated Press said
Shilts's story in the *San Francisco Chronicle* "quoted unnamed sources as saying
health problems had forced the couple to cease marital relations for several years
before Mrs. Bauer received the contaminated blood transfusion. The newspaper
said health officials said the case raises the possibility that the deadly disease
was transmitted from the wife to her husband through saliva—which, if confirmed, would be the first such documented case. The *Chronicle* did not name
the officials."[26]

Kinsella wrote an expansive review of media coverage of the AIDS crisis and
captured the anger and eventually outrage that Shilts's story had inspired. Just
as AIDS researchers and advocates for people battling the disease thought they
were making progress with their findings about the limited transmittable nature
of the virus that caused AIDS, Shilts revived the saliva scare. Most experts in 1985
were convinced that the virus causing AIDS was not able to survive in saliva long

enough for transmission and that the primary means of transmission remained either unchecked blood transfusions or sexual intercourse that resulted in contact with human blood. "Any reader breezing through the *Chronicle* [the day Shilts's original story appeared] had good reason to be alarmed," Kinsella wrote. The experts casting doubt on the claim by Donald Bauer and his doctor that he had contracted AIDS through kissing his wife were buried back on page 16, while the startling claims were on page 1. Kinsella added, "Officials at the CDC said they had tested Donald Bauer's blood and found he did not even have antibodies to the AIDS virus, much less the full-blown disease. Despite the CDC's heavy-hitting denial, Shilts went on to describe the fear among Bauer family members about catching AIDS from their grandmother or grandfather. Another *Chronicle* reporter followed up the next day on Shilts's sensational story as it spread across the nation via news wires; that reporter quoted medical experts who cast serious doubt on the possibility of transmitting AIDS via saliva. Two weeks later, Kinsella noted, the *Chronicle* printed another story indicating that Donald Bauer did not have AIDS. Kinsella said the Bauer story highlights "the contradictory nature of America's best-known AIDS reporter" and summarized: "Shilts is an openly gay man whose strong connection to the story prompted him to cover it from early on. . . . He is also known by many of his colleagues as the reporter who most wanted to make his career with the AIDS story. Shilts was driven by the scoops the epidemic provided. So driven, in fact, that he sometime[s] played too fast and loose with the facts or overdramatized the news. The Bauers from San Bruno were just one example."[27]

Shilts also made waves inside newsrooms across the country by openly proclaiming his disdain for American media coverage of gay-related issues and the AIDS crisis. His critique of his fellow journalists was on full display in an August 3, 1985, *Chronicle* article carried on the news pages (as opposed to the editorial or opinion pages and in the days before Shilts was given an opinion column) in which Shilts complained about the "recent explosion in media coverage of AIDS" in the days following the July 25, 1985, disclosure by famed Hollywood leading man Rock Hudson that he had contracted AIDS. Shilts concluded, "The new-found interest in AIDS only highlights the sorry truth that most American media have given the AIDS story only haphazard attention from the start"—but Shilts would somewhat contradict himself later when he would point to Hudson's HIV disclosure as an important "demarcation point" in the American understanding and awareness of AIDS. At the time, Shilts's anger and bitterness slipped in, although he reflected the views of many at the time: "It should not have taken the diagnosis of a movie star to nudge the nation's television networks, newsmagazines and national dailies into serious AIDS coverage. By anybody's standards, more than 12,000 Americans dead or dying from a disease nobody even heard of just four years ago is a giant news story. Still, outside San Francisco, the subject has evaded the kind of thorough coverage any comparable threat to public health would engender."[28] Expanding on his theme, Shilts told *San Francisco Focus* magazine, "I think history will record the news media's response on AIDS as one of the darkest chapters in our profession. After Vietnam and Watergate, reporters became very aggressive in their pursuit of the truth. We stopped settling for press releases. We were going to find out what the truth was. Not the official truth, but the real truth. But in covering AIDS, we've generally had newswriting by press release."[29]

By any standard or measure, Shilts was an incredibly productive newspaper writer. His editors and colleagues marveled at how much copy he was able to churn out on a regular basis and not just on topics that had captured his interest. His drive to always do more served him well in "feeding the newsroom beast," which is rarely satiated.

In the middle of Shilts's growing portfolio of articles about the AIDS crisis, the destructive and deadly Loma Prieta earthquake struck the San Francisco Bay area just after 5:00 p.m. on Tuesday, October 17, 1989. Shilts was at his desk at the *Chronicle* in his new role as assistant city editor, and along with reporter and friend Susan Sward he coordinated the literally hundreds of news reports and updates pouring in from *Chronicle* reporters and outside sources as the scope of the 6.9 magnitude quake became known. In the end, sixty-three people died, more than thirty-seven hundred were injured, and many thousands more were left homeless.

Editors at the *Chronicle* later asked Shilts to lead the compilation of the newspaper stories and photographs of the quake in a book entitled *The Quake of '89*. Shilts's essay "Lessons," which introduced the text, was a classic showcase for his strong views about shared responsibility. The earthquake's destruction "posed troubling questions, not only for the Bay Area and not only about earthquakes, but also for the nation and for the great social conflicts that churn beneath the seemingly tranquil surface of society." Focusing on the collapse of large portions of Interstate 880 that were known as the Cypress Street Viaduct in economically challenged Oakland, where forty-two of the sixty-three fatalities from the quake occurred, Shilts said the collapsed two-tier section of the freeway was a "social and political metaphor for our era." Noting that experts had often questioned the safety of the freeway in a big quake (the freeway was constructed in 1957), Shilts said the sharing of the blame for the tragedy should be widespread.[30] Friend and fellow journalist David Israels said he was impressed at Shilts's ability to pull such a large and developing story together: "I remember talking to Randy about that, asking him 'How the hell did you do that?' He just looked blasé about it and just said, 'That's what I do. They picked me because I write so fast.' Here he was at the computer, and he was getting how many reports from out in the field, sending in reports, and he pulled it all together. That is a pretty amazing accomplishment."[31]

The distinguishing characteristic of Shilts's reporting, however, beyond covering general assignment or other local stories, has to be the direction or outline that reporting provides for Shilts's overall scholarship on AIDS, gay civil rights, and gay military service during his tenure as a reporter for the *San Francisco Chronicle*.

Although Shilts would later assert that "not one bad thing happened" to him in the *Chronicle*'s newsroom, he did describe a short struggle he had in getting one of his very first articles printed about the new "gay cancer" that was to become the AIDS pandemic. Angered that his story about a local support group known as the Shanti Project had languished on an editor's desk for three weeks and hearing rumors that the story had been the butt of a joke by someone in an editors meeting, Shilts went into overdrive. Visiting the *Chronicle*'s morgue and the local library, he compiled a growing stack of articles the paper had run about the widely reported public health issues of Legionnaires' disease and toxic shock syndrome that affected a relatively small number of Americans. Media scholar Edward Alwood reported that the expected confrontation with the *Chronicle*'s editors never occurred—before he could present his counterargument with coverage afforded Legionnaires' disease and toxic shock syndrome, Shilts's article ran, and he quickly moved on to his next assignments, all of them increasingly focused on the growing issue of "gay cancer" and its widespread implications.[32]

Shilts's mostly positive assessment of his personal interactions at the *Chronicle* left out a painful incident that occurred not too long after his arrival in the newsroom. Jerry Roberts, who later would become the paper's managing editor, retold the story of a meeting of the NewsGuild–CWA, the union for newspaper journalists, one afternoon when Shilts rose and asked the local guild to consider endorsing health benefits for domestic partners of *Chronicle* staff. "One of his colleagues shouted, 'Sit down, you little faggot,'" Roberts said. "Nobody stood up to defend Randy, who left the meeting in tears, which tells you something about the enlightened views of the San Francisco press corps about gay rights at the time."[33]

Years later, Shilts took up the domestic partner benefits issue again, lobbying his bosses on behalf of issues important to him, including hammering out a friendly but direct letter to both William Randolph Hearst III, the publisher of the *San Francisco Examiner,* and Richard Thieriot, publisher and editor of the *San Francisco Chronicle.* The letter petitioned both men to consider backing adoption of a nondiscrimination statement for their newspapers based on "sexual or affectional orientation" that was currently being discussed by members of the NewsGuild and the papers' owners. He told Hearst and Thieriot, "I have never before had to bring any issue to your attention or in any way intervene in your handling of the paper. This largely reflects the fact that I feel I have consistently been treated with respect and professionalism by every level of *Chronicle* management as well as by my colleagues. As far as *Chronicle* employees go, I'm pretty much a happy camper." Shilts wrote about his years of struggle before joining the *Chronicle:* "I often felt the sting of job discrimination" while being rejected by newspaper editors and TV news directors who wouldn't hire an openly gay reporter. Shilts believed the *Chronicle* could take the lead in removing that sting: "Non-discrimination is not an industry standard when it comes to the news business. Even in San Francisco. It needs to be, and *The Chronicle's* endorsement of [nondiscrimination] would send a strong message that a new day is at hand in regards to their personnel."[34]

Roberts recalled Shilts as a reporter during his "pre-AIDS fame" and a series of reports he wrote about alleged physical brutality against gay citizens and others by members of the San Francisco Police Department. Shilts's "original tip [for the story] came from complaints from gays about being harassed by cops," Roberts noted, "but by the time he was done, it was in no way, shape or form a 'gay piece,' just a good, solid investigation of an under-the-radar problem in city government that affected everyone."[35] Another one of his earliest *Chronicle* stories also gained notice after Shilts voluntarily spent the weekend locked up in the Queen's Tank, a special cell at the city's jail for cross-dressing and obviously gay inmates.

Shilts's book editor, Michael Denneny, said he believed Shilts was "in love" with the idea of being a journalist. "I think of him as a classic journalist," Denneny said. "Somebody who took the almost romantic notion of being a journalist, totally believed it, and lived it out." His love affair with the role of journalism was at the heart of a lot of the criticism leveled against him by fellow gays, many of whom labeled him an assimilationist because "he chose to write about gay issues for the mainstream press precisely because he wanted other [heterosexual] people to know what it was like to be gay. If they didn't know, how were things going to change?" said Shilts's literary assistant and friend Linda Alband.[36]

Neither Shilts nor his editors at the *Chronicle* seemed to make much of an effort to separate his news reporting on various topics from his opinion pieces from a weekly editorial column he was granted under the title "AIDS: The Inside Story." A classic example is the *Chronicle*'s coverage of the sad "milestone" achieved as the number of US AIDS cases recorded by the Centers for Disease Control topped one hundred thousand in July 1989. Shilts wrote poignantly: "Someday this week in suburban Atlanta, the AIDS program of the federal Centers for Disease Control will receive a phone call from a state health department providing its latest statistics on the disease. The calls come in every day of the week, but this one will mark the watershed in the history of acquired immune deficiency syndrome: it will put the number of diagnosed AIDS cases in the United States over 100,000. ... And still the disease rages." Shilts recorded that the "march" of AIDS across America had been swift: in six and a half years, the epidemic had reached fifty thousand cases; the next fifty thousand cases occurred in just the eighteen short months that followed. "There have been no new, novel, or surprising outbreaks of the disease. Indeed, the people who have tended to get AIDS are just getting it in far greater numbers." Shilts signaled other problems, however, that reflected his growing fear that the AIDS story had been tuned out by many Americans: "Although heterosexual AIDS is emerging as a dark and chewing problem for minorities in inner cities, the national heterosexual epidemic some experts feared several years ago has not materialized. Although AIDS is turning into a disease of the underclass on the East Coast, it remains largely a disease of gay men in most other parts of the country."[37]

At the time of Shilts's story, gay men made up 61 percent of all AIDS cases in America, one in five cases in California alone. Shilts said the feared "second epidemic wave" of HIV and AIDS had not materialized to any great extent in the heterosexual community, although intravenous drug users, their partners, and their unborn children were at high risk. Even the feared risk to heterosexual populations via prostitution or other portions of the sex trade had not surfaced in any great way. "The bulk of white heterosexual cases in the coming years will be less likely coming from sexual contact than from blood transfusions dating back to the early 1980s," Shilts wrote. Shilts chose to quote AIDS expert June Osborn as noting the possibility of a "bleak nightmare" in which forty thousand new cases of AIDS would emerge each year, but because those cases were among gay men and other underclass segments of society there would be widespread acceptance of AIDS as just a reality for some Americans.[38]

Shilts's boyfriend and live-in lover during this period, Steve Newman, recalls that covering the AIDS beat was taking a great toll on their lives. Fully engaged and convinced that HIV and AIDS was "the story" of the gay liberation movement for a generation, Shilts had trouble letting loose of the stories he wrote. Newman said,

> He would say to me, "If I don't report this, no one will, and people will just keep on dying." But it really took a toll on him. He would come home from reporting and be very beaten-down and quite devastated from the reactions he would get from some people. He would come home night after night and take a Quaalude and then start drinking heavily, and by the end of the evening, he was just blasted, and day after day it was no fun watching such a brilliant person drag themselves down in such a way in order to deal with what people were saying about him.[39]

Newman said he decided to confront Shilts about the situation and met with a brief flash of anger at the suggestion that he give up the AIDS beat and let someone else do some of the writing. "He was furious with me," Newman said. "He felt like it was the most important subject of our generation and that it was happening to a very marginalized population and that no one was going to report about it."[40]

Shilts stepped outside the AIDS story in one column that foreshadowed a homosexual debate yet to gain traction: that of gay marriage or domestic partnerships for same-sex couples. Using his column to explore a local domestic partners proposition that would apply only to San Francisco—Proposition S—Shilts linked the desire of some gay couples to register their partnerships with the city via Proposition S as helpful to building understanding of AIDS. Once again, Shilts revealed his worldview that words via journalism could perhaps change minds, quoting local activists and health officials about their belief that promoting stable relationships among gays could further understanding and support for AIDS funding. "By allowing gay partners to get some form of official recognition for their relationships," Shilts wrote, "[activists] feel it will help reinforce the message they've been dispensing throughout the AIDS epidemic: Reduce sexual contacts and don't spread this disease." Shilts downplayed the more controversial aspects of Proposition S that would provide bereavement benefits for unmarried couples (such as work leave) and requirements for hospitals to grant the same visitation rights to same-sex couples that they do to married couples. Using the personal stories of gay men who had lost partners because of AIDS and other causes, Shilts called opponents to Proposition S "vicious" and "callous" and concluded, "There is a cruel incongruity here. On one hand, some conservative clerics have fiercely criticized gay men for not rushing into monogamous relationships with the advent of AIDS. Now the same clergymen are violently opposing a law that could foster such pairings. Gay men quite literally are damned if they do and damned if they don't."[41]

The measure ultimately failed in a razor-thin vote margin of just 1,686 votes on Election Day, November 7, 1989, failing 50.4 percent to 49.5 percent, with just 168,178 votes cast citywide amid low voter turnout.[42] This loss caused grave disappointment in Shilts and others who worried that it signaled a weakening of gay political strength in the city. Mainstream media had covered Proposition S, but with the election coming just a month after a devastating earthquake, coverage of and, apparently, voter interest in the matter had faded.

Perhaps inspired by a growing concern that AIDS was becoming an old story with no new angles, a noteworthy shift appears in Shilts's work at the *Chronicle* during a particularly prolific period in October 1989. He produced four weekly columns of about a thousand words each and five major byline stories in addition to coordinating the *Chronicle*'s extensive coverage of the devastating Loma Prieta earthquake. The earthquake and its aftermath were not separate from the realities of AIDS for Shilts, as evidenced by his column one month after the deadly shake. He opined, "Death, an issue once so comfortably distant, suddenly becomes an imminent threat," and linked the fears of thousands of Bay Area residents amid aftershocks rattling their homes with the fear people with AIDS must feel. "Death becomes a preoccupation," Shilts wrote. "Sleeping is difficult, nightmares are frequent. A vague, nameless depression sets in"—feelings all too familiar to an estimated thirty-five thousand gay men in San Francisco (one in twenty city residents at that time) living with HIV and AIDS. Buttressing his provocative analogy, Shilts noted, "Experts say the psychological stresses imposed by the earthquake bear striking similarities to those raised by infection with a virus that can kill you."[43]

One expert quoted by Shilts compared living with AIDS to suffering the trauma of a massive earthquake every day and noted that while earthquakes may have a widespread impact on the entire community, a virus such as HIV leaves some of its victims feeling isolated and targeted. "HIV-infected people typically must work and live within a larger society that barely recognizes the huge numbers of HIV-stricken people in its midst. This leads to a depressing sense of isolation," Shilts wrote. While Shilts's column explored an interesting direction in which to take the *Chronicle*'s ongoing coverage of the Loma Prieta earthquake and the AIDS epidemic, both of which were dramatically impacting the city, the tone and basis for the column must have struck some readers as a rather odd correlation held together by a rather thin string of relevance.

In a subsequent news article and in his opinion column, Shilts led criticism of federal funding for AIDS, which trailed resources allocated for drought relief for farmers. His critique came as part of his coverage of the American Foundation for AIDS Research Conference, which drew twenty-five hundred doctors, nurses, and researchers to San Francisco.[44] *Chronicle* readers were given a second day of coverage for the conference, with Shilts reporting that federal officials expected a "dawning age of intervention with AIDS" that could help reduce the number of cases expected in the coming decade.[45] Shilts's article covered remarks from Dr. Anthony Fauci, associate director for AIDS research with the National Institutes of Health. Fauci, who would earn Shilts's particular scorn for the manner in which the NIH approved AIDS treatment drugs, told Shilts, "We have proven conceptually that you can control HIV infection. We can't cure it yet . . . but the skeptics who said that we could never find a cure or control of it have already been proven incorrect." Shilts contextualized Fauci's optimism with a prominent reminder that no vaccine to prevent HIV infection was forthcoming anytime soon.

Coming on the heels of these reports, two days later Shilts then offered a nearly six-thousand-word story that explored the federal government's role in helping force down the cost of expensive drugs for AIDS treatment such as AZT. Shilts quoted a top US Department of Health and Human Services official questioning the "social responsibility" of some drug manufacturers, focusing specifically on the ongoing battle with massive drug maker Burroughs Wellcome, the manufacturer of AZT.[46] Shilts followed up this article with another piece just weeks later, further exploring the AIDS drug-pricing wars. He noted that some manufacturers had earned the title "the great Satans of the AIDS epidemic" and focused his vitriol particularly on a small company known as Lyphomed Inc., makers of an aerosolized version of the antibiotic drug pentamidine, used to treat pneumonia and other lung infections. Consistent with his normally balanced approach, Shilts told of the struggles to get AIDS treatment drugs into the hands of those who needed them, but he warned that "many public health officials and AIDS researchers are worrying that the politicization of drug pricing may drive pharmaceutical companies away from manufacturing AIDS medications."[47]

In early December 1989, in three articles of more than four thousand words each, Shilts attempted to link the struggle of people living with HIV to include hemophiliacs. His analysis of the responses to people infected with HIV via their needed blood products rang familiar. He noted that more than 60 percent of the nation's twenty thousand hemophiliacs carried the HIV virus. He reported that special problems existed for hemophiliacs, including lack of knowledge of HIV treatment by their physicians, who were unaccustomed to dealing with the emerging virus.[48]

Perhaps inspired by the calls for reduced drug costs for people living with AIDS, Shilts churned out additional editorial columns that explored the fact that the need was not for altogether new treatment programs but for more parity in how they were accessed by all those in need. He also warned about the fact that as long as access to basic health care coverage eluded more than thirty-one million Americans (by federal estimates), coalitions to bridge gaps in health care for all needs—not just AIDS—would be necessary.[49]

For all of Shilts's columns championing the need to lower costs for AIDS treatment drugs and the need for more government-supported research for a vaccine or "cure" of some sort, he still could win and influence enemies perhaps quicker than any reporter who ventured to cover any gay issue. His December 11, 1989, column, "Patiently Tiptoeing through the World of Word Twisters," took on a "helpful glossary of politically correct terms" handed out to reporters at a recent AIDS conference. His attempt at humorous commentary would win him even more scorn, especially among gay leaders. Declaring the efforts "gobbledygook" and recording the arrival of the "AIDS Word Police," who sought to enforce "AID-Speak," Shilts openly bemoaned the effort by some to change the nomenclature of language from "AIDS victim" or "AIDS sufferer" to "person with AIDS," or "prostitute" to "sex industry worker," or "IV drug abuser" to "injection drug user." He noted, "In no medical crisis has the politics of language become such a central issue, leaving journalists and researchers to tiptoe their way through a minefield of linguistic sensibilities." Shilts said the problem with this form of "word doctoring" was that it represented what he saw as "well-intentioned eagerness to use the language to bend the public mind" as a tool of manipulation rather than illumination. "What's most troubling about all this grousing from AIDS groups, however, is that it distracts attention from the truly profound issues confronting our society in the HIV epidemic," he wrote. "At a time when the federal government is not devoting anything resembling adequate resources to prevent the epidemic's spread and to speed the development of treatments—both issues that are life and death matters for hundreds of thousands of people—it's difficult to take the complaints about the word 'sufferer' very seriously."[50]

Shilts's column mirrored the article he wrote for *Mother Jones Magazine* in November 1989 titled "The Era of Bad Feelings," which reviewed the highly contentious International Conference on AIDS, held in June 1989 in Montreal. In that article, Shilts turned his attention to both ACT-UP and another ad-hoc protest group, People with Immune System Diseases (PISSED): "The age of gentility between activists and researchers had passed, perhaps forever. It had been coming for more than a year, this 'Era of Bad Feelings.' If the scientists had been less keen on analyzing the statistical parameters of their research papers and had fleshed out the human dimensions of their studies, they probably could have seen it coming."[51]

While Shilts's article pointed out the controversial tactics protestors had used to interrupt the proceedings at Montreal, he showed some alliance with their efforts. "Many of [the protesting men] had waited, patiently and politely, through these conferences before," he wrote. The protestors had "wait[ed] for word of some breakthrough. Wait[ed] for the scientists to produce results from their hundreds of millions of dollars in research grants. Wait[ed] for hope. But hope was long in coming." He said that, as a result, protestors could no longer wait for hope. "They went to the conference themselves to tell the scientists that it was no longer enough for the world to understand science; it was time for researchers to understand the world and what the world expected from them." His report for *Mother Jones* took on a religious tone, Shilts writing that conference presenters used "slides, curves and calculations, the Scriptures of the scientific faith," that the "clicking of the slide projector echoed through the hall like the rapping of rosary beads," and that "as the slides clicked by, a jaw occasionally dropped open, as if to receive the host. But the slides offered no hint of absolution."[52]

While Shilts continued to take issue with the overall news media coverage of AIDS, his criticism bypassed his employer, the *San Francisco Chronicle*. Shilts set his bosses out as the exception, noting that he and his editors had decided early on to move the AIDS story from "just" a science or medical story to one that also had social and public policy implications. The *Chronicle* was not shy about promoting Shilts's growing prominence as "the AIDS reporter" in mainstream journalism, running full-page advertisements in its own publication and in *Editor & Publisher* magazine. The ads trumpeted Shilts's work "as the nation's first full-time reporter covering the AIDS story," adding that "for five years San Francisco read his AIDS reporting in our paper. . . . Long before the government, the general public, and most newspapers began taking AIDS seriously, one reporter, and one paper, wrote about AIDS day in and day out. . . . We're proud of Randy Shilts. And proud we were printing his stories, even when not everyone was ready to listen."[53]

Through his stories for the *Chronicle*, Shilts was honing his later thesis that "the groups most victimized by acquired immune deficiency syndrome are not exactly an honor roll of America's favorite minorities." Shilts wrote, "It is noteworthy that San Francisco is both the only city where the local media have most consistently covered AIDS and the city which boasts the best public AIDS educational and treatment programs." This statement affirms again Shilts's belief in the power of journalism to shape and even change realities.[54] Shilts said that mainstream journalism struggled so much with covering AIDS because of the nature of its transmission, primarily via anal intercourse among gay men. "The media has never been comfortable with anything homosexual," he said. "The media's job is to be the watchdog of government, but it didn't do that, so the government was left to do things as they saw fit."[55]

Belva Davis, one of Shilts's colleagues from his TV reporting days at KQED, said Shilts had strong opinions about AIDS and its transmission among gay men: "I don't know of any good reporter who works on a story that doesn't have an opinion of some sort. If a story is worth doing, they feel strongly about it. It is our job to inform people about the good, the bad, and the ugly. I know that is a horrible cliché, but that is what Randy should have been doing. He was making people aware of a real life-threatening danger."[56] Shilts's own words seem to affirm such ideas. He told gay historian Eric Marcus in a 1989 interview, "I have a very strong point of view and I think most journalists in general, and particularly in the gay community, don't have a point of view because they're too afraid. They don't have the courage to say, 'Here's my analysis of the situation.'" He added that he "felt strongly that if you laid out all the facts that there is obviously one side that is right, but it was my job to do both sides," causing friction with activists and advocates who struggled with independent analysis of gay issues. Gay leaders often foisted upon him an expectation that he should "articulate the gay point of view," but Shilts insisted, "That's where I think a lot of people are just very naïve."[57]

When Alan Mutter joined the *San Francisco Chronicle* as city editor, Shilts's "big personality" surprised him. Mutter had only known about Shilts from reading the explicit and prominently placed articles Shilts was churning out on the AIDS crisis. He soon concluded that Shilts was bound to be a journalistic star. "At first I thought he was quite unlike anyone I had ever known, but then the more that I got to know him, I realized he was a lot like the many other great reporters I have known," Mutter said. "I came to admire him enormously. He was a bit more theatrical than the average reporter, but he was very head down, hard-nosed and hardworking. He was very serious down underneath this veneer of showmanship." Mutter found himself "shocked" and "amazed" at the frank nature of the AIDS reporting Shilts and fellow writer David Perlman were doing. He said, "Before I left Chicago the idea of us covering gays at all was almost unthinkable. The idea that a newspaper would write about gay sex was unbelievable. The idea that a newspaper would write about gay sex in gay bathhouses, or gay diseases, was simply out of the question." Back in Chicago, a health reporter there had approached him about a doing a story on immune-system related illnesses striking some of the city's gay men, but it received little attention. The stories and headlines Shilts was producing for the front page of the *Chronicle* were "about things that people don't talk about. That was the environment that we were in," Mutter said.[58]

Shilts seemed to share the same view about the novelty of what he was able to write about at the *Chronicle*, noting, "It was a matter, always, of breaking barriers of what was permissible to say," he said. "If you had told me 10 years ago that we were going to have something about anal intercourse in the paper every day, the way we do today, I never would have believed it."[59]

As part of his growing influence in San Francisco as a leader on AIDS-related issues, Shilts joined a group of community leaders for a special trip to Africa and filed noteworthy stories about how AIDS was affecting communities far across the globe, including a two-thousand-word article from Rakai, Uganda. Shilts identified central Africa as "ground zero of the AIDS epidemic" and noted, "Health officials consider the region's hot and dusty villages to be at the front line of the international war against the deadly disease." Contrasting the fact that AIDS was impacting primarily heterosexual individuals in Africa, Shilts declared that "it is here, in the equatorial belt of central Africa, that the disease is believed to have begun. It is here that the AIDS virus has become more entrenched than anywhere else on Earth."[60] Shilts's assuredness about the starting line for AIDS in Africa won him scorn not only among some social scientists but also among his African hosts. According to Davis, who was on the trip representing her new bosses at KTVU-TV, the tour group's African hosts grew insulted by Shilts's running dialogue, which made similar claims while on the ground in Africa. "I thought I was going to have to save his life," Davis said. "He had come on this trip to learn about the genesis of AIDS. He was traveling with an all-black group, and he was just being Randy, just saying what he thought, and the last thing these people wanted to hear was Randy's thoughts about whether AIDS could or should be traced back to Africa. Their attitude was that this was another example of Americans trying to blame someone else."[61]

Despite these personal miscues, Shilts's reporting from Africa was typically detailed and comprehensive, considering AIDS not only in Uganda but also in Burundi, Kenya, Malawi, Rwanda, Tanzania, and Zaire. He paid particular attention to the radical changes in sexual lifestyles and cultural mores that had helped to stem the transmission in Africa but had not altogether stopped it. It was a familiar theme for Shilts, who had written about similar ideas in the gay community for many years.

FIGURE 1. An elementary school photo of Randy Shilts from Aurora, Illinois. (Photo courtesy Gary Shilts)

FIGURE 2. Brothers Randy and Reed Shilts dressed for church at the Calumet Street house in Aurora, Illinois, circa 1962. (Photo courtesy Reed Shilts)

FIGURE 3. Randy Shilts shown with members of the National Forensics League debate team at West Aurora High School, circa 1966. (Photo from West Aurora High School Eos Yearbook)

FIGURE 4. A 1974 photo of Randy Shilts writing a story on a typewriter in the newsroom of the *Daily Emerald*, the student newspaper at the University of Oregon. (Photo by Beth Van Deesen, *Northwest Gay Review*, December 1974)

FIGURE 5. Randy Shilts and his one-time partner Steve Newman on the Pacific Coast. (Photo courtesy Steve Newman)

FIGURE 6. Randy Shilts interviews San Francisco City Supervisor Harvey Milk in early 1978 for a report on KQED-TV. (Photo courtesy KQED / San Francisco State University)

FIGURE 7. A 1982 photo of Randy Shilts for a story about the release of his first book, *The Mayor of Castro Street*. (Photo by Gary Friedman, *Los Angeles Times*)

FIGURE 8. Shilts waits to use a Geary Street bank machine on a rainy day in San Francisco. (Photo by Steve Newman)

FIGURE 9. Shilts poses along the Pacific Coast on a weekend getaway. (Photo courtesy Reed Shilts)

FIGURE 10. Randy Shilts in the newsroom of the *San Francisco Chronicle* circa 1988. (Photo by E. Luge, *Bay Area Reporter*)

FIGURE 11. In Houston in November 1987 promoting *And the Band Played On* with Buddy Johnston, host of a groundbreaking LGBT radio program, *After Hours*, on KPFT-FM. (Photo courtesy Buddy Johnston)

FIGURE 12. Randy Shilts on a tour of the USS *Constitution* at Charlestown Naval Yard as he researched his third book, *Conduct Unbecoming*. (Photo courtesy Reed Shilts)

FIGURE 13. The Shilts family gathered in 1984. *Top row, left to right*, Bud (and his second wife) Pat, and Reed Shilts. *Front row*, David, Randy, and Gary Shilts. (Photo courtesy Reed Shilts)

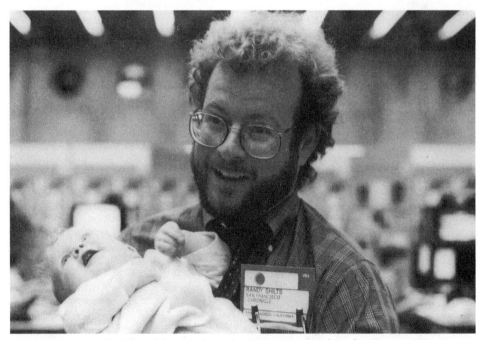

FIGURE 14. Randy Shilts holding a baby at the 1990 International Conference on AIDS in San Francisco. (Photo courtesy Dr. Will Schlotterer)

FIGURE 15. Posing with his beloved dog, Dash, Shilts in 1993 a little more than a year before he died. (Photo by Phyllis Christopher)

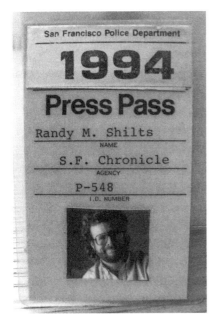

FIGURE 16. Randy Shilts's press pass, issued by the San Francisco Police Department. A copy of the pass was attached to his casket for his February 1994 memorial service. (Photo by Andrew E. Stoner)

FIGURE 17. Posing with his beloved dog Dash and his partner Barry Barbieri, Shilts in one of his annual "Shiltsmas" holiday cards. (Photo courtesy of Reed Shilts)

FIGURE 18. Artist-illustrator David Levine created this image of Shilts for the *New York Review of Books*. (David Levine Archives)

FIGURE 19. Randy Shilts's image was among the first twenty installed on the Rainbow Honor Walk in San Francisco. Shilts is memorialized near the corner of 19th and Castro Streets. (Photo by J. Wesley Cunningham)

FIGURE 20. Randy Shilts's February 1994 funeral drew protestors from the Westboro Baptist Church and counter-protestors, such as those here outside Glide Memorial Church. (Photo by Andrew Ferguson)

# CHAPTER 7

# Bathhouse Daze

Shilts settled early on the idea that ground zero for the emerging AIDS battle in the United States was to be found inside gay bathhouses, once a symbol and artifact of an achieved level of independence and freedom (particularly for gay men) but now a dark corner of an increasingly troubling saga. Author Ira Tattelman noted the role bathhouses played in the "emergence of the gay male community in the latter half of the twentieth century," explaining that they "provide[d] a public place where a wide mix of strangers [could] come together.... Tolerant of difference, open to a diversity of issues, the public territory of the bathhouse [gave] men the space to define, support, or flaunt their sexual interests.... As one factor in the development of a gay identity, the baths [offered] variety and opportunity, and propose[d] new ways to explore relationships between men."[1]

Nowhere was the battle for the continued role of the gay bathhouse more in play than in San Francisco. Shilts's *Chronicle* colleague David Perlman believed that Shilts's role in the emerging bathhouse battle was "fascinating" and took note of the fact that as a member of the gay community he was "a participant in the life of that community [and] remained a good reporter throughout, no matter how conflicted he may have been personally or felt personally. He never lost his sense of journalistic integrity, which is another quality that isn't always apparent in other people."[2] Analyzing his own role, Shilts cast his writing as a means of saving the lives of gay men:

> To be writing about a sexually transmitted disease and not write about the bathhouse institutions that everyone had sex in every weekend, where lots and

lots of people were having lots and lots of sex, would just have been dishon-
est. Here I was, writing stories about the failure of the Reagan administration,
[and] I felt it was my equal responsibility to write about the failure of the gay
community as well. When I started writing about the bathhouses—that did
not make a lot of people very happy. It was definitely the most painful period
of my life, because here I was trying to do something that I felt was trying to
save people's lives, and I was being called this malicious sellout who would do
anything to advance my career over the dead bodies of other gay men.[3]

Shilts's reporting on the bathhouse issue had consistently run head-on into what
journalist John-Manuel Andriote described as a challenge to the existing gay
establishment, which "refused to distinguish between sexual license and gay liberation." Amid accusations that Shilts and the activists who took up sides against
the bathhouses were tools of the heterosexual establishment, the fight wore on,
and Andriote noted that Shilts quickly became "a lightning rod for the wrath
of those in the community who considered themselves sacrosanct. Shilts was
demonized for daring to question the judgment of some gay people in the pages
of a so-called 'straight' newspaper, rather than simply caving in to pressure of gay
activists to keep it[,] as it were, 'in the family.'"[4]

Shilts earned the scorn he acquired. He admitted to purposefully timing his
articles to coincide with events in the gay community, including publishing one of
his very first AIDS articles before the start of Gay Pride in San Francisco in 1982.
He tried timing his articles on AIDS to get placement in a Friday edition of the
*Chronicle* in order to reach gay men before they went out for a weekend of anonymous sex in the bathhouses. "I wanted everyone to have the fear of God in them,"
Shilts said.[5] Shilts's November 15, 1983, article for the *Chronicle* under the inflammatory headline "Some AIDS Patients Still Going to the Baths" was emblematic
of the kinds of stories that incensed his critics. The story's intent was to explore
the complicated municipal ordinances that prevented the mayor of San Francisco
from directly closing the bathhouses, but its headline focused on people infected
with HIV or living with AIDS and their alleged sexual activity at the baths. The
bottom line was that no simple answer existed, but the headline of Shilts's story
bore little resemblance to the insider political discussion of how to handle bathhouses. Dr. Selma Dritz said that she had heard "through informal community
channels that some [AIDS patients] were going to the baths." His story also raised
the specter of quarantine for people with AIDS, a deputy city attorney saying that
while the city opposed people with AIDS going to bathhouses, there wasn't suf-
ficient evidence to quarantine anyone. In a show of balance, Shilts added a quote

near the end of his story from Martin Box, an AIDS patient who volunteered to work with the homeless and who asserted that the bathhouses filled a need for the homeless, allowing them a place to take a shower and clean up.[6]

Shilts often concerned himself with when his stories appeared, working editors not only for placement in the newspaper but also for particular days. One example of Shilts's effort to do so is in his June 15, 1984, "Political Scene" commentary, titled "On Bathhouse Politics." Shilts declared, "Among the only–in–San Francisco attractions to amaze delegates to the Democratic National Convention next month will be a new civic donnybrook over gay bathhouses," noting that "gay Democratic activists already are cringing at the possibility of a nationally-televised debate which will detract attention from more serious civil rights concerns." Shilts quoted an unnamed "prominent gay Democrat" as saying, "The cameras will be pointed at a bunch of crazies arguing for our right to commit suicide in sleazy bathhouses."[7] Shilts was completely overstating the attention the assembled Democrats from across the nation would pay to a specialized and localized story such as whether gay bathhouses should remain open. The DNC and its presumptive nominee, former vice president Walter Mondale, weren't in any way concerned about the bathhouse issue in the face of a daunting fall election against a popular incumbent president. It was an obvious overreach. In reality, how many DNC delegates descending on San Francisco that summer lived in a community where a gay bathhouse operated or had even heard of one? Further, in this instance Shilts's focus did not seem to be on how to curtail or prevent out-of-town conventioneers from exploring the gay bathhouse experience; instead, his intent was to foment the simmering political—albeit local—battle over the bathhouses' future.

Clifford L. Morrison, organizer of the AIDS Ward at San Francisco General Hospital, said he felt pressure from Shilts and others to join in the effort to force closure of the bathhouses. "I thought the bathhouses should have been closed," Morrison said. "It was obvious; we had enough information at the time. I essentially agreed with Randy Shilts; I just didn't agree with his message completely." Morrison said he felt caught between Shilts and one of his primary sources, Dr. Mervyn Silverman, the controversial San Francisco public health officer. Morrison said Shilts's anger with Silverman was because "Merv barred [Randy] from Grove Street [the administrative offices of the Department of Public Health]. Randy couldn't go in there and interview anybody, because Randy was constantly attacking Merv." Morrison recalled an "awful confrontation" between Silverman and Shilts at the 1989 International AIDS Conference in Montreal in which "Merv and Randy wound up yelling at each other." Morrison said, "Randy could be like an old dog with a bone. He was a fascinating person, but when he was on to something, he wouldn't let go of it. He was a journalist in the true sense of the word."[8]

*Chronicle* editor Alan Mutter affirmed that Shilts was convinced AIDS was spreading via unprotected sexual contact and used that as a starting point for most of his stories. Mutter said that Shilts "made sure that the story never went away" but did so "in the proper way that a reporter needs to when the story is this important." Mutter said it is his belief that good reporters continue "poking around" on stories that are important, because "we have seen people win Pulitzer Prizes at the tiniest of tiny newspapers because they saw something that just wasn't kosher and they pursued it. That was the level of engagement that Randy had. It wasn't about taking a point of view about the morality of things or the seediness of something. It was because he was a great journalist, and he could see that this was a great story. And it *was* a great story." Mutter believes it is important to remember that Shilts's enterprise in following a "non-AIDS story" at the height of the bathhouse battles of 1984 produced one of the only real "news" stories emanating that year from the upcoming Democratic National Convention in San Francisco. Mutter recalled that since Mondale had sewed up the nomination long before the convention, the only open question was whom he would select as a running mate. Shilts picked up information that the Mondale camp was seriously considering US representative Geraldine Ferraro of New York, the first woman named on a major party ticket for president or vice president. Shilts promptly jumped on a plane heading east to research Ferraro's background and as a result positioned the *Chronicle* to break the story of the barrier-breaking Mondale-Ferraro ticket. "Ferraro was not gay, so this was not a gay story at all," Mutter said. "This was a national political story, and Randy got that story for us. I still get chills when I think about it, because we would have looked like fools [with the convention in our city] if we had missed the story. Instead, Randy was spot on the story, and we had it."[9]

Among criticism and controversy with his coverage of the bathhouse issue, Shilts continued to score major stories that won him praise. On June 1, 1984, Shilts broke the story that Mayor Dianne Feinstein had ordered undercover police investigators to go into as many as fourteen of the city's bathhouses and report back to her on what they found. Shilts quoted Feinstein as saying that the probe was "entirely justified," as she was "increasingly alarmed at the politicization" of the bathhouse issue. He said Feinstein was "impressed" by the degree of high-risk sex that continued to take place according to the police reports she received. "My concern with this has nothing to do with anything I may or may not think about morality," Feinstein said. "It has to do with life versus death."[10] To the degree Shilts wanted to move forward with closing the bathhouses, the mayor's comments were helpful to that end, all the while scoring points for him with some activists who applauded his calling out of city officials for their clandestine investigation of gay sex in the city.

Shilts bulldozed forward into analysis to end his story by noting that Feinstein's actions highlighted a growing rift between her and the city's public health director, Dr. Silverman, who had been slow to order the bathhouses closed. Silverman defended his actions to Shilts, saying he was seeking the answer that was best for public health, not what was popular. Feinstein lacked the power to fire Silverman because of bureaucratic city rules that officially made him an employee appointed by the city's administrative officer. The mayor again sounded her concerns about keeping bathhouses open and operating during the upcoming Democratic National Convention in the city and cautioned: "People are coming here, get carried away by the nature of the environment and [will] carry [AIDS] back with them when they go home—they will carry it with them all over the world. This isn't just a local problem."[11]

Nearly three decades later, Silverman still defended his cautious approach on the bathhouse issue:

> My goal was to try and relate to the gay community, not politically, but I was trying to work with them because I knew we can do a lot better by working with them as partners rather than as a policeman. Probably only 10 percent of the gay community regularly went to the bathhouses. No question that the majority of the activities taking place there placed you at risk of HIV, but there was some 90 percent of the gay community [that] was not going there on any regular basis. The last thing that I wanted to do was to put a wedge between the health department and the gay community. The gay community couldn't elect me or hire me or fire me . . . but we needed to work together.[12]

Silverman's goals notwithstanding, a pending conflict was at hand with Shilts and others who either openly or secretly wanted the gay bathhouses to close. Silverman said he knew that "Randy was passionate and had a really strong feeling about the bathhouses from the get-go" and that "I was never one who was ever really thrilled with the bathhouses either." Beyond the open sexual activity occurring in the bathhouses, a variety of public safety issues were present, such as poor lighting and few if any fire exits beyond the main entrances to the establishments. In addition, the focus on sexual activity in the bathhouses completely ignored similar activity occurring inside gay adult theaters, bookstores, and public parks elsewhere in the city. Gay leaders had succeeded in getting bar and bathhouse owners to install additional fire exits, "and I wanted to get that same thing started on AIDS, a sort of community-based drive," Silverman said.[13] Few gay leaders were willing to stand with Silverman in the effort, some telling Silverman privately that they supported him, but then they backed out of any public disclosure of their support, leaving Silverman twisting in the wind.

The CDC's Dr. James Curran recalls accepting an invitation from Silverman to come to San Francisco to meet with local public health advocates, including representatives of the gay community. The supposed "top secret" meeting was to be at 8:00 p.m.—long after the health department offices closed—in order to avoid public or media scrutiny. "Our position at the CDC generally at that time was that bathhouses were primarily state and local issues, and it was up to the state and local jurisdictions to deal with these issues. It was not like the blood bank policies, which was a federal issue. Dr. Silverman just wanted me to come and share the latest data and be a sounding board," Curran said. "Well, when I got off the plane, there was Randy Shilts greeting me at the gate at the airport. The so-called big secret meeting wasn't a secret at all, at least not to him. He asked me, 'Are you going to the secret meeting?' and the very next morning the *San Francisco Chronicle* reported that a representative of the CDC had attended a meeting about how to close the bathhouses."[14]

Shilts didn't live long enough to make his full peace with Silverman, though Silverman expresses respect and admiration for Shilts to this day. During the time of the bathhouse controversy, Shilts spared no words when it came to what he thought of Silverman:

> Political concerns have continued to triumph over the need for public health. . . . [Dr. Silverman] didn't close the bathhouses when he should have because he didn't want to make a decision that would make anybody mad. What's so tragic about his stance is that studies show that at least a third of the gay men who were infected with this virus were infected between late '83 and late '84. In that period, a huge proportion of gay men were still going to the bathhouses. And I'm absolutely convinced that a lot of those infections could have been entirely avoided if those bathhouses had been shut down.[15]

Shilts's friend Linda Alband believed Shilts was one of the first "to see the hand-writing on the wall." He manifestly curtailed his own bathhouse activities and became vocal that others should do so as well. "He was very prescient about that," Alband said. "He wrote a lot about these topics when he was still at the *Advocate* and again at the *Chronicle,* and he could see the trajectory of sexually transmitted diseases in the gay community."[16]

Beyond the bathhouses, Silverman and Shilts also clashed over the level and type of public health education about sexually transmitted diseases such as HIV. Shilts found critics of the program who declared it "lackluster," angering Silverman, who was proud the health department was trying to take the lead. Silverman had had enough. "I called his editor [at the *Chronicle*] and I said, 'Why don't you put him on the opinion page because he is making and wants to take positions. And that's OK, but when you're reporting, I think it should be as objective as it can be.' It was my feeling that he was not being that objective," Silverman said. Not satisfied that Shilts's bosses took Silverman's complaints seriously enough, Silverman said, "I cut him off from the health department" and ordered colleagues and subordinates to cease cooperating with Shilts for news stories until the tenor of those stories changed.[17] Silverman recalls that his relationship with Shilts deteriorated so far that it prompted a rare show of humility from Shilts, who sent Silverman a personal note in an attempt to regain access to health department sources. "He ended up writing me a note saying, 'I'm sorry, you're right, I shouldn't do this, and I promise not to do it again.' [He was] not promising not to be critical, but promising not to be so biased and one-sided."[18]

Dr. Marcus Conant, one of the founders of the local AIDS Foundation, which raised some of the very first dollars for research and treatment of AIDS in America, had been quick to jump on the side of closing the bathhouses. He said he came to that conclusion while riding an older roller coaster at an amusement park in Santa Cruz, California:

> I was scared shitless, and I was sure we were going to fly off the track. My boyfriend said to me, "Listen, if it were dangerous, they would shut it down." And I said, "Who is they?" And it's the same as with the bathhouses. If they are dangerous, they would shut them down. Well, some poor kid coming here to San Francisco from Sioux Falls, Iowa, would say, "Well, I've heard about AIDS, but if the bathhouse was dangerous, they would close them down." I mean, it wasn't like there were signs over the doorway that said, "Ye who enter, beware, you can catch AIDS in here."[19]

The other incident that prompted Conant's outspoken support of bathhouse closures was an interaction with a patient suffering from AIDS-related illnesses who grew impatient waiting for the doctor. Conant said the patient wanted to get the appointment over with so he could go out to the bathhouse later.[20] Conant's account of a patient with AIDS-related problems still patronizing a gay bathhouse was a theme repeated by Shilts in his writing—a bitter pill for gay leaders to swallow.

Most of the bathhouses would eventually close, either failing to meet new regulations or collapsing from a lack of business. In either event, the forces that saw the bathhouses as throwing gasoline on the already burning fire of AIDS had won a victory. James Curran of the CDC thought that by the time the bathhouses finally did close, the risk they presented for the transmission of HIV had greatly diminished. "It's not as if people are going to stop having sex just because the bathhouse closed," Curran said. "People will just go somewhere else to have sex. The question is, does the bathhouse make it more conducive to dangerous sex? Clearly, it did earlier in the epidemic, but I never thought [that closing the bathhouses] would be any magical fix." Curran said one caution at the time supports Silverman's stated concerns about working *with* gay leaders, not *against* them. "The risk is when you are working with a marginalized group like the gay community, you can easily lose their cooperation and their attention," Curran said. "There was a real risk of driving the gay community even further underground with certain social control mechanisms—that's why we had anonymous [HIV] testing initially."[21]

Shilts said the bathhouse issue was not one of morality regarding homosexual contact:

> The baths exist solely for the purpose of promiscuous sexual activity and—when you have a disease which is most certainly transmitted by a single agent—a bathhouse sticks out like a very large erection. You just can't ignore the role it plays. No other newspaper in the United States has more aggressively pursued the bathhouse issue than *The San Francisco Chronicle*. It involved some very aggressive journalism, and I'm quite proud of the fact that I'm an aggressive journalist. Although I hate to admit it, I think Dianne Feinstein was right when she said that if AIDS were an epidemic among straight people and an institution like the baths existed, they would have been closed two years ago. Gay activists may be able to bullshit some reporter from *The Los Angeles Times* by telling him that the baths don't play any role in the AIDS epidemic, but they can't bullshit me, because I know what goes on in the bathhouses. I used to go there myself. I even had a job as a towel boy when I was working my way through college.[22]

Looking back, Cleve Jones, an early campaign and staff aide to Harvey Milk and later the creator of the NAMES Project AIDS Memorial Quilt, thinks Shilts almost unknowingly stepped into an incredible public relations nightmare on the bath-house issue. "I still feel uncomfortable when I talk about this," Jones said nearly thirty years after the controversy. "It was such a bitter and pathetic little stage. It was really fucked up on so many levels. . . . To this day, I feel some ambivalence about it. I went to the baths. I liked the baths. The baths were really an important part of my social life, but it was more of a social thing for me than a sexual thing. . . . It was where I networked with people." A real concern, however, was with closeted gay men (some of them married to women with children at home) who would engage in sexual activity that could make them susceptible to a variety of sexually transmitted diseases, including eventually HIV. Shilts "really was push-ing the issue" during his days at the *Chronicle,* and "he would confront people, he confronted me, and he pushed me to the point where I came down on it, and I'm not proud of this, but I just wanted the issue to go away."[23]

Shilts's reporting style often matched his personal style, frank and direct, with a strong commitment to telling the story of people and issues with all their faults and failings present and never compromising just to save someone's feelings. It likely reflected the world Shilts had known throughout his life. There wasn't much room for error, and a "gotcha" mentality surrounded him often and, in turn, was broadcast to the world, including his story subjects. There were bumps in the road along the way. Whether he intended to or not, Shilts was good at inspiring hard feelings in his sources and his readers. Two of Shilts's prominent news sources in the bathhouse battles of 1984 eventually turned on him publicly. Curran, a coor-dinator and researcher on the CDC's AIDS task force, said Shilts misquoted him about his desire to close all bathhouses. Curran told other reporters that Shilts had it wrong and that what he said was that he wouldn't be "disappointed" if the baths were closed, but he was not advocating that federal or local units of government get into the issue of "legislating sexual behavior." At City Hall, Supervisor Harry Britt, an openly gay man who succeeded the assassinated Harvey Milk, also took issue with Shilts's reporting and use of quotes on the bathhouse issue. "[Randy] wants to shut down the bathhouses, and he tried to get someone to say that," Britt told a reporter. Shilts seemed to be feeling the heat. He wrote a first-person account for *Native* magazine in which he declared that "a homosexual McCar-thyism has descended on San Francisco's gay community" and that "even now, the thought police lurk in the sweet summer shadows of these balmy evenings. Hysterical inquisitors stand on the corner of 18th and Castro, ready to guillotine heretics from the True Faith."[24]

If Shilts thought "making it" in mainstream journalism at one of the nation's largest dailies would lift him from the sometimes blistering criticism he had come to know firsthand during his days as a writer for gay publications, he surely was disabused of this idea quickly. Gay people in San Francisco had strong opinions about Shilts and what he wrote, and it didn't matter where he published his stories. While letters critical of Shilts and his work were somewhat rare on the opinion pages of the *San Francisco Chronicle*, letter writers to the *Bay Area Reporter*, a weekly gay newspaper, didn't hold back in their views. His reporting on the bathhouse issue was in fact the match that ignited a long-burning firestorm of anti-Shilts sentiment. Under a letter titled "Shilts Is a Sellout," one writer accused Shilts of "manufacturing the gay bathhouse / AIDS issue" as a cause close to his so-called objective heart and continued, "Shilts proves that power politics is alive and well and all gussied up in journalistic drag at the *Chronicle*."[25] Another writer accused Shilts of engaging in "blue-nosed morality" and noted, "What I find even more intolerable is the *Chronicle*'s use of biased reporting and the presentation of one reporter's opinions as news in this, and other articles on the subject by Mr. Shilts. If the *Chronicle* wishes to take a stand on this issue, it should do so on the editorial page as appropriate."[26]

Additional letters followed Shilts's long article for the *Chronicle* about the two-day party and auction that marked the end of one of the city's oldest and most popular bathhouses, the Sutro Baths. In his story, titled "A Farewell 'Orgy' at Sutro Baths," Shilts noted that the city's famed "bisexual bathhouse threw in the towel" as "another casualty of the city's changing sexuality during the AIDS crisis."[27] He relayed that while gay customers still frequented the Sutro, patrons who identified as either heterosexual or bisexual had sworn off the baths in the midst of the AIDS crisis. Five hundred guests attended the "orgy," which apparently was a provocative term Shilts and his editors used to mean meeting or gathering rather than sexual activity. Among the activities were remarks "by an AIDS victim who praised Sutro, a singer who mourned the baths' demise," and a ceremonial burning of AIDS prevention brochures by five bathhouse employees who were losing their jobs. Letters quickly popped up in the *Bay Area Reporter* taking Shilts's coverage to task. In a letter titled "Shilts without the L," a *Bay Area Reporter* reader asked, "Why does the *Chronicle* continue to keep a writer with a history of irresponsible journalism, especially when he continues with this behavior? I am referring to Randy Shilts and his recent article on the closing of the Sutro Bathhouse." The letter continued, "The Sutro closing that Randy Shilts described was a far cry from the type of event that actually occurred. . . . He completely de-emphasized and distorted the reason for the actual closing. It was not because of the AIDS crisis, but because of political maneuvering . . . [causing] the public to be misinformed and misled." The writer concluded that the bathhouse closure was a "political injustice that has occurred surrounding the scapegoating of the bathhouses," and "apparently Mr. Shilts continues to be unaware of the damage that is caused by his insensitivity to issues which dramatically affect peoples' [sic] lives."[28]

The criticism perhaps hit its target. For a subsequent report on the Sutro bathhouse closure for the New York Native, Shilts adjusted the story a bit, noting that the ceremonial burning of AIDS prevention brochures by the bathhouse staff had been staged for TV reporters and that he, as a newspaper reporter, "came later, to confirm the facts."[29]

The owner of the Sutro Baths, Bill Jones, joined the chorus with a letter titled "Randy Got It Wrong Again!" and denounced him: "If you want to know why the gay community dislikes the Chronicle's token fag so much, just look at the headlines for his story on the closing of my bathhouse. . . . The headline said, 'A farewell orgy at Sutro Baths,' . . . No one attending our party could possibly define it [as an orgy] and Randy [Shilts] was not there. Our Grand Closing Party was fun, but not that much fun and Randy Shilts has again sensationalized a very human story into something grotesque and fearful."[30]

Deep in the middle of the AIDS crisis, everyone's frayed nerves and edges started to show. "For the past year," Shilts wrote, "the San Francisco gay community has been characterized by vengeance, vendettas, and arguments arising out of the AIDS crisis."[31] His remarks prompted one Bay Area Reporter reader to comment:

If Randy Shilts truly thinks that he is a "journalist first"—presumably being one who impartially records facts and events—he is under a major misconception about himself. He is a commentator first. Read his articles. Read his interviews. How about his slur against gay leaders on page one of the Chronicle, which he later rationalized as he did because he honestly thought it was funny? But don't condemn excessively. Mr. Shilts at worst is only right in there with the rest of the pack who report about gay events. . . . It is a sad loss for the community that Mr. Shilts and others can't get beyond the drag queen level. So he's a commentator . . . and a knowledgeable observer.[32]

One reader's letter in support of Shilts appeared on the editorial pages of the Bay Area Reporter days later:

I am tired and angry to hear the continuing sarcastic, critical remarks related to Randy Shilts by the gay press. The bottom line of his message to us is—take responsibility for yourself and others. I have mixed feelings about closing the baths, but I do not have mixed feelings when I talk with other gay men who could not give a damn about who they sleep with, could care less what their health status is, mine, or others in the community. As Randy pointed out in his article of March 7, the epidemic is growing.[33]

The wording of the letter, remarkably, reflects how Shilts's reporting had come to be viewed by many—the phrase "his message to us" reflects that at least some members of the gay community were beginning to view Shilts's words as cautionary, instructive, and certainly directed toward specific positions as opposed to others. A truly "objective reporter" would have winced ever so slightly at the open suggestion that his reporting carried a "message" to the community that went far beyond any role as watchdog journalist. The letter writer also praised Shilts as among a small group of "gay brothers" who were "helping sound the alarm about AIDS so long ago, very often at great ridicule from the very people they were trying to protect."[34]

Criticism of Shilts was not limited to the opinion pages of the *Bay Area Reporter*. Addressing the political issues surrounding the proposed closure of gay bathhouses in San Francisco, the *Bay Area Reporter* devoted most of its April 5, 1984, edition to covering the kerfuffle. Reporter George Mendenhall analyzed the news coverage the bathhouse issue was receiving in the mainstream press and noted, "While television and print media appear to be balanced [on the issue of closure], there is increased criticism within the gay community of the coverage by gay reporter Randy Shilts of *The San Francisco Chronicle*. Increasingly, activists were openly calling Shilts prejudicial in his bathhouse articles."[35]

Two weeks later, an April 19, 1984, front-page story in the *Bay Area Reporter* reported that the Alice B. Toklas Lesbian/Gay Democratic Club had voted to "denounce *San Francisco Chronicle* reporter Randy Shilts who is responsible for the wrong message" on gay bathhouses. The story quoted Toklas Club president Randy Stallings as naming Shilts "the most homophobic person in the Bay Area," and "I am sick to death that he continues to victimize the gay community in the name of objectivity . . . [via his] continuing blasts and inaccuracies written against our community." A voice vote determined the "denouncing" of Shilts, with few people in the crowd dissenting, the newspaper reported.[36] The Toklas Club vote followed an earlier "nonbinding" vote of the Stonewall Gay Democratic Club, which had chastised the bathhouse closure process but stopped short of opposing outright closure and made no mention of Shilts or his reporting.[37] Toklas Club members had always been weary of Shilts because they knew that his private allegiances ran more closely with the members of the Harvey Milk Democratic

Club, including their views on the bathhouse issue. Author James Kinsella faulted Shilts's editors for failing to recognize the quagmire created by Shilts's previous (and perhaps ongoing) political allegiances with the forces remaining from Milk's movement. "Many in the gay community thought Shilts had stepped over the line," Kinsella wrote about Shilts, pointing out the differences in positions on the bathhouse issue between the Toklas and Milk Clubs. "No one had aired the gay debate in the straight press, but now [Shilts] was editorializing in the news pages. . . . *The Chronicle* editors might have recognized the problems [Shilts's connections to the Milk Club raised] if Shilts had been covering almost any other brand of politics. Despite the paper's interest in reporting on gays, the editors did not pretend to understand, or want to understand, gay politics. They kept hands off."[38]

Brian Jones, a reporter at the *Bay Area Reporter*, also took issue with Shilts's coverage of public health statistics regarding the rate of sexually transmitted diseases among gay men. Jones focused his story on the more than 60 percent drop in infection rates for all forms of STDs among gay men: "The unprecedented drop in [venereal disease] rates indicates that most gay men have made dramatic changes in their sexual behavior as a response to the AIDS epidemic." Jones noted that the statistics showed that rates of rectal gonorrhea, for which gay men were particularly susceptible, had risen dramatically between 1979 and 1983 but that a "statistical plateau" appeared to be forming, with about eighteen hundred reported cases each quarter. "That changed early this year when a slight rise in venereal disease became the centerpiece for a major article in *The San Francisco Chronicle*. Under the headline, 'AIDS Expert Says Bathhouses Should Close,' gay reporter Randy Shilts's February 3 story stated, 'A new study by the San Francisco Department of Public Health shows that rectal gonorrhea among gay men is surging again.'" Jones refuted Shilts's reporting for its lack of statistical data to make relevant comparisons. Apparently not satisfied at that and again placing Shilts in the context of being part of the news story and not just reporting on it, Jones wrote, "Questioned by *The Bay Area Reporter* after his article appeared, Shilts said he had not reviewed the statistics. He said he had relied solely on an interview with then-director of the health department's Bureau of Communicable Diseases, Selma Dritz. Shilts's article—and the slight upturn in VD rates it recorded—are widely regarding as having initiated the latest campaign to close the city's bathhouses, sex clubs, and bookstores."[39]

Jones's analysis of VD rates among gay men in the city—whether one believed those rates were going up or were on a "statistical plateau"—seemed oddly fixated on Shilts's reportage and its implied impact. Jones did quote local public health officials about the VD rates, but including Shilts's story and casting doubt on its accuracy reflected Shilts's new role as a major voice in gay politics in San Francisco (whether he wanted to remain just a newspaper reporter or not). Jones would later take to the "Viewpoints" page of the *Bay Area Reporter* to criticize Shilts and the *Chronicle* for its coverage of a recent census of gay men in the city. Shilts's story had emphasized that the census was one of the first of its kind to measure how many gay men and women actually lived in the Bay Area. Jones's relationship with Shilts had a bit of a history—Jones, along with Shilts, had been one of ten college journalists honored years earlier in writing contests sponsored by the William Randolph Hearst Foundation. Shilts says that Jones "became my nemesis over the bathhouse issue and he just hated me. I think he was jealous because we had known each other going back to college and I was so successful."[40]

Shilts's coverage of a 1984 recruitment drive by San Francisco County sheriff Michael Hennessey, which included a pitch for job applicants at Chaps, a gay leather bar where patrons often dressed as cops anyway, drew additional disgust from some gay leaders for allegedly portraying the gay community in a bad light. Shilts wrote his story about Hennessey's effort in a sardonic tone, noting the irony of a sheriff trying to recruit new deputies among gay men who liked to dress as cops. The controversy Shilts's story stirred, however, seemed to bite gay activists most painfully because the *National Enquirer* picked it up and used it in a splashy story that ridiculed the unusual ways of San Francisco life. The *Bay Area Reporter* reported that Hennessey later apologized to his department and the community for the event but quickly blamed Shilts and his overemphasis on Hennessey speaking to a group of gay men partially clad in leather outfits, resulting in the heavy use of Shilts's article by reporters from the tabloid. Hennessey joined in the focus on Shilts and his reporting and declared that he would not have held the recruitment forum at the gay leather bar if he had fully understood that it was a gay bar and if he had anticipated "the portrayal and light that it has [brought to the sheriff's department] by *The San Francisco Chronicle*."[41] After the *National Enquirer* had fun with the story, titled "City Hell-Bent for Leather as Sheriff Recruits in Gay Bar," another reporter at the *Bay Area Reporter*, Dion B. Sanders, was back with another story that noted that the *Enquirer* "has never made any attempt to conceal its hatred of gays" and emphasized that it had its article in the first place thanks to Shilts's reporting. Sanders wrote, "*The Enquirer* repeatedly referred to a story in the *Chronicle*—while neglecting to mention that the story was written by a gay reporter, Randy Shilts." Sanders's story reflected the ire and embarrassment Shilts had inspired by broadcasting a gay leather stereotype to a readership of more than seven million via the pages of the *Enquirer*.[42]

Shilts subsequently told reporter Gary Schweikhart of the *Sentinel* (an early gay newspaper in the city published by Charles Lee Morris) that he had written hundreds of positive stories about the gay community and attributed the controversy to the lack of a sense of humor on the part of gay leaders:

> The people who are the maddest are those gays who are very concerned about how straight people view them. In other words, they have a major psychological investment in getting approval from straight people. Well, I have been living in this world as an openly gay person for so many years that I forget that there are people like this. So, I think a lot of gay people read the article and said, "Oh my God, look what he is saying about us to straight people." I have long ago ceased to care about what straight people think.[43]

Criticism of Shilts and his reporting popped up elsewhere; his name was a topic for discussion at some of the earliest AIDS-related public forums in San Francisco. An April 1984 forum organized by the San Francisco AIDS Foundation brought out several Shilts critics—among them Supervisor Britt, now the city's only openly gay official. Britt walked a tight line between his call for "some very basic changes in how we conduct our sexual activity if we are to survive as gay people" and his caution that "we must fight back against moralistic messages that say gay sex is wrong or immoral. We must advocate for our sexual freedom as much as we ever have done."[44] The kind of raucous public comment section that one would expect in San Francisco followed the bathhouse forum, which presented speakers from the AIDS Foundation, the city's health department, and the Northern California Bathhouse Owners Association.

Speaking on behalf of the bathhouse owners, Sal Accardi, owner of a city bathhouse, took aim at Shilts, accusing him of "misquotations, lack of context, and an overzealous position": "To Mr. Shilts, who calls for urgency and an alarmist approach [to stopping the spread of AIDS], we say that such approaches didn't work for Chicken Little and I doubt it will work for Randy Shilts. While Randy Shilts, and those who think like him, may be sincere and well-intentioned, they are wrong, along with Jerry Falwell and his ilk, and they are fueling the fires of bigotry and repression. They are not thinking, they are only reacting."[45] Accardi noted that closing bathhouses would do little to stop so-called unsafe sex practices and would just result in new locations for sex practices to occur, and he chastised city leaders for their lack of attention to curtailing sexual activity in the city's gay adult movie theaters and go-go clubs.

Bathhouse owner Bill Jones said he was unconvinced bathhouses played any greater role in the spread of AIDS than anywhere else in the city. Jones attempted to use quotes attributed to Supervisor Britt in articles written by Shilts (ascribing bathhouse activities as not associated with pleasure but with death) as evidence that Britt was not serious in his support of ongoing gay sexual liberation. Jones said he worried Britt would try to "wiggle out" of his statements reported by Shilts. He had called Shilts directly, and "he verified what he reported was what you said. He said that he had witnesses who also heard you say these things, but that he does not have tapes of you saying them."[46] Britt seemed rattled by Jones's assertions, noting, "Randy Shilts very much wants someone to say that the bathhouses should be shut down. He is trying very hard to find someone to say that. I have not said it, and I am not going to say it. In the particular interview that you are referring to, I spent the better part of an hour trying to convince Randy that we should talk about sexual practices, not about where they take place."[47]

Britt fell back on the fact that "Mr. Shilts does not carry a tape recorder" and "writes down about every twenty-fifth word you say. . . . He then fits those into what thesis he had laid out. . . . I think that tells you an awful lot about how he works and what his motives are." Britt had noticed Shilts's self-styled manner of "quickhand" notetaking (as Shilts dubbed it), which perhaps lacked the precision in quotes that other reporters achieved. His criticism notwithstanding, Britt described Shilts "as my friend a large part of the time" but said that "on this particular issue, he is trying to get the community divided."[48]

LGBT historian Edward Alwood noted that "in my conversations with Randy Shilts, he made it clear to me that he does not allow the incoherence of someone to get in the way. He reconstructs what the person is *trying* to say." Alwood acknowledged that this was "within the realm of new journalism" but also subjected Shilts to the same sorts of questions about source accuracy that have followed other writers, such as Truman Capote and Tom Wolfe. "I am not saying that anything Randy wrote was misleading or biased, but I think he was definitely more focused on the ways of storytelling."[49]

In a rare example where a working journalist got to give back a little bit of the criticism he had suffered throughout 1984, the November 21, 1984, front page of the *Bay Area Reporter* featured a large photograph of Shilts smiling under a provocative headline: "Shilts Calls Gay Leaders 'Inept,' 'Bunch of Jerks.'" Shilts's interview with *Stallion*, a gay porn magazine, offered up "strong words from the reporter who is assigned to cover those leaders for his newspaper." Shilts clarified right off the top: "Whenever a hot issue comes along, I'm going to become an unpopular guy, because I'm always going to be a journalist first and a gay person second.... Look, you can do two things in journalism: You can tell people the truth or you can tell them what they want to hear. Given a choice, most people would far prefer to hear what they want to hear. They really don't want any bad news." Shilts said he resented the presumption that "the only mode for being a correct homosexual in this society is to be a political activist" and that "those people will never understand the difference between being a newspaper reporter and being a paid propagandist for the gay community. The reason I get screamed at so much by such movement people is that I will not be a gay activist. I'm a professional who chooses to be open about being gay." Shilts accused gay political leaders of being "immature" and said, "Let's not kid ourselves, the local gay political scene is a loony bin. This community is top-heavy with chiefs and not an awful lot of Indians. You're not dealing with normal people—these folks are crazy." Not finished yet, Shilts noted that the gay leadership of San Francisco "looks like all these naked emperors walking around trying to appear clothed. The people currently running the political aspect of our movement are a bunch of jerks who wrap themselves in silly, dogmatic rhetoric." Shilts said he believed the AIDS crisis sweeping the gay community had found many of its organizations wanting, and "if anything, AIDS is forcing gays to do something which we have resisted for a long time; to start dealing with each other on an ethical basis beyond sex. Before, everyone was spending his nights picking up one-night stands in the bars. Every man you met was weighed by his sexual status. ... Lord knows, I did it too. But it was a very immature and adolescent stage to go through."[50]

The damage done and Shilts's personal views apparently aired once and for all, in an unusual move, Shilts wrote a follow-up letter to the editor of the *Bay Area Reporter* to comment on the new controversy his blunt remarks had created. Shilts said that reading the story had convinced him that "I made too many broad generalizations about the gay leadership. There are a number of political leaders and gay organizers—of diverse political perspectives and gay activist organizations—who are firmly and primarily committed to the pursuit of a better world for lesbian and gay people. Not all are motivated by thoughts of selfish political gain." He added, "Looking back on what I said, I feel my broad brush blurred over the many people who have demonstrated sincere altruism.... I apologize for this oversight in my comments."[51]

Response to the article showed up days later in the *Bay Area Reporter* and seemed split, with one reader saying they found much to agree with in Shilts's remarks and another noting that while his reporting could be maddening, he may have spurred a necessary debate about the nature and diversity of leadership in the gay community. Shilts was one of the first to ask, "What is this movement, this community, all about?" He was also among the first to attempt to describe the dichotomy that had grown inside the gay community. "The political direction of the gay movement in the 15 years after Stonewall seemed clear," Shilts declared. Borrowing from the civil rights efforts of blacks and women, "the message was fairly simple, since the ignorance was so great: boot out the stereotypes and show we're just like anybody else, undeserving of the slights meted out to social pariahs."[52]

The cutting nature of the criticism Shilts received, especially from within the gay community, had its effect. Partly blustering, Shilts said he felt he attracted such responses because he had strongly held beliefs (or at least expressed them strongly at every turn) and that others lacked the courage to do otherwise. In a retrospective moment in a 1989 interview with researcher Eric Marcus, he said, "People say to me that 'You must like controversy,' and really, I hate it. I'm very sensitive and my feelings get very easily hurt. So they're hurt a lot. But having my feelings get hurt is not enough to change writing about something I think is right." His remarks reveal the classic survival skills of the child of an alcoholic—easily hurt feelings—and an almost simultaneous desire and ability to excuse, explain, or codify the basis for the hurt. He added, "I do internalize it too much. I spent a lot of time with my therapist talking about this. I don't get any better but then the other part of me thinks, well, I think the reason my writing is good is because . . . the sensitivity comes out. If I become thick-skinned about that, then I'd be thick-skinned in my writing. . . . I want to be the kind of writer who still connects to people on a human level."[53]

Shilts understood that the gay meccas of America, San Francisco and New York, had grown out of a driving desire to break free of the repression felt by most gay men and women in their hometowns across the United States, resulting in a free-for-all "adolescent accent on sex" that reflected "a lot of catching up we needed to do." Pulling the curtain farther back, Shilts explained to Marcus, "It was comforting to assure ourselves that we weren't cavorting any more than heterosexual men would if they had willing partners. We were just men being men." While some saw sexual promiscuity—or freedom—as a step toward broader political liberation, others emerged focused more on a gay reality that included a basic set of values, including monogamous relationships. "It's always easier to cast off old values than create new standards," Shilts surmised. "The gay community drifted for many years" and refused to discuss the issue of whether bathhouses could make a sexually transmitted pandemic worse. "To discuss the issue, however, implied that gay people might also have to talk about something alien: values. Gay leaders are extraordinary in discussing politics but not values. The notion of moral absolutes is largely repulsive to them."[54]

# A Balancing Act for Shilts

Despite the wildfire of hard feelings surrounding the bathhouse closure issues, which was ignited in part by Shilts's reporting, he seemed to gain more confidence shifting comfortably between the almost inescapable dual roles of a journalist and an activist. The *Los Angeles Herald Examiner* reported on a January 1988 meeting in which local officials in West Hollywood and elsewhere in Los Angeles County discussed closing twelve bathhouses in the community, establishments drawing an estimated ninety-six hundred patrons each week. Shilts spoke before an audience of six hundred Los Angeles activists and political leaders, urging that closing the bathhouses was "crucial to the wildfire spread of the [AIDS] epidemic in this community." Shilts continued, "Support for closing the bathhouses affirms one thing: that we want to save our lives." Failing to act would turn back the progress the gay community had made to prove that "we're not a bunch of sex-craved lunatics that will do anything for an orgasm." Shilts predicted that the Los Angeles bathhouses would eventually close. "The question is how many people will have to die" before that happened.[1]

Fellow journalist David Israels believes there is no question that Shilts abandoned a portion of his objectivity when it came to the bathhouse story. "I would say he *was* advocating a position those days," Israels said. "This is the most obvious example of where he used his position to advocate a position that can be identified. I think he took the position he did on the bathhouses based on the reporting he had done. I think he used his ability to write stories to function in the role of at least a semi-advocate." Shilts encountered a strong backlash from portions of the gay community, but as Israels noted, "He felt that he was disseminating information that needed to get out there. I think he also had come to a feeling at this point that the bathhouses represented a negative force in the community." Some of the criticism against Shilts in this era may have been fair, Israels believes. "Some people might say, therefore, he violated the journalism craft's admonition that you shouldn't be advancing your own personal opinions. But it's important to remember that his personal opinion was based on hard reporting that he had done on the subject, and he had reached a conclusion."[2]

Israels is one of many who attempt to "qualify" Shilts's apparent abandonment of objectivity because it was based on a record of research and information that he had been gathering through years of reporting about AIDS. Israels admits, however, that Shilts's own "randy" past of visiting and having sex in San Francisco and New York City bathhouses in the 1970s undercut some of his credibility among some gay leaders on the bathhouse issue. "I don't think you can discount that criticism," Israels said. "He was quite sexually active, he went to the bathhouses and all that, he had multiple partners at one time, and people saw that as hypocritical of him." Israels adds, "But that argument doesn't fly when you take into account what we knew before and what we know now. When he was out there being sexually promiscuous or whatever, we didn't know about the virus."[3] Shilts's one-time partner Steve Newman confirms that he and Shilts visited gay bathhouses together during their intimate relationship: "We would go out to sex clubs together, and we would have a good time, and he enjoyed it," Newman said. "But there comes a point when that becomes lethal, and it probably really should be highlighted." Newman thinks that any criticism that flows to Shilts because of his previous patronage of a bathhouse is meaningless. "If you look at what he was reporting, he was emphasizing what medical experts and scientists were saying about what they knew at that time about HIV and AIDS," Newman said. "He was writing news articles that quoted scientists and experts and making sure people understood that if this were in fact a communicable disease or a sexually transmitted disease, that people knew about it."[4]

Shilts complicated the reporting on the growing AIDS problem because of his sometimes openly hostile relationship with Dr. Mervyn Silverman, who had risen in stature nationally because of his role in combatting AIDS and was serving as chair of the US Conference of Health Officers via the US Conference of Mayors. Despite dustups and disagreements along the way, CDC researcher James Curran hails Shilts as "the first, best and most important everyday reporter covering the AIDS issue. He was at every single event, every conference or meeting, everywhere in the country that had to do with AIDS. His book on AIDS was not the result of some list of purposeful interviews after the fact, because he was interviewing me and everyone else all of the time."[5]

Not everyone agrees, of course, on where to place Shilts in terms of the bathhouse battles. James Kinsella, a noted researcher on the media's coverage of the AIDS crisis in America, concedes that the bathhouse issue "could not, and should not, have been avoided by Shilts or any other journalist" but says that Shilts's "play" and "politicization" of the story "made progress in preventing AIDS much more difficult. By focusing on the bathhouses as though they were primary sources of infection, he tended to discount the more basic problem: changing individuals' sexual behavior."[6] Kinsella's review is one that would sting—Shilts viewed his work as critical to helping save the lives of gay men who had come so far to gain their freedom and emancipation from the closet, only then to risk being destroyed by the specter of a deadly virus spread through their intimacy.

It wasn't just bathhouse owners and their patrons who loathed Shilts, however, as his sometimes contrarian views inspired vitriol from some of the most motivated gay activists ever, the AIDS Coalition to Unleash Power (ACT-UP). ACT-UP, formed in New York City in 1987, served as a direct-action advocacy group for people with HIV and AIDS. Playwright and activist Larry Kramer, who employed an in-your-face approach to demanding governmental action to combat AIDS, inspired ACT-UP members with his words. Highly unstructured in its governance, ACT-UP grew to be a worldwide phenomenon with thousands of members demonstrating beneath its famous "Silence = Death" banners. ACT-UP, not surprisingly, was successful in generating widespread news coverage of its provocative protests in San Francisco and was a force to be reckoned with. Members demanded a more militant and progressive approach to addressing AIDS and found themselves at odds with many mainline gay rights and AIDS activists. Among those loathed by ACT-UP (in what appeared to be a "mutual loathing society") was Shilts. Michelangelo Signorile, a New York–based journalist who was a cofounding editor of the sometimes-militant *OutWeek* magazine, said, "Randy was someone that many people in ACT-UP were infuriated with, seeing him and his [writing] as, rightly or wrongly, contributing to the AIDS hysteria in the media. . . . He also advocated for closing bathhouses, something that many civil libertarians and AIDS activists opposed."[7]

In his reporting on ACT-UP and other protestors at the International AIDS Conference in Montreal in June 1989, Shilts wrote that activists shared the belief that in the fight against AIDS anything that "does not hasten its prevention or treatment cannot be justified. This credo presents a standard by which dissenters as well as scientists must be judged." Shilts, however, had formed his own credo about what the purpose of such confabs were, noting, "The international conference was not a therapy session, but a moment that was supposed to move the fight against AIDS forward. Just as it was no longer enough for society to have compassion, it was no longer enough for protestors to have only anger." Shilts granted that ACT-UP had aided in the effort to speed up key drug treatments for treating people with AIDS and for lobbying for more money for research: "Confrontational tactics have succeeded where years of polite lobbying from more moderate AIDS organizers failed." He believed that "past success and the justifiable anger will be to no avail if future protests do more to alienate their targets than persuade them."[8]

In the pages of the *Chronicle*, Shilts extended his critique of ACT-UP by taking on its provocative forms of protest, especially its interruption of Catholic masses and vandalization of Catholic churches. Shilts posed typically pointed questions in his narration: "What if Catholic militants vandalized the headquarters of the San Francisco AIDS Foundation? Wouldn't ACT-UP be screaming 'Nazis!'? ACT-UP says every act of science should be based on the standard of saving lives, but does the blocking of the Golden Gate Bridge do anything to save lives?"[9] Shilts's battle with the leaders of ACT-UP continued to reside at the center of several of his columns, including a December 18, 1989, effort that scathingly declared, "If I didn't know better, I'd swear that the AIDS protestors who have been disrupting services and vandalizing Catholic churches . . . were being paid by some diabolical reactionary group dedicated to discrediting the gay community."[10] Shilts deemed their actions the embrace of a troubling yet understandable double standard, given the Catholic Church's opposition to distribution of condoms to prevent HIV, opposition to any sexual relations except those contained within the confines of a heterosexual marriage, and financing of a strong campaign to defeat a domestic partnership ordinance (Proposition S) in the November 1989 election in San Francisco.

Despite all this, gay protestors did not have the prerogative to deny Catholics the right to their own worship and beliefs, he declared. Shilts said the ACT-UP protests targeting churches were "not only morally wrong, but strategically stupid." With the ink barely dry on Shilts's blistering editorial-page analysis of the ACT-UP protests, editors at the *Chronicle,* interestingly, didn't see any conflict with Shilts writing up a news story on the same topic ("ACT-UP's Acting Up Gets Mixed Reviews"). The decision by the *Chronicle* to continue to allow Shilts the freedom to navigate between opinion columnist and news writer on the same subjects (such as the ACT-UP protests) served to overshadow and undercut, for some, the credibility of a well-written, four-thousand-piece analysis of "the year in AIDS," also published on Christmas Day 1989.

As 1989 ended, KQED-TV announced that it had tapped its former *Newsroom* reporter Randy Shilts to host and narrate a major documentary titled *Wrestling with AIDS*, dubbed a comprehensive look at six challenging issues expected to emerge in the AIDS battle of the 1990s. *San Francisco Chronicle* entertainment writer John Stanley declared, "If anyone is qualified to talk about the shifting issues of AIDS, and the new dilemmas that the 1990s will bring, it is probably Randy Shilts." Shilts told Stanley that the program would move beyond his oft-stated central thesis that the government and researchers weren't doing enough to address AIDS and move toward "broader social issues" that AIDS had introduced, including many matters related to health care and the future of gay and AIDS-related political activism in a clearly decimated gay community. Shilts promised that the ninety-minute special would move beyond TV's usual role of being "a diary of the obvious" and said, "What I like about this show is that it's ahead of the story; it's dealing with issues just now emerging and accelerating."[11] A long portion of the program was devoted to suicide pacts or "euthanasia cocktail parties" organized for those with no hope of any further quality of life under the crushing reality of AIDS. During this segment, in which Shilts profiled a young gay couple in San Francisco who had already made elaborate plans to commit suicide together, Shilts acknowledged knowing twenty-five other people who had similar plans or had already carried them out. He said that most of them "didn't commit suicide out of despair. The experts call it 'rational suicide' because the decision to die is fairly well thought out, weighing the risks of life against the benefits of death."[12]

Shilts's work on the *Wrestling with AIDS* documentary came as Shilts and the *Chronicle* announced he was taking "a year's sabbatical from his coverage of the AIDS story" and that he would turn his attentions elsewhere. Having written more than sixty thousand words in stories and columns on the pages of the *Chronicle* in a flurry of activity in 1989 alone, Shilts stated, "I'm feeling completely depleted. Until this year, I hadn't felt burned out, and [in the past] I didn't have a lot of sympathy for those who said they were burned out. I thought they were weak. Then I started having nightmares. In my dreams, I was wandering around funerals, screaming, 'I can't take it anymore!' I've spent eight years recording the decimation of my generation. I need a break."[13] Shilts's regular editorial page column, "AIDS: The Inside Story," ended in 1989, and his regular contributions to the news pages of the *Chronicle* on the AIDS topic were limited to major events, such as the Sixth International AIDS Conference, held in San Francisco in June 1990, for which he produced daily stories and columns. The conference was again the center of controversy, however, as Republicans in Congress had successfully pushed the Immigration and Naturalization Service to tighten the rules on allowing people with HIV or AIDS to obtain entry visas to attend the conference. "At least 85 countries called for a boycott of the meeting, prompting the INS to agree to temporarily waive the policy for those seeking a brief, 10-day entry to attend medical meetings," wrote Katherine Bliss in her history of the International AIDS Conferences.[14] Shilts covered an opening session featuring Academy Award–winning actress Elizabeth Taylor's appearance for the International Fund for AIDS. He followed up his news coverage of Taylor's brief stop with an editorial page column labeled "Analysis & Opinion" by taking a tongue-in-cheek look at the "AIDS celebrity circuit." His story drew attention to the fact that the major researchers, eminent virologists, and scientists from around the world were the stars, while the actual Hollywood stars, such as Taylor, were a secondary consideration. "It's a world where a man can be called the world's leading expert in treating AIDS patients but he doesn't really treat many patients because he's too busy giving speeches and interviews about treating patients," Shilts wrote. He did not spare himself, however, noting that it was also "a world in which you go on TV to talk about covering a story that you're not really covering because you're on TV talking about covering it."[15]

Although his regular opinion column had ended, Shilts's desire to express his opinions had not. His most pronounced criticism of AIDS-related issues and the gay community (and its journalists) came at one of the earliest meetings of the National Lesbian and Gay Journalists Association in 1992. Shilts didn't hold back and referred to some of the gay reporters as "lavender fascists" interested in forcing their ideology on everyone—comments that fostered lingering resentment of Shilts among gay journalists. "There is a fundamental fallacy in preaching diversity but rejecting the most important form of diversity of all, which is diversity of thought," Shilts said.[16] Some perceived Shilts's comments as evidence that battles with gay leaders had left him bitter and angry. Others dissected his comments even further, suggesting they were perhaps an artifact of a deeper, ongoing personal struggle they believed raged within him to fully accept himself as a gay man, despite his open disclosure of his homosexuality from an early age. Those promoting the idea that Shilts was a self-hating gay man pointed to his self-effacing humor offered in interviews: "I'm not a very good homosexual—I can't keep house, decorate, cook or dress," he told a *New York Times* reporter for a profile story.[17]

The National Lesbian and Gay Journalists Association meeting at which Shilts spoke drew three hundred journalists to San Francisco in the summer of 1992, and by then Shilts had already become one of "the most famed gay journalists" in America. Some of the assembled journalists would not provide their names to a reporter from *Editor & Publisher* magazine writing about the convention; they feared losing their journalism job back home. The conference attempted to move beyond the need for newsroom "coming out" and explored gay journalists' identities and their potential power and influence in mainstream journalism.[18]

Shilts's reputation for being outspoken and blunt had won him few friends in the gay and lesbian media, for while Shilts had earned the respect of straight journalists, "many of his gay and lesbian colleagues continue[d] to regard him with suspicion, if not hostility," journalist John Weir wrote. Weir suggested that this criticism of Shilts was symptomatic of a "peculiarity" of the LGBTQ community, which closely monitored Shilts's work after he "crossed over into the mainstream press and that many of those watching have been men controlling the gay press who might also have successfully worked and advanced in the mainstream if they'd remained in the closet."[19]

In an interview for the *Washington Journalism Review* in 1990, Shilts addressed the reality of an ongoing struggle mainstream media had in covering gays and particularly the propriety or fairness of outing someone as gay in the media: "What bothers me is the media piously talking about private lives. They just find homosexuality so distasteful and don't want to write about it. They don't have a problem lying about it; their problem is telling the truth about it." There were limits, however, and Shilts restated his abhorrent feelings about outing, telling a reporter for *Gentlemen's Quarterly* magazine that "when the threat of outing is employed [by gay leaders] to pressure a public official to vote a particular way, it amounts to nothing more than blackmail, plain and simple."[20]

Ironically, Shilts revealed in his biography on Harvey Milk that Milk was responsible for one of the earliest and most noted outing incidents in the media. Somehow, Milk had learned the sexual orientation of ex-marine and Vietnam vet Oliver Sipple, who became a national hero on September 22, 1975, when he blocked the gun of Sara Jane Moore as she attempted to assassinate President Gerald R. Ford outside a San Francisco hotel. Sipple later unsuccessfully sued the *San Francisco Chronicle* and other publications for invasion of privacy for naming him as a homosexual, thus outing him to his family and friends, though Sipple never denied he was gay.[21]

As researcher Edward Iwata reported, "For many gays, the debates [over outing] took on a real-life urgency. As several speakers at the NGLJA [*sic*] confab observed, it was dangerous to be gay in an American newsroom. Attacks from conservatives, rising street violence against gays, and the hysteria around AIDS make life risky for politically active gays."[22] The notion of "politically active gays" working as journalists begged the obvious question: If gays were fighting a cultural war for overall survival in society, what role, if any, should the first mainstream journalists who are gay play in that war? The debate among the journalists present for the NLGJA meeting ranged from advocating more and better coverage of gay rights issues, to those who saw a conflict of bringing their personal interests into their work. Still others opened the long-debated question of whether overall journalistic objectivity even mattered at all.

Outing was at the center of the discussion for many of the stories Shilts would write in the coming months about the struggle for openly gay men and lesbian women to continue serving in the US armed services, as the very act of disclosing one's homosexuality had serious ramifications for members of the military. Shilts was no fan of outing, even if he faced accusations of practicing it himself. Criticism similar to that which Shilts endured from gay advocates regarding the closing of gay bathhouses would return around his position opposed to the practice of outing closeted gays. Spurred on by the editors of *Out* magazine and activist journalists such as Michelangelo Signorile, another open war between Shilts and the Left erupted. Shilts conjoined the practice of outing with the AIDS crisis and said that the times were "becoming less congenial for covert homosexuals" but that outing tactics presented a variety of "ethical quandaries." Shilts returned to his commitment to mainstream journalistic values, declaring that outing of politicians or celebrities based solely on gossip or rumor had no place in "a legitimate news story": "As a journalist, I cannot imagine any situation in which I would reveal the homosexuality of a living person who was not a public official engaged in voracious hypocrisy."[23]

Appearing on *CBS This Morning* opposite Gabriel Rotello, editor of *OutWeek* magazine, which had just outed deceased millionaire and gadfly Malcolm Forbes, Shilts embodied the mainstream journalist expert, while Rotello represented the gay media interested in outing closeted gays. Shilts acknowledged, "I've got several opinions on this issue, some of which are contradictory. I would agree . . . that the world would be a much better place if every person who was gay would say so publicly. . . . What I have a problem with is as a journalist using my professional role to make other people's moral choices for them." Shilts added criticism of newspapers and other media that willingly accepted "planted" stories by publicists that implied that certain people were heterosexual when they were not but then feigned disgust at the prospect of outing someone. "I think there is a contradiction in the media," Shilts said. "That contradiction fuels anger, and I think that anger is something that's leading to this trend among some gay publications."[24]

Shilts was more animated and more pointed in his remarks on the Malcolm Forbes outing when he appeared opposite Signorile on CNN's *Larry King Live.* Shilts openly defended the position of his bosses at the *San Francisco Chronicle* to ignore reported stories about the alleged homosexuality of Forbes (as well as similar outing reports surfacing about Pentagon spokesman Pete Williams). Signorile noted that instead of fully exploring the issue of whether the mainstream media should or could have reported on outing issues earlier, "Shilts did as he had always done in the past, he blasted the radicals," engaging in what Signorile viewed as a self-loathing commentary. Signorile believed that Shilts's remarks to King and his national cable TV audience were ample evidence of a growing distaste by Shilts for gay leaders supporting outing. According to Signorile, Shilts concluded that in regard to the nastiness of outing, whether outing is done to army privates by the Pentagon policy or to prominent officials by the gay press, "it's still a dirty business that hurts people." Signorile and other gays openly seethed at Shilts's elevated positions, with Signorile declaring that Shilts's remarks "reeked of self-loathing."[25] Richard Rouillard, editor of the *Advocate,* described Shilts's commentary on outing by the gay media as "particularly vicious."[26]

The controversy over Shilts's remarks reflected the same battles he had faced before when he was doing what he thought mainstream journalists should do: offer up straightforward, unvarnished commentary that reflected an objective point of view, but include a critical analysis of gay politics and society. Repeating an optimistic theme he had rolled out before, Shilts said:

> I don't consider myself an activist or an advocacy journalist. I feel that prejudice in our society [against homosexuals] is born less out of malice than out of ignorance, and that if you just inform people . . . you can do more to erase prejudice than any other kind of action. Because [straight people] just don't know any better, they're just dumb, and they live in a society where we weren't talked about, where all these silly images of us exist, the fantasy images, really, and you try to replace that with some facts.[27]

Amid the growing concerns about how to handle outing a closeted gay person via a newspaper article, Shilts kept the drumbeat reporting going by writing up for the *Chronicle* a congressional study that estimated the cost of rooting out and replacing gay military personnel at $27 million a year, with more than seventeen thousand service members discharged for being gay between 1980 and 1990, according to the Pentagon's records.[28] Shilts focused attention on a new reality of the military's policy: lesbian women were far more likely to be discharged than gay men were. (Women made up 11 percent of the armed forces in 1990 but represented 22 percent of all gay-related discharges. These numbers were even worse in the Marine Corps, where women were 5 percent of the force but 28 percent of gay-related discharges.)

The role gay journalists could or should have in covering day-to-day news was at the heart of author Ransdell Pierson's exploration of Shilts's earliest reporting at the *San Francisco Chronicle*. Pierson particularly looked at stories Shilts wrote about murders and assaults targeting some of the city's gay population and profiles of a local lesbian judge and an openly gay cop. Pierson quoted Shilts as saying that his presence in the newsroom had helped improve the perception of the *Chronicle* with gay readers and had created no problems with his editors or readers about his objectivity.[29]

Scholar Cynthia Tucker reported that ideas about objectivity and the matter of who was reporting the news began to change during the 1970s as women and racial and ethnic minorities began to make headway in gaining newsroom jobs. Tucker said the issue was clear: "Can a reporter from a segment of society which has long been discriminated against resist the temptation to become an advocate?" Tucker raised even more interesting questions when she explored the issue of what stories minority reporters were given, noting that breakthrough African American reporters were often assigned to cover stories in the "black community" and that "by putting black reporters into a news ghetto, where they covered only black politicians and 'black' issues, white news managers helped create an environment in which too many black reporters were protective of those politicians."[30] Ironically, the exact opposite claim often came against Shilts, insisting that he was not favorable or amenable to providing positive coverage of gay political leaders.

Scholar K. A. Nishikawa and colleagues have suggested that it is still unclear whether the increased presence of minorities in the newsroom has any actual effect on coverage afforded to minority communities, although minority reporters self-reported that they believe they are making a difference despite the constraints of "journalistic norms." These journalistic norms are often built around long-established "rules" for gathering news from authoritative sources, such as political and government leaders, and a resulting marginalization and/or exclusion of divisive or minority voices.[31]

Shilts's one-time TV colleague Belva Davis knew something about breaking barriers in journalism. Hired in the early 1970s by KQED-TV during a push by local TV stations to add more on-air talent that included blacks and other minorities, she quickly rose to be the first female black TV anchor west of the Mississippi River, becoming host of *Newsroom*. "I had no role models to follow, but fortunately for me, I worked for people who allowed me to do stories that I found of human interest. I covered everything," Davis said. "In Randy's case, I got myself involved because I wanted to come into the struggle of gay reporters to cover gay communities because that was a problem that they had. Some of my colleagues then thought that if you had gay reporters, they needed to be barred from covering certain issues. I have always said no to that. I would have quit if they told me I could not cover black stories. Otherwise, why was I hired?"[32] Davis, a heterosexual, believes Shilts's journalistic struggle for acceptance was perhaps greater than hers:

> I can't draw a line between my singular experience coming out of an era where the government was encouraging and asking people of color to end segregation in the media. I, at least, had my country's backing, the FCC, encouraging stations to hire minorities. Gay people did not have that kind of front-door support system from the government. They just sort of had to figure it out on their own. There was all of this uncertainty. [A gay reporter such as Randy] couldn't know how people would react to them. With me, I had no choice. They could see that I was brown right away.[33]

The question and debate about what the role was for a gay news reporter reflected how far gay journalists had come. It was Shilts himself who had queried the editors of the *Columbia Journalism Review* in the 1970s about the idea of reporting on the existence of gay men and lesbian women in the mainstream media. Shilts's story idea faced rejection in a kindly worded letter to Shilts from James Boylan, editor of the *CJR* at the time. Boylan said he and his fellow editors "like the subject" and found Shilts's proposed article "readable" but added, "If this were the one major treatment we were likely to do on this issue for a while, it really ought to be definitive. While you present the professional problems of gays, I feel the lack of solid documentation." Boylan said Shilts's story needed more coverage of any legal protections gays may have against workplace discrimination via local or federal statutes, whether any gays had challenged hiring or firing decisions based on sexual orientation, and consideration of gay employees in trade and union contracts with journalists. "Have there been any recent trends in the handling and treatment of gay-rights news that ought to be documented?"[34]

At first blush, Boylan's reply appears to be eliciting more information, but on further consideration, it displays a tremendous amount of cynicism. Boylan and any editor at his level at the time would (or should) certainly know that little to no workplace discrimination protections existed for gay journalists then (or now) and that even if legal challenges had gone forward, they would have failed miserably under local and federal laws that ignored the rights of homosexuals in the workplace. Boylan offered a predictable approach: he encouraged Shilts to "severely shorten" his suggested piece and transform it from a piece of reporting about journalism into an opinion piece that Boylan might consider for publication.[35]

Back at the inaugural session of gay journalists in 1992, Shilts urged his fellow gay journalists to fight the inclination to engage in "political conformity that snuffs out diversity of thought and opinion."[36] His description of some gay journalists as "lavender fascists" for their practice of what he termed "the politics of petulance" and "journalism of rage" that threw objective standards out the window caused a big stir. Signorile highlighted that Shilts "didn't seem to catch the irony of his remarks. He, a man who had called for government-imposed curtailing of sexual activity years earlier, was attacking others as fascists."[37] Signorile said the remarks reflected what he had previously noticed with Shilts: "I'm not sure if he was able to have open disagreements with others or not. He seemed, with me and other gay journalists and activists, to position himself as the moral authority and as the 'professional,' diminishing us as the 'unprofessional' and people of questionable ethics."[38]

Signorile countered Shilts's provocative "lavender fascist" label by noting that gay journalists working for gay publications "are journalists in the best sense" and that "we're reporting the truth, not controlling thoughts or pushing a political agenda."[39] Shilts would be reminded of his artful yet provocative use of the words "lavender fascists" for the remainder of his life, including in the ongoing debate about whether closeted gays in public positions should be outed, a position Shilts opposed in most circumstances, again placing him at odds with more radical gay journalists. Signorile labeled Shilts "arrogant" in his effort to elevate himself to the level of professional journalists and to demote gay journalists "as rag tag activists whose ideas were not mainstream." Signorile added, "I sensed a desperation [from Shilts], perhaps a fear, that the ACT-UP perspective, and that of many new gay journalists and activists, was catching on, being embraced by even those in the mainstream. He seemed to raise the alarm, truly demonizing us by calling us 'lavender fascists.'"[40]

For Shilts, it seemed, to be militant was to be an advocate and thus not a legitimate journalist. In a freewheeling 1987 interview with freelance writer Rich Grzesiak for a Philadelphia gay newspaper, *Au Courant*, Shilts was in full tilt in his assumed role as gay leader and ordained critic, putting in question whether anyone beyond himself still could view him as a solely objective journalist. Shilts expressed his amazement that gay bathhouses had continued to operate for years in some cities after he had helped shutter them in San Francisco. He excoriated gay leaders on the issue: "How dare we go and demand that the federal government pull out all stops for treatments and vaccine research [for AIDS], when we're not willing to do even so much as to close a business? It's a travesty on our part and politically stupid to boot. It makes us [gay people] look incredibly irresponsible." A more palpable example of Shilts engaging in discourse as a "gay leader" perhaps doesn't exist—and there was more to his critique, which included gay-owned and gay-operated newspapers. Shilts accused existing gay leaders of "misguiding us by always talking about civil liberties. The most important thing for most gay men in the next five years, particularly in urban areas, is going to be just keeping sane in the face of all this suffering, because what I do know is going to happen is that we are going to be facing an incredible amount of untimely death." Gay leaders weren't the only subject of his wrath; he noted that gay men in particular seemed reluctant to get involved in politics. "So much of the gay community remains so incredibly apathetic to politics," he said. "It seems that so few people in our community have opened up to the importance of politics in our lives, so they're reluctant to become involved in these gay political groups."[41] Irony seeped in, however, because while Shilts used a wide brush to paint over many gays as politically naive and inactive, to their own detriment, he didn't spare his wrath for those who did dare to get involved and just happened to disagree with him.

*Au Courant* reporter Rich Grzesiak asked Shilts directly about an editorial by *New York Native* and *Christopher Street* publisher Charles L. Ortleb that urged gay readers not to read or follow Shilts's work because of its open criticism of homosexual leaders and gay bathhouse owners. Ortleb, who earlier had been a Shilts advocate and backed his writing of the biography of Harvey Milk, disagreed with Shilts on a variety of issues in the decade that had passed since Milk's death. Shilts and Ortleb certainly disagreed over the closing of gay bathhouses. Shilts, an aficionado of bathhouses in his early days in San Francisco and during visits to New York, hadn't always seen them as a problem, Ortleb was quick to remind others.[42]

Shilts and Ortleb later disagreed over varying theories about what was causing AIDS. Shilts placed a lot of faith in doctors and researchers at the Centers for

Disease Control and the National Institutes of Health, including his friend Dr. Don Francis. Ortleb had been more open to alternative causes of AIDS (beyond the quickly growing belief that it was caused by the identified human immuno-deficiency virus) and had expressed as much often on the pages of *Christopher Street* magazine. Ortleb agreed to feature a story and excerpt of Shilts's new book, *And the Band Played On*, in *Christopher Street,* but with an editorial eschewing the book as unworthy. "Ortleb is a lunatic," Shilts bluntly asserted when asked about the mixed messages coming from *Christopher Street* and Ortleb and then made it even more personal: "I think most people in the gay community recognize his bleatings as the result of probably some viral infection of the brain." Ortleb had made it personal as well, suggesting that Shilts was a self-loathing homosexual taking out his frustration on the gay community.

Michael Denneny said the friction between Shilts and Ortleb was not unusual—fights popped up in lots of corners as AIDS continued to wreak its devastation among gay men. "This was a very heated time, and everyone was under a lot of pressure," Denneny explained. "Consequently, relations were very complex and freighted, with disagreements erupting constantly." Denneny said the relationship between Shilts and Ortleb was no more out of the ordinary than many others at the time, "and above all, their relationship changed under the pressure of events and the various interpretations of them people had. To untangle all these controversies would be like cleaning the Augean stables. Good luck, I say."[43]

Shilts seemed to hold out little hope for the gay media ever growing in credibility and journalistic integrity. He complained that most publications showed little concern for the standard of ethics promoted by either the NLGJA or the Society of Professional Journalists, although he acknowledged that the gay press was sometimes successful in digging up story ideas for other reporters in the mainstream media, including himself, to capitalize upon. "It's so disappointing, though, . . . that you can't trust an awful lot of what's said there. . . . That [personal bias] undermines the credibility of these newspapers and it limits their acceptance both within the gay community and among straight people. The gay press would have a lot more influence on policy, both local and federal, if it were a credible press. You don't need a huge circulation to have influence; you just need to be telling the truth."[44] Shilts's open questioning of the motives of the gay media mirrored their questioning of his—one of many dissonances that would remain unresolved.

143

# CHAPTER 9

# Clean and Sober

Not surprisingly, as Shilts did battle with a vocal—and sometimes cruel—group of critics within the gay community, his long-standing need to address his almost insurmountable addiction to alcohol and marijuana became unavoidable. Shilts's personal diary revealed the struggle he faced in getting sober. "I'm sitting here with my root beer in my new apartment with all my new stuff in it and feeling free and relieved at long last. . . . Day 29 living sober, no alcohol since four weeks ago last night," he wrote in March 1984. "I can see now the dramatic changes which I had hoped would come in my life." Concerned that he was stuck in a rut that would never free him from drinking, he wrote, "I have new confidence, but too much drugs [marijuana], however, [and] I have a fight ahead."[1] In November 1984 Shilts wrote an entry in the diary indicating he was beginning to question his self-medicating: "What are all these changes? . . . Am I addicted to marijuana? Am I fooling myself? Examples—car left in reverse at the bank; small forgetfulness; driving things sneak up on me (I'm spaced out); standing dazed, disoriented, paranoid. Get out of it before I make a big mistake—be clear again."[2]

Randy's brother Gary took note that Randy quit drinking first but took another year before finally giving up pot. "Randy told me once that the first time he smoked marijuana he said to himself, 'I'll never be lonely again.' He really, really liked the drug [and he thought] it had a good effect on him."[3] Shilts's diary reflects he understood, perhaps even as a college student, that getting drunk or getting high held too much importance in his life. A 1972 diary entry from his college days found him self-assessing: "I am changing radically. I am structuring my life less and less and trying to free myself. More marijuana smoking. I feel a new freedom and yet at times I become so totally confused and vulnerable—I often sit and feel that I can only wait for additional things in my life to unfold, a life in which I am only a pawn. Will I fulfill these insanely creative ambitions of mine?"[4]

A wide gap in Shilts's diary ended with a dramatic announcement on April 6, 1986: "It's been two years without alcohol, and in nine days, one year without any drugs. No pot. No coke and that has helped me see how success is my drug now." Noting that he was tired from a burst of writing and editing his forthcoming book, *And the Band Played On,* Shilts wrote, "Suffice it to say, that somewhere, I hoped to have a hand in making a better world and [most lately] in saving some lives. Life gets so much more serious than we ever expect it to be and all our youthful scheming can look pretty petty in retrospect. I do hope I do a better job of all this life business in my second 34 years."[5]

Personal counseling and a growing sobriety had enabled Shilts to gain greater perspective and understanding about his life. His new life view was on full display in the hours after his mother's funeral, when he led a small group of family members "in the know" in a short chorus of "Ding-Dong! The Witch Is Dead" from *The Wizard of Oz.* While he no doubt loved his mother, Shilts was unapologetically open about the abuse he believed he suffered from her—so open, in fact, that among the many writing "sidebars" he undertook was an assignment to contribute a chapter to actress Suzanne Somers's anthology *Wednesday's Children: Adult Survivors of Abuse Speak Out.* Somers, who gained fame as part of the 1970s "jiggle" craze on ABC's situation comedy *Three's Company,* seemed an unlikely conduit for such a serious topic until the release of her best-selling memoir, *Keeping Secrets,* in which she revealed her own battle as an abused child. Shilts's chapter appears among a varied mix of celebrities recruited for the work, including Gary Crosby and Desi Arnaz Jr. (both sons of two famous Hollywood families), Patti Davis (youngest daughter of President Ronald Reagan and his wife, Nancy), TV and film actress Angie Dickinson, and porn actress turned legitimate performer Traci Lords. Declaring that "abused children grow up feeling a deep sense of shame about their abuse," Somers said Shilts's words further the understanding that "shame helps promote secrecy. The abused child is too ashamed to tell anyone what's really going on. Randy Shilts carried two secrets. His first secret was about his mother. . . . Later on Randy recognized that he was gay, which entailed keeping another secret."[6]

Shilts opened his chapter with a painful disclosure: "My mother was given to horrible rages for as long as I can remember. I have clear memories of her drinking through my junior high and high school years. The alcohol really worked her up. Not only would she act crazy and get mad unpredictably, but she beat us all the time—almost every day. Not a swat on the head, she beat us with a belt. It was very ritualistic." The ritual, Shilts wrote, involved inflicting pain more than embarrassment. "I remember going to school after being beaten on those crazy mornings and trying to act as though everything was all right," he wrote. "I didn't want anyone to know my terrible secret, so I had to pretend things at home were normal." His approach to life didn't go unnoticed—he was awarded for three years of perfect attendance in junior high school. Shilts stayed equally invested in school when he moved across Plum Street from junior high to West Aurora High School in the fall of 1966. "With things so tough at home, school became my escape. My teachers were substitute parents. I'd be very good in school and was always going after extra credit as a way of currying teachers' favor. In turn, I would get their approval."[7]

Gaining the approval of adults would remain a major focus of his life, a young Shilts recognizing as early as age eight that he was somehow different from other boys, but it would take many more years for him to fully understand the differences inherent in his sexuality. "Nobody talked about [being gay] back then," he wrote. "There weren't words for it. There wasn't a sense that gay people were a minority group that deserved civil rights, so there was no one I could talk to. It was my secret alone." Many young homosexual boys and girls learn quickly that the closet is the best place to be because they risk the scorn and rejection of their parents and all of society. Shilts wrote, "By the time I was in junior high, I was keeping two horrible secrets. . . . I thought I was a bad person because I was being beaten nearly every day. Add to that this secret knowledge I had that something was unspeakably different about me, and you can begin to understand why I wanted to shut out my feelings."[8] The beatings at the hand—or belt—of his mother didn't stop until Randy was sixteen years old, when he threatened to hit her back.

The forthcoming nature of Shilts's commentary in the Somers book was noteworthy and reflective of the period he was going through: he had entered counseling to finally understand his personal demons and challenges. One of the issues he sought to put behind him was nearly daily intoxication. It was familiar territory for him, as substance abuse was something he had witnessed firsthand as a child, and it created a growing fear that being drunk or high could destroy his burgeoning journalism career. The counseling he sought and the self-examination it entailed opened the floodgates. Shilts was an open person for much of his life, and his book chapter for Somers's anthology blew apart the last barrier of secrets to understanding his life. For his family and other midwesterners more accustomed to families who keep their secrets tightly wrapped up, his disclosures were startling. Randy's older brother Gary remembers standing in a suburban Chicago bookstore—in the self-help section—looking for a book to give as a gift to a friend. There he stumbled across Somers's anthology and Randy's name on the front cover. A wave of shame and embarrassment rolled over him as he read his brother's words: "My mother was given to horrible rages for as long as I can remember."[9] "My first thought was I needed to buy up all of the copies of that book they had," Gary said, realizing that he had only fifty dollars in his wallet and might need to steal the remaining copies in order to prevent customers from reading about the Shilts family secrets on display in a handsome text.[10] Giving it more thought, Gary quickly gave up on the idea of buying up all the copies of the book. He had long before come to live with the openness with which his brother led his life, whether in print or in person.

Randy's brother Reed wondered if the accounts Randy put to words in the book were overstated. "My reaction was, 'Was Randy being a drama queen?' I mean, that was the 'in' thing in the '80s when Randy came out, to talk about your childhood," Reed said. "Our childhood wasn't perfect, I mean, but we were fed, we didn't have cigarette burns on our bodies like other kids I have heard of. So, okay, we got spanked a lot, and we were spanked aggressively, but we were six boys."[11]

The gaps Randy Shilts felt between his hopes and his reality exist at the center of his relationship with his mother. Randy's friend Linda Alband recalled hearing stories about how tough Norma could be on her sons at times. "I think she was just really frustrated and sometimes took that out on the boys," Alband said.

Norma Shilts had some initial reservations about homosexuality, particularly so as related to her son, her feelings often so near the surface that she would abruptly leave the room whenever the subject of homosexuality came up in conversation. As time went along, Norma settled into a familiar position—protective and supportive of her son Randy, gay or not. For his part, with the help of a therapist, Randy finally came to better understand that the relationship with his family—particularly his mother—would always have limitations. The tension between Shilts and his mother, however, was nowhere in sight when she wrote a breezy, newsy letter to him in July 1980, just before his twenty-ninth birthday. The letter, written in the years after she had curtailed her drinking, was loving and funny. "Dad's out in the back yard digging a hole trying to fix the Galesburg-type sewer system," she wrote, setting the scene from the family's new home in Michigan. "In 1980, you can put a man on the moon, but in Galesburg [Michigan], they still have fucking septic tanks!" She mentioned watching a morning news show as she jotted down her thoughts and added, "Dad and I each tossed you a bill for your birthday—in case you need the money worse than a dumb present! If you rather have a dumb present, go buy it dummy!" She concluded, "I'd better close and go out in the kitchen so I can keep an eye on Dad, I don't want him to fall in the fucking septic tank on his head!!" She added a two-page postscript in which she mused about the financial problems of some of her sons because of their growing affection for marijuana, noting that her sons "love their pot and that can get expensive."[12]

Gary asserts that his younger brother had mixed feelings regarding his mother: "There was a lot of ambivalence toward her." Gary believes the Shilts boys learned to navigate their mother's shortcomings, recalling his mother demanding that her husband, Bud, "beat" Gary once when he had misbehaved when he was just a young boy. Gary recalls his father taking him upstairs and having him pretend or fake noises to make it seem like he received his punishment. Over time, "I certainly could feel sorry for my mother and in a lot of ways empathize with her more so than my father," Gary said. "I think ultimately we all do the best we can with what we know at the time, and all the rest I guess goes into therapy and analysis later." "My mother really never accepted Randy's homosexuality, in my view, and she just never really wanted to talk about it. My dad was really cool about that, but she just never said anything about it," Gary said. "However, when Randy would be on television and talk about a gay issue or his books, she would just love it, but if it was a discussion afterward about a gay issue, she would just walk out of the room."[13]

Dealing with the remnants of a tough childhood wrapped up in his mother's rage and his father's frequent absences sent Randy Shilts through various difficult stages of life as a young boy and adolescent. In the first two or three years after he fled home, he responded by essentially cutting off all contact with his family. Moving beyond that, however, he settled too easily (for his own comfort) into a "minimizing" stage in which he attempted to explain away or downgrade the seriousness and ugliness of the reality of the Shilts home. Years later, he said a caller to a radio talk show helped add some context. "I was on a talk show promoting my book when a woman called in saying she was my mother's sister," Shilts said. "After the show I called her up. We hadn't had any contact over the years, but I remembered her once having babysat me. Something told me we had to get together. When we did, she indicated there had been a lot of unhappiness in her family—my mother's family. . . . She told me that from the age of three years old [my mother] had been sexually molested." The estranged aunt—cast out for more than thirty years for having revealed her own childhood molestation—said Shilts's mother joined the rest of the family in cutting off all contact with her. "Having this knowledge about my mother explains why there was no possibility that she could have a happy marriage," Shilts wrote. "She and my dad had six children, but there had to be a lot of anger tied up with just the sexual act itself. . . . I feel pain now when I think of what her life must have been like. She had to live with those memories. I now can understand her unexplainable rage when I would get caught playing doctor as a child. . . . It helps in the healing process . . . [and] knowing what I know now about my mother has really helped me to come to understand her."[14]

The sharp edges others often noted in Shilts's personality reflected the personal challenges he was facing, primarily with falling into the same alcoholism that had been at least a part of his youth. Beyond dealing with the scars of childhood, Shilts addressed his own alcoholism head-on. He was not the first, and certainly not the last, member of the fourth estate to come to the realization that drinking and drugging can destroy many things. Shilts confessed a moment in his career—one that only he knew about—when he came back from a dinner break at the *San Francisco Chronicle* lit up from a quick stopover at a local bar and scared himself into thinking he was placing his career and even his life at risk. He promised he'd never do it again. Shilts "got sober" through a brief in-patient stay at a rehabilitation facility and via a group he had reported on in the past, Alcoholics Anonymous. His commitment to getting sober, however, didn't come until he took risks that could have endangered his career. In the weeks following the death of his mother, a ton of unresolved issues never broached, growing criticism of his coverage of gay bathhouses, and news of the death of his friend Gary Walsh from AIDS-related complications on February 21, 1984, sent Shilts over the edge on that dinner break. He found temporary solace in six shots of Jack Daniels and then tried to return to work. Shilts said the incident "terrified" him because "I realized that I had worked so hard, and it was a struggle to get to the point where I could be at the *Chronicle*, to be at a major newspaper, and I was just going to throw it away for this cheap high? And that was the last time I had a drink."[15]

Shilts knew he was self-medicating: "As I got older, my drinking became very pronounced. . . . I worked 12 to 14 hours a day, but I still found time to get drunk four or five nights a week." Kicking pot, however, would be a tougher sled. Shilts told family and friends he was convinced marijuana was a very good mix with his personality and body. The drug made him feel good and didn't seem to slow him down appreciably in his ability to churn out large volumes of words. "I smoked marijuana every day and did for the next year" after he quit drinking but finally went "clean and sober" in March 1985. During this period, however, deadlines and the demands of writing *And the Band Played On* while he was still a staff writer and columnist for the *Chronicle* precipitated the need for sleeping pills. Within months he was addicted to those as well, not being able to shed his dependence on them until November 1986. For the Somers book chapter he wrote six years later, he proclaimed proudly, "Since that time I haven't used any mind-altering substances. I have become very serious about recovery. I go to support groups several times a week." He understood that "I have an addictive personality, and I think it's been about abating pain."[16]

"Being an alcoholic was a great gift to me," Shilts told one reporter. "My own recovery from substance abuse helped me see some of the things that were going on in the gay community. People lose their judgment when they are drunk. Recovery has even clarified my writing."[17] Shilts's friend David Israels affirmed Shilts's decision to get sober, recalling, "He was a pretty heavy drinker and not a particularly fun drunk."[18]

Gay fiction author Daniel Curzon encountered a drunken Randy Shilts once and reported he believed Shilts well personified the vacuous drunk gay man who inhabited gay bars and bathhouses across the Castro. He described Shilts as "a cherubic, bright eyed . . . boy reporter" but also recalled him as an arrogant, even verbally abusive drunk. Curzon said Shilts came across as "a prime example of the young literate but totally unlettered generation."[19] Curzon's criticism of Shilts upset him considerably, Shilts admitting to friends that he struggled with internalizing criticism he received because of his own belief that his writing showed a lot of sensitivity. "If I became thick-skinned about my writing, I would not be the kind of writer I want to be, the kind of writer who still connects to people on a human level," Shilts said.[20]

Among the changes Shilts made when he joined AA was to break up with his live-in lover and partner, Steve Newman, an on-air weatherman for KRON-TV. Their meeting wasn't an immediate match. Newman recalls Shilts, flush with alcohol, holding forth at a party about the silliness of local weather forecasts because of the already existing work of the National Weather Service. Newman recalled that it was "Randy being Randy": he sometimes enjoyed insulting others without stopping to think about the impact of his words. Privately, however, the two men hit it off, and a sexual relationship soon blossomed into living together in a high-rise condo on Cathedral Hill overlooking the San Francisco Bay. Newman recalls that in private, Shilts would say that the *Chronicle* newsroom could be quite stodgy, but "Randy always just had a lot of effervescence about anything that he was doing. I'm sure that took some adjusting to on their part at the paper, but when they began to see the quality of reporting that he could do, it was not a continual concern. I know that they could see that when he was truly enthusiastic and committed to a subject or story idea, that he would produce some truly significant reporting."[21]

Shilts's friend Cleve Jones "took the cure" along with Shilts, both of them transitioning for a time from being buddies who prowled around south of the Market Street bars in San Francisco to being compatriots attending Alcoholics Anonymous meetings. "He was dealing with alcohol issues that I was sort of always peripherally aware of," Jones said, "and then I remember the change was pretty dramatic after he got into the program. His house, his apartment was always filthy, and suddenly it was all clean and organized. I know the [AA] program was really important to him."[22]

"Randy [Shilts] can't be understood without understanding his alcoholism," declared Shilts critic John Preston, a former editor in chief of the *Advocate* who knew Shilts professionally and personally. Preston believes the twelve-step process of sobriety advocated by Alcoholics Anonymous highly influenced Shilts's writing and his tendency toward what Preston believes were "puritanical positions" on certain issues, including gay bathhouses, which he helped shutter at the height of the AIDS crisis in San Francisco. Preston believes Shilts viewed bathhouse owners as comparable to bar owners who exploit the compulsions of gay men to the detriment of those men.[23] Shilts openly confirmed this view via a May 1991 interview with *Progressive* magazine as he defended his commitment to writing about HIV transmission in the gay community, despite calls from other gays to back off. On the bathhouse issue in particular, Shilts said: "In my mind, it was always a business issue. Here were greedy businessmen who would kill anybody to make 25 cents. But the gay community did not interpret it as a business issue. It interpreted it as a civil rights issue. My reporting was aggressive, sometimes overly so. There was this perception that I was out to subvert gay rights and I didn't care about civil liberties and civil rights. To me, the overriding issue was that civil rights wouldn't do us any good if we were all dead from this disease."[24]

Shilts's growing prominence and respect as a national journalist not only showed in the amplified authority that came through in his written voice but also allowed him to briefly meet two of his heroes along the way, Bob Woodward and Carl Bernstein. The influence of those two *Washington Post* reporters, who were credited with unearthing the secrets of the Nixon administration, held a long and significant sway over Shilts's writing process. Woodward and Bernstein and their style of reporting loomed large for many young journalists entering the field in the 1970s. Shilts was a fan of the book *All the President's Men,* which followed the efforts of "Woodstein" to untangle the myriad lies that eventually engulfed President Nixon, and he sought to employ a similar journalistic style in his own writing process. For his first book, *The Mayor of Castro Street: The Life and Times of Harvey Milk,* friends recall Shilts employing the writing process depicted in the film version of *All the President's Men.* Shilts typed *The Mayor of Castro Street* on an electric typewriter (this was before personal computers), a decidedly burdensome task, because edits and changes required large sections of the text to be retyped. "I remember visiting him at his apartment and being amazed at all the pieces of paper that he had taped up on the walls," Cleve Jones recalled of Shilts's work in 1980–81 in preparing the Milk biography. "I was fascinated by the physical work of making the book. It was kind of intriguing for me to see him operating in this sort of new way that was a very different type of writing than what he did as a column or a twelve-paragraph news story. He was extremely conscientious."[25]

Dr. Don Francis, one of the earliest scientists researching the onset of HIV and AIDS (and still today a researcher looking for a vaccine to block or prevent AIDS), said he saw a twenty-to-thirty-foot-long row of note cards in Shilts's apartment as he made his way through the complicated issues of his second book, *And the Band Played On.* Francis recalled, "He had all these three-by-five cards, and they were all in chronological order with all the information that he gleaned. . . . But this was his whole book, the outline of his book, which was written out on these cards, and they were standing upright, so they were all across the room, hundreds of them, all handwritten." Shilts asked Francis to look at several of the cards, on which there were questions or issues: "Randy had these sticky notes that he would stick to them and he would pull them out and ask for a clarification or wonder whether he had something right."[26]

David Israels was in an elite group of friends and associates who were mailed copies of the earliest drafts of both *The Mayor of Castro Street* and *And the Band Played On.* "He had a number of us, I think it was three or four of us, who got copies of the manuscript as he produced it," Israels recalled. "He made copies for us to read and talk to him about it as he wrote it, but it was also to protect it in case the original copy got destroyed, there would be multiple copies in different locations. This is still in the typewriter days, so when he finished a chapter, or multiple chapters at a time, he would give each of us a copy. . . . By then we were good enough friends and he respected my opinion and he wanted multiple reactions to the book." Israels cannot recall making any significant suggestions for changes. He viewed Shilts as a mentor and always respected his writing style—"I just gobbled it up," he said. His biggest suggestion, that of changing the name of the Harvey Milk biography to something other than *The Mayor of Castro Street*, was advice Shilts ignored. Israels thought Castro Street was too obscure for most people to know anything about.[27]

Jones thought a book about Milk's life made perfect sense at the time and credits Shilts's book and the 2008 feature film *Milk* from director Gus Van Sant for keeping Milk's legacy alive. Van Sant, an Academy Award–nominated director, had previously expressed interest in a film treatment of Shilts's biography on Milk, introduced to him by Jones, a mutual friend. "I remember this weird, really sad meeting we had with Randy up at his condo," Jones said. The meeting came in the midst of a rough patch healthwise for both Shilts and Jones: "I took Gus up there, and Randy and I were both sick, and I remember feeling like this was just so weird. It was like [Gus] has come to interview these two dying people who were sort of the last survivors of this particular chapter in history."[28] After their meeting, Van Sant split his time between San Francisco and Los Angeles and began working on producing the biopic treatment, but eventually he abandoned the project at that time because of wrangling with studio executives and producers. A big-screen dramatic interpretation of Shilts's biography would eventually fail.

Van Sant didn't give up, however, and revisited the topic more than a decade later. Van Sant engaged a young, up-and-coming screenwriter, Dustin Lance Black, a writer gaining notice for his contributions to HBO's successful dramatic series *Big Love* and an earlier documentary, *On the Bus*. Black befriended Jones and others to create from whole cloth the Milk story. Film rights to Shilts's book were still under option with Warner Independent, a part of Warner Bros. Entertainment, Inc., where producers Neil Meron and Craig Zadan had tried for years to get their own version off the ground.[29]

On November 26, 2008, Focus Features released *Milk*, a $20 million feature directed by Van Sant and produced by Dan Jinks and Bruce Cohen. Packed with a "name" cast, including Sean Penn in the role of Harvey Milk, the film was a box-office and critical success. It won eight Academy Award nominations, eight Critics' Choice Movie Awards, three Screen Actors Guild Award nominations, a Golden Globe nomination for Penn, and a Directors Guild of America Award nomination for Van Sant. The Directors Guild Award went to Van Sant, as did an Oscar for best screenplay for Black.

The success of the 2008 film on Milk's life notwithstanding, the film left Shilts behind, with no mention of his original work in the film's credits. Shilts had experienced nothing but frustration in his own efforts to get a movie version of his book made. The interest Hollywood had shown in his work (primarily via options and rights purchased to produce a dramatic work on Shilts's writing) never grew. Shilts himself even took time off from his reporting job to try his hand at screenwriting, a skill that everyone generally agreed eluded him. Eventually, director/writer Rob Epstein and producer Richard Schmiechen debuted *The Times of Harvey Milk* as a documentary, winning an Academy Award for best documentary feature in 1984. Shilts was absent from the frames of the documentary, though archival film footage from stories he had prepared for KQED were included—sans Shilts.

Despite such setbacks (and with the knowledge that his book had sold well and that he had been paid options fees for a film that would never be made), Shilts moved on to his next book project while remaining a full-time reporter at the *San Francisco Chronicle*.

# CHAPTER 10

# Strike Up the *Band*

hilts's editor at St. Martin's Press, Michael Denneny, said there was never any question that Shilts would write a second book and that it would be about HIV and AIDS. As a result, all of Shilts's work researching and writing on the issue for his daily news stories in the *Chronicle* formed valuable research and background material. Denneny recalls: "We knew that was going to be his next book, but this was at the very beginning, and we did not know when the 'event' would resolve itself. . . . I cannot remember when Randy decided that he should do that, but it must have been 1983 or 1984. I remember that I thought it was too early and that we didn't have the story yet and there was no ending. Randy and I had a lot of arguments, but he finally convinced me that we had to go ahead anyway." As expected, St. Martin's editors weren't interested and passed on a chance to publish Shilts's work.[1]

Shilts viewed writing *the* book about the AIDS pandemic as a required task. Frustrated that his articles in the *Chronicle* weren't having any influence beyond gay circles and San Francisco proper, he was convinced the political aspects of the disease must be covered. His desire to be the definitive reporter covering AIDS coincided with visions he entertained of becoming a best-selling author and Pulitzer Prize–winning journalist (the latter goal was never realized). As Shilts explained, "Writing a book was the way to get over the heads of the *New York Times* and the other papers that weren't covering this issue, in terms of the political components of it. . . . I had such a clear vision of what had gone wrong in the early years of the epidemic, one shared by hardly anyone, except the very people who were involved in it."[2]

The complexity of writing a story as big and broad as the advent of an infectious disease pandemic—the arrival of HIV and AIDS—cannot be understated. It was, as many warned Shilts, a story without a known ending. It was a story, even, without a known scope. How many people would die of AIDS before it was over? How would societies around the world respond? Brilliantly, Shilts took up the very barriers that seemed to argue against taking up the story and made them work as the guiding principle of the book. One understandable and manageable way to cover the chronicle of AIDS was to provide excruciating details about the growing infection rate and death toll. "The story of these first five years of AIDS in America is a drama of national failure, played out against a backdrop of needless death," Shilts wrote as he attempted to introduce the overall themes that would drive his book *And the Band Played On.*

> *People died* while Reagan administration officials ignored pleas from government scientists and did not allocate adequate funding for AIDS research until the epidemic had already spread through the country. *People died* while scientists did not at first devote appropriate attention to the epidemic because they perceived little prestige to be gained in studying a homosexual affliction. *People died* while public health authorities and the political leaders who guided them refused to take the tough measures necessary to curb the epidemic's spread, opting for political expediency over the public health. And *people died* while gay community leaders played politics with the disease, putting political dogma ahead of the preservation of human life. *People died* and nobody paid attention because the mass media did not like covering stories about homosexuals and was especially skittish about stories that involved gay sexuality.[3]

Shilts found a writers' agent, Fred Hill of Los Angeles, who went shopping for a publisher for the story of AIDS after Denneny delivered the news that St. Martin's Press said no to publishing the book and to Shilts's hefty advance demand. Denneny said Hill tried to pitch the book to twelve other publishers, all without success. Shilts said publishers all had similar responses—that the AIDS story was one without an ending, since a cure had not been found; that its total impact was unknown, as infection rates continued to climb; or that the story of a disease required a doctor or someone with a clinical background to write it.

Undeterred and with no publisher lined up, Shilts continued writing. Denneny later said that he was feeling a personal and professional conflict of interest. Over the course of working on *The Mayor of Castro Street*, Denneny and Shilts had become friends, yet Denneny still was professionally obligated to represent the views and interests of St. Martin's Press. As a result, the two worked out an "at work" and a "not at work" communication system in which Denneny stood firm in the "no" for a book by St. Martin's on AIDS but privately coached Shilts on how he might be able to shoehorn in an agreement to get it published. A first step was getting Hill and Shilts to drop their $80,000 to $100,000 advance proposal, and a second step involved getting Shilts to sharpen his pitch for an AIDS book down to a crisp eighty-eight-page proposal. "It was the best book proposal I ever read," Denneny said, but it still lacked an ending, since the outcome or scope of the AIDS pandemic was unknown. Finally, moved by the book proposal's quality and Denneny's lobbying, St. Martin's relented and agreed to publish the book, but with a very small advance, only $15,000. "They were not convinced there was any arc to the story, no shape, and no ending," Denneny said. "I got on my high horse and said, 'This is a literary question and I am the editor, and I guarantee that it will have an arc and an ending!'"[4]

Shilts balked when Denneny delivered the St. Martin's offer. Shilts said the $15,000 advance was an insult, and he wanted to pass on the new offer. Denneny went into his "not at work" mode: "I went home and had dinner and called Randy up and said, 'I am now talking to you as your friend,' and I said, 'You're being an asshole.' I said, 'This is the book that you were meant to write. I don't care if we pay you $2,000. I don't care if it costs you $5,000 to write it. If you don't realize that this was the book that you were put on Earth to write, then you are a bigger fool than I ever thought you were. Money is irrelevant. You have to write this book.'" Shilts took some convincing, but with the backing of his bosses at the *Chronicle* and the knowledge that he would be able to write the book and keep a weekly salary coming in from the newspaper, he agreed. Denneny said, "The *Chronicle* had been, and continued to be, very supportive. Basically, they allowed him to keep working only exclusively on the AIDS beat, and that meant that they were essentially paying him a salary as he wrote the book. He kept writing stories on AIDS and doing research for the paper, but always with the book in mind overall."[5]

Shilts's writing style for *And the Band Played On* created a variety of heroes and villains, with the virus that caused AIDS as the biggest antihero presented. Dr. Don Francis, once an obscure scientist at the Centers for Disease Control and Prevention in Atlanta, became one of Shilts's heroes. Francis gained fame in part because of the HBO film adaptation of Shilts's work, which cast a convincing Matthew Modine as the crusading Dr. Francis trying to fight his way through a bureaucratic maze that was unable to respond to AIDS.

The idea for Shilts's book—and his desire for Francis to help him—was not one Francis was initially excited about, however. "He said he was thinking about writing a book and wanted to know if I would help him," Francis said. "At that time, we were just so wiped out working on AIDS that I was very reticent to get involved in anything of that sort."[6] Francis forgot about Shilts's book idea until months later, when drafts and outlines came his way, convincing him that Shilts was not only very serious about writing the book but also smart enough to write it correctly. Shilts set up his work in a foreword that declared that his book was "a work of journalism" and that "there has been no fictionalization." His journalistic claims, however, were problematic for many, especially given the influence of fiction techniques employed by writers such as James Michener. Shilts explained, "For purposes of narrative flow, I reconstruct scenes, recount conversations and occasionally attribute observations to people with such phrases as 'he thought' or 'she felt.' Such references are drawn from either the research interviews I conducted for the book or from research conducted during my years covering the AIDS epidemic for *The San Francisco Chronicle*."[7]

For many traditional journalists, Shilts's approach causes dissonance, but it accurately reflected the style popularized by Truman Capote, Tom Wolfe, Gay Talese, Norman Mailer, Joan Didion, and others as Shilts was coming of age in journalism. Regardless, with the releasing of *Band,* few challenges to his words arose, in part because Shilts was always so comfortable and confident about his claims. His confidence grew, it seems, out of the fact that few writers could or would "outwork" him. Over a five-year period he conducted hundreds of interviews in support of *Band.* Of those, Shilts held a "special reverence" for those living and dying with AIDS "who gave some of their last hours for interviews, sometimes while they were on their deathbeds laboring for breath. When I'd ask why they'd take the time for this, most hoped that something they said would save someone else from suffering. If there is an act that better defines heroism, I have not seen it."[8] The story underneath the reams of statistics and government bureaucracy was always a personal one, including Shilts's selection of his friend Gary Walsh as an early spotlight in the book. Walsh, who would succumb to AIDS before the book was completed, knew Shilts from the bars and from shared carousing in the gay mecca. Shilts was a loyal friend to Walsh and agreed to accompany him for an ultimately painful and awkward live television satellite interview discussing AIDS. The interview was classic for TV journalism, pitting Walsh and Shilts against the Reverend Jerry Falwell, founder of the so-called Moral Majority and president of the ironically named Liberty University. Walsh and Shilts struggled against Falwell's relentless quoting of scripture to justify his argument that gays had violated "moral, health and hygiene laws" and as a result had "reaped the whirlwind."[9]

Francis, a scientist and clinician and not a trained journalist, believes Shilts's approach fit the story he was attempting to tell, noting that the "club of knowledge" about HIV and AIDS in the early years was quite small. The number of "club members" who knew about the history of the growth in reported cases of sexually transmitted diseases among gay men was even smaller. Shilts was among those who knew, Francis said, recalling that he had talked to Shilts by telephone during his earliest days at the CDC as Francis and his colleagues were busy mapping a Hepatitis B study among gay men in New York City in the late 1970s. Francis made this point, he said, to emphasize that not everyone agreed to or supported the idea that a transmittable or communicable agent was behind the growing exotic illnesses affecting gay men (initially known as GRID). He believes Shilts understood this important fact from a very early point. Another fact that Shilts understood, likely because Francis shared it with most anyone he could, was the rising level of frustration and anger among CDC employees about the federal government's response to AIDS. Francis said:

> In all the time that I spent fighting infectious diseases, I was appalled and shocked, and so was everyone at CDC. We were quite a bit discouraged by having essentially the disease of the century in terms of severity in our hands, and we still didn't know how big it was going to be, and we're being told that we can do nothing. We pushed everybody we could politically, but there are limits when you are in a government setting. You have to go up the government channels to operate. There was really tremendous frustration. We got fairly sophisticated politically. We would send around our prevention plans, and when they said no, we would just do a little bit of calling around asking others to help us. But you couldn't come up against these Reaganites and do anything. They were truly evil people.[10]

Francis likes to ask, "Where would we be on the issue of AIDS without Randy's book?" and answers his own question with a declaration that Shilts "chronicled the pain, the society and the people who were involved with AIDS and what they went through, and he did that in a beautiful way, and you can really see the misery and the successes and the failures."[11]

Beyond the unprecedented attention Shilts was able to provide AIDS via the pages of *And the Band Played On*, he also highlighted other emerging gay rights issues, including ongoing struggles gay couples encountered with hospitals unwilling to allow partners to visit their dying lovers. Shilts noted that Ward 5B at San Francisco General Hospital would have none of that, allowing all "significant others" and partners of patients to have full visiting privileges: "As far as [the hospital] was concerned, the definition of the American family had changed. It should be the right of the patients to define their families, not the right of the hospital."[12]

Shilts's friend Carol Pogash, a reporter at the *San Francisco Examiner* during the time Shilts was at the *Chronicle,* wrote a 1992 Pulitzer Prize–nominated book about the AIDS ward at San Francisco General Hospital entitled *As Real as It Gets.* Shilts, who wrote the foreword for Pogash's book, admired her work. According to Pogash, "This was a time when people were just petrified of AIDS. . . . [I]n the early days people just didn't know how it was transmitted, and that led to all kinds of fears." Some of those fears were so strong that a surgeon at San Francisco General was reluctant to perform surgeries on people with AIDS, Pogash uncovered.[13]

A frequent Shilts source during his days covering the emerging "AIDS beat" for the *San Francisco Chronicle* was Selma Dritz. Dritz would become a key link between Shilts and the most controversial aspect of his upcoming book. She was among the first who hypothesized that one man, an Air Canada flight attendant, could represent some sort of hideous sexual monster who was infecting his sexual partners with the virus linked to AIDS. She described to Shilts (and later to Harry Reasoner and the entire nation via CBS's *60 Minutes*) her face-to-face confrontation with a beautiful young gay man, Gaëtan Dugas, and her efforts to get him to stop or at least alter his sexual practices. By this time, Dugas was long gone and unable to tell his side of the story. Dritz's version cast Dugas as openly defying logic; he said he didn't care if he was infecting others with a still unknown infectious agent. Dritz's story about Dugas—confirmed by variations of it from others—would form a critical and ultimately highly controversial point in Shilts's book. It's clear the Dugas story told by Dritz had captivated Shilts, who wrote to her early in 1986: "I'm going to nag you about 'Patient Zero' since he has such a unique role in both the epidemic and by epitomizing [in one body] so many of the public health issues which defied knee-jerk response. What to do about a 'Patient Zero' remains something the gay community has yet to face up to—and such patients will certainly arise again."[14] His cavalier, almost excited tone about the concept of a "Patient Zero" at the heart of the AIDS crisis would prove revealing to Shilts's later writing motives and methodologies.

Shilts pursued Dugas's presence with many sources, both medical and personal. From his interactions with Dugas, CDC epidemiologist Dr. William Darrow indicated that Dugas simply could not understand how a person with cancer—as he had been told his Kaposi's sarcoma was—could be a communicable threat to anyone.[15] Dritz said she confronted Dugas at her office about changing his sexual behaviors, and "I never saw him again. It was a pity, because he was apparently an intelligent man, except on this one point. And he was very, very sexually active. He was *a presumptive proof* that AIDS was something transmissible from an infected person directly to the uninfected person."[16]

Dritz not only shared with Shilts her interactions with Dugas and her growing concern about his sexual behavior but also was instrumental in connecting Shilts to Darrow, a respected epidemiologist with the Centers for Disease Control and Prevention for three decades. It was Darrow, through his use of "disease detection" interviews and qualitative research methods, who drafted the landmark 1981 "cluster study," which attempted to determine the basis for an outbreak of Kaposi's sarcoma among a growing number of gay men, mostly in San Francisco, Los Angeles, and New York City.[17] In 1982 Darrow and Dr. David Auerbach undertook another study based in the gay community, focusing on a hypothesis that linked the outbreak of KS infections to sexual contact. As part of their study, Darrow and Auerbach investigated thirteen of the first nineteen KS cases reported in Los Angeles and Orange Counties in southern California and found that nine had reported sexual contact with one common partner within five years before their onset of symptoms.[18] Darrow reported no problems in getting the mostly qualitative study published:

> Even though it was self-reported data, we had set stringent criteria. We were not going to consider the context of our data to be valid unless we could get another person to validate it. In other words, if Person A named Person B as a sexual partner, then we would go to Person B and ask them who they had had sex with, and if they did not name Person A, then we could not be certain that there was a relationship between the two. . . . Even the most rigorous bench scientists, when we started telling these stories, were quite convinced that they were true, especially our colleagues at the CDC.[19]

Later, the study was extended to include ninety patients from across the country representing about three-quarters of the reported cases of KS or *Pneumocystis carinii* pneumonia among gay men alive at the time. The result found that forty of the ninety patients in ten US cities had sexual contact with one man, supporting the original theory that sexual transmission played a part in the spread of opportunistic diseases and infections among gay men with suppressed immune systems. That one man buttressed the suspicions of Dritz and others that the

Canadian man they had encountered was not only an early victim of the new disease of AIDS but perhaps a key player in spreading infections. After the fact, critics have suggested that Shilts and others settled too quickly on the role that one man could play or was playing in the spread of the disease, somewhat like a homicide detective who focuses on one suspect to the exclusion of all others.[20]

Darrow recalls encountering Shilts long before Darrow's first-ever studies on the origins of HIV and AIDS became public. Shilts telephoned him for a 1978 report Shilts was preparing on sexually transmitted diseases impacting gay men but only used Darrow's information on background: "He would call me on and off over the years, but I would not describe myself as a major source for him. I'm not a physician; I am kind of unusual because I'm a sociologist, and I come out of social science. . . . So if Randy wanted to get a different slant on an issue, he would call me."[21]

Darrow said he developed a strong working relationship with Shilts, even to the point of Shilts agreeing to forgo audio recording interviews when asked to. "He agreed to do that and he was under no obligation to do so," Darrow said. A disagreement arose, however, based on Shilts's insistence on trying to learn the names of the men included in Darrow's groundbreaking studies. Shilts had used his sources in the gay community and among health professionals to unearth the names of most of the men, the most controversial of course being Gaëtan Dugas, whom Shilts later infamously identified as "Patient Zero" (an identification that was later questioned). Darrow said he begged Shilts to use pseudonyms for the men in the study but said Shilts refused: "Randy made the decision that he had to use the names, he said that this was the only way we were going to affect the [Reagan] administration. He told me that if you're going to have impact on the public, the kind of impact he believed we had to have in order to change things, you had to name names. He was concerned about 'the band playing on,' and that nothing was going to change unless he started to name names, and talking about people in all of their various dimensions."[22] Darrow's colleague James Curran said that some transparency was necessary in the pursuit of what he called "a public health emergency." "We felt justified, at the time, in sharing names with other patients [but not with reporters such as Shilts]. We were trying to figure out what was happening and what was causing it, and we didn't know of any other way."[23] Perhaps more importantly, however, Darrow and Curran maintain that Shilts terribly misinterpreted the original cluster study as an attempt to find the origin of AIDS rather than an attempt to further researchers' understanding of disease transmission.

Shilts's decision to identify any of the men in the earliest studies about the disease that would become known as AIDS was instantly controversial and remained so as Shilts went so far as to write about Dugas in significant detail in *And the Band Played On*. Shilts did so within a fully understood tradition of journalistic adherence to protecting confidential sources, including those gained via medical or scientific studies. Researcher Isabella Awad undertook an interesting analysis of how issues of confidentiality play out in journalistic investigations versus other types of social science queries such as anthropology. Awad noted that while most social sciences must adhere to federal and university-level regulations regarding research involving human subjects, journalists have sometimes moved outside these restrictions because of their larger adherence to First Amendment protections for a free press. The study of human subjects "requires the assessment of costs and benefits, the informed consent of informants, and, in general, researchers' protective and responsible attitude towards them," but journalists sometimes forgo such requirements. Journalists, she said, argue that "news is non-generalizable knowledge, [and therefore] journalism exempts itself from this regulation." Beyond inherent conflicts some journalists perceive as arising with the watchdog role of the press, "the apparent conflict between confidentiality and credibility, and journalists' reluctance to take responsibility for the consequences of what they publish," raise serious questions about "news professionals' understanding of truth in terms of facticity and of their job as the transmission of such truths," Awad concluded.[24]

The ethical responsibility of violating patient identifications in the various early studies on HIV and AIDS (all occurring in the years before strict patient confidentiality laws existed via the Health Insurance Portability and Accountability Act of 1996) by Shilts was controversial from the start. Darrow and his CDC colleagues didn't like Shilts's approach, as they were strict in their adherence to privacy involving the gay men who willingly participated in their studies, including Dugas. Shilts apparently felt no such restrictions and let no reservations cause him to keep Dugas's name private. Through his various sources—many suspected primarily Dritz—Shilts matter-of-factly set about finding the men in the CDC studies.

Shilts's process in identifying the one man found to be at the center of many cases of KS infections is of particular importance. Darrow said his process in writing the cluster studies focused on identifying cases based on where they lived. "In the Los Angeles cluster, I talk about cases LA-1, LA-2, LA-3, and so on," Darrow said. "This reflected the order in which the cases were reported. But then there was this one out-of-California case, so I called him 'O' for 'outside of California,' but when everybody saw the 'O' they translated that to zero, which became 'Patient Zero.'" Among those who made such a translation was Shilts. "It was a misinterpretation of what I'd shown and what I'd written, and it became common folklore, this so-called 'Patient Zero' that connected cases in Los Angeles and also connected cases in New York, San Francisco, and elsewhere in the world," Darrow said. Darrow said Shilts's interpretation, along with that of others, was "a complete misrepresentation" that the "O" case was the first case or an origin of the infections. "He was not being interpreted by us to be the origin," Darrow declared. "We never meant to say that he was the first case. We never had any evidence that he was the first case." Darrow is still convinced, however, that "Patient Zero" (as dubbed by Shilts) *was* among the very first cases diagnosed with Kaposi's sarcoma in Toronto in May 1979, two years before any cases were reported in the United States, and that he *was* at the center of this particular cluster of cases.[25]

Complicating the likelihood of Dugas as an original patient, however, is the eventually determined incubation period for HIV, which can be as long as a decade, meaning that Dugas would have had to become infected as early as 1969 or 1970 (when he was only sixteen or seventeen years old) to be any sort of "original" AIDS case—a likelihood that seems narrow, given what is known of Dugas's life as a boy and an adolescent. Darrow determined, in direct contradiction to Shilts's conclusion, that Dugas "easily was among the very first 100 or 200 cases in North America, but never would I argue that he was responsible for every single case." Despite the conflict of conclusions, Darrow defends Shilts's supposition and believes a careful reading of Shilts's text indicates that Shilts viewed Dugas as *representative* of how the AIDS pandemic could have started but not as solely responsible for all cases occurring. "I don't think Randy Shilts ever intended to deceive anyone," Darrow said.[26] University of Cambridge historian Richard McKay disagrees: "By the time that Shilts was writing his book . . . researchers had extended the incubation period for AIDS from several months to several years of asymptomatic infection. This extension cast doubt on the significance of many of the links depicted in the cluster diagram" created by Darrow and used by Shilts. The "Patient Zero" concept, however, survived to the final version of the book because Shilts was unable to resist "the storytelling potential of the cluster study's central figure," which had "captivated" him, McKay believes.[27]

Curran believes Shilts "got it wrong, certainly": "We did the study and we knew that [Dugas] was not the first patient to anything—he was just the patient who was at the center of this particular cluster. It didn't even necessarily mean that the same virus was being transmitted to all of the other people, even in that cluster; we didn't even know that. You would have had to isolate the virus to know that, and we didn't know that."[28]

Dr. Marcus Conant believes Shilts's intent in using the Dugas story was to tell the larger story of AIDS. Conant, who personally treated Dugas on more than one occasion in his dermatology practice, was one of the sources Shilts called repeatedly, trying to place a name with a case number—"Patient O." Conant refused to budge on disclosing the name. It didn't matter. Shilts went about working the phone with a variety of other sources and eventually called Conant back and told him, "I've got it." Conant contends that Shilts used Dugas as

> a metaphor, for Christ's sake! If Dugas hadn't done it, someone else would have, and probably many others were. The thing about Dugas was that he became infected early on. Dugas became infected and he was traveling often between Paris, Brussels, as well as Montreal, New York, San Francisco, and Los Angeles. Clearly, he was *one* of the people responsible for infecting a lot of people. As far as picking up people, and as far as giving people this disease, [Dugas] had no compunction about that. Randy Shilts made a metaphor of him and could personalize the story, and I see that as nothing but good journalism. I don't see that as any kind of nefarious plot.[29]

Cleve Jones recalls having many conversations with Shilts, now back among friends and away from official sources, about the use of the "Patient Zero" concept and naming Dugas publicly. Jones, like Shilts, had visited with Selma Dritz at the county health department, and she wove a very interesting story about what could be causing AIDS among gay men. "Dr. Dritz down at the health department had this blackboard in her office that actually showed squares and circles that represented various houses and neighborhoods where people were either getting sick or who had died," Jones said.

> This is very, very early on in the process, when no one had any sort of information about transmission of this disease or how long someone could live without symptoms. So we knew almost nothing. She had this map on her blackboard, and you'd go in there and see, "OK, well, here's this house on 18th Street where three roommates in the same house have come down with it." And then we learned that one of the guys who lived in that house dated a guy who lived in another house over on Douglas Street. And then there was somebody else who lived in that house, and so this blackboard had circles with lines connecting them, and I think it was really the first epidemiological mapping of what would

165

become the AIDS pandemic. I remember hearing about this flight attendant [Dugas], and he was on that map. So when Randy started investigating Gaëtan as a part of the research for his book, he believed that Gaëtan was the guy who brought the virus to our city, and I think most of us believed that too. You know, there was this guy who appeared and people thought he was very good looking, and people he had sex with got sick.[30]

Jones said he recalled challenging Shilts, who by then was deep into his writing for *And the Band Played On*, about the concept of a "Patient Zero" and raised with him his doubts about whether such an idea held up, given new knowledge about the potentially long incubation period for people exposed to HIV before they developed AIDS symptoms. Jones said, "I am quite certain that we had a conversation about that. I think that it made him [Randy] uncomfortable. It was a very interesting story, but I felt that it was unfair. . . . We quarreled about that. I cannot remember the words of the conversation, but I did raise that with him, and he decided to go ahead with it."[31]

# The Sum of Zero

W hile research notes for Shilts's book clearly indicated that Shilts himself had originated the idea to use Gaëtan Dugas in his book as the alleged "Patient Zero" for AIDS in America for its storytelling value, it wasn't Shilts's idea to make "Patient Zero" a major focus of promoting his work until he and his St. Martin's Press editor, Michael Denneny, found that an audience for the book was remaining elusive. What followed would be some of the most controversial decisions about *And the Band Played On* that would haunt Shilts for years. As Denneny worked to promote and sell the finished work, major newspapers and others were taking a pass on reading it—most notably, the book reviewers at the *New York Times*. Subsequently *Time, Newsweek,* and the *Washington Post* all indicated that they too would pass on reviewing Shilts's book in any prominent way.[1] Desperate and facing pressure from his St. Martin's colleagues who had given in to Denneny's push to get the book published, Denneny called on a former press agent he knew and asked him to read the manuscript and provide ideas on how to get it some publicity. The idea hatched by the agent was one Shilts would come to regret. Denneny said, "The press agent told me, 'Look, there is only one way you're going to get any publicity. I can tell you exactly how to do it, but you're not going to like it. It is really yellow journalism. The only way the media is going to cover a story like this is if you mix together glamour and death, and all of these are tied up in this "Patient Zero" character in the book.'"[2]

It was a pitch that the editors of the *New York Post* couldn't resist—and one that would guarantee the whole front page of the tabloid *Post,* known for its screaming headlines. Born was "The Man Who Brought AIDS to America" 90-point head-line, which filled the top third of the *Post*'s front page on October 6, 1987, with a hammerhead that offered, "Triggered 'Gay Cancer' Epidemic in U.S." The actual article appeared inside on page 3 under a separate headline, "AIDS: The Man Who Started It All!" and declared, "Homosexual Gaëtan Dugas, who died of the killer disease in 1984, is a modern-day Typhoid Mary, says *San Francisco Chronicle* reporter Randy Shilts." (Shilts is never quoted in the story, which includes only short excerpts from his book that mention Dugas.) The story highlighted that Dugas was allegedly linked not only to 17 percent of the first 248 reported cases of AIDS in the United States but also to the first two known AIDS cases ever in New York City. Skipping the portion of Shilts's thesis that took on the political and medical failures found in society in its response to AIDS, the *Post* instead reported only on Shilts's suggestion that the treatment of AIDS was viewed as a public relations problem by the gay community rather than as "a medical problem rooted in promiscuity."[3] The *New York Daily News* followed with its own scream-ing headline, "The Man Who Flew Too Much."[4]

A day later, the *New York Times* picked up a six-hundred-word news story on Shilts's book (after having previously declined to cover the book's release) under a calmer heading: "Canadian Said to Have Key Role in Spread of AIDS."[5] Days later, the weekly tabloid gossip magazine the *Star* offered its own version of the story under another alarmist headline, "The Monster Who Gave Us AIDS," although the text of the story itself was far less inflammatory than the headline.[6] By this point, the editors at *Time* magazine had changed its mind as well and ran a story on Shilts's book on its Medicine page under another ugly headline, "The Appalling Saga of Patient Zero," though the story itself quickly dispatched with details about "Shilts's discovery" of Dugas as "Patient Zero" and instead launched into the growing political disagreements simmering among members of President Ronald Reagan's advisory commission on AIDS.[7] The same week *Newsweek* took a calmer approach: "The Making of an Epidemic: A Reporter Pursues the Origins of the AIDS Crisis."[8] So did *Maclean's* magazine with a story titled "'Patient Zero' and the AIDS Virus" and a half-page photo of Shilts over the cutline: "Shilts: Blaming the AIDS epidemic on one man, a Canadian airline steward."[9]

The *Washington Post* offered a lengthy book review titled "The AIDS Epidemic: A Report from the Front Lines" and noted that "Dugas is a character who would have had to be invented [by Shilts] did he not already exist." According to the paper, the focus on Dugas is "pivotal to Shilts's account."[10] The *Chicago Tribune* paid Shilts for lengthy excerpts from his book for its Tempo section for three days between November 1 and 3, 1987, which included a reprint of Dugas's obituary from a Quebec City newspaper. The subhead of the *Tribune*'s story was particularly troubling: "Wherever Gaëtan Dugas Paused, Gay Men Began to Sicken and Die."[11]

The *Times* of London put the focus on the failure of US officials to get their arms around the AIDS crisis and praised Shilts's work as "a chilling and disturbing book" that "details the way ignorance, ideology, political expediency and prejudice have contributed to a pandemic in the world's richest and most powerful country while the government fiddled, the risk groups played on, and America sank into misery and death."[12] In Scotland the *Sunday Mail* focused directly on Dugas as a "sex-crazed air steward who brought AIDS to the western world after taking an incredible 250 male lovers each year" and labeled him a "randy Air Canada steward [who] sentenced thousands to death."[13]

A review of both LexisNexis and NewsBank archive databases reveals that the tone of the wire stories concerning Shilts's book were equally alarming. William F. Buckley Jr.'s conservative vehicle, *National Review*, didn't question Dugas's role in the spread of AIDS but piled on by indicating that "AIDS's primary tie is to homosexuality" and that Shilts's book had simply confirmed long-held conservative concerns about rising rates of sexually transmitted diseases, "a direct result of the so-called Sexual Revolution. Medical researchers wondered what would happen if a new element were dropped into the disease equation"—such as a killer virus—and "now they know."[14] By year's end the "Patient Zero" story had grown so large that *People* magazine named Dugas one of the most intriguing people of 1987.[15]

Not unexpectedly, Canadian media focused more on questions being raised about the validity of Shilts's claim that Dugas was the originator of HIV and AIDS. The *Toronto Star* offered, "MDs Doubt Claim Canadian Carried AIDS to Continent."[16] A month later the *Toronto Star* ran a lengthy excerpt of Shilts's book titled "Patient Zero: The Airline Steward Who Carried a Disease and a Grudge" and let its readers read for themselves the claims made in Shilts's book.[17]

Topping off the hysteria whipped up by the *New York Post*, gay publications quickly pounced on the coverage and the scapegoating of Dugas. An ad in *California* magazine (which paid to excerpt large portions of Shilts's text at its release) hit a particularly sour note with a growing faction of Shilts critics among gay leaders as it displayed a copy of Dugas's Air Canada employee ID card with the provocative claim, "The AIDS epidemic in America wasn't spread by a virus. It was spread by a man."[18] San Francisco–based ACT-UP members were incensed about the advertisement and urged their members to flood the magazine's editors with complaint phone calls. The controversy grew; for some, it was based on the idea that one man had brought AIDS to the United States all by himself, while others were outraged that someone had been so bold as to make such a claim. Four days after its breathless headlines about "Patient Zero," the *New York Post* ran a follow-up story, "Doc Confirms 'Patient Zero' Began Plague," quoting one of Shilts's regular sources, Dr. Marcus Conant, who confirmed the idea that Dugas "probably brought the deadly virus to North America." Conant, labeled a pioneer AIDS researcher, was quoted by *Time* magazine saying that if it wasn't Dugas, "it would have been some other" man.[19]

The *Chicago Sun-Times* examined the role of "Patient Zero" in telling Shilts's story, changing Dugas's epithet to "Victim Zero" but offering a subhead for its story that did little to improve the Dugas aura: "Victim Zero Left Tragic AIDS Trail: Airline Steward Played Key Role in Spreading AIDS in America." If the blame placing on Dugas wasn't complete from the headline, graphic artists at the *Sun-Times* offered a crude locator map that showed a large arrow from France to Toronto and then to Los Angeles, San Francisco, and New York purporting to represent that "Gaëtan Dugas probably contracted AIDS from an African in France, then infected men in New York, Los Angeles, San Francisco, and Toronto." *Sun-Times* writer Andrew Herrmann quoted Shilts as waffling a bit—"Only God knows if Dugas was the person who brought AIDS to the United States"—but then qualified his balancing act: "And God would have to be a pretty good epidemiologist to figure that one out. But a number of researchers have said to me that of all your likely candidates, he'd be your top nominee as the person who did."[20] Later, Shilts tried working both sides of the issue again: "Sex wasn't just sex to Gaëtan, it was the basis of his identity."[21] He then told Herrmann that Dugas's sex life "is not at all typical" of gay men and that Dugas was "a bizarre, troubled individual."[22]

Beyond logical concerns about whether any *one* person could be responsible for the transmission of a deadly virus to an entire continent of people, writer George S. Buse and the editors of the *Windy City Times*, a Chicago-based gay newspaper, raised questions about advertising for excerpts of Shilts's book planned for *California* magazine. They noted that the ads referred to Dugas as a "young egocentric" and "the star of the homosexual jet set" and labeled him "a promiscuous man with a deadly disease. A disease that may eventually threaten an entire nation." Editors at *California* magazine ducked attempts to explain the provocative nature of their ad, which struck many as homophobic in its reinforcement of placing singular blame for the AIDS epidemic on gay men. Shilts talked to Buse and denied he had characterized Dugas as the person who brought AIDS to America. "AIDS is an act of nature, not of people," Buse quoted Shilts from a phone interview. He said the ad by *California* magazine for his work was "a bizarre interpretation of the excerpt from the book. Never in my book do I ever say anyone brought AIDS anywhere. It is irresponsible to make such a claim" and said the ad touting his work was a distortion with "homophobic undertones."[23]

Shilts *had* made extensive references to Dugas in his book as a means of explaining the epidemiology of a communicable disease, even labeling him as the first person in Canada to test positive for HIV/AIDS and as "the Quebecois version of Typhoid Mary." But he had also done extensive interviews with people who knew Dugas from Canada and across the globe, people who had been his sexual partners, and some who had just tried to be his friend. Shilts had talked to doctors and researchers who knew Dugas professionally in order to create his version of the man that emerged. Shilts drew some strong conclusions: "From just one tryst with Gaëtan, therefore, 11 GRID cases could be connected. Altogether, Gaëtan had a connection to nine of the first 19 cases of GRID in Los Angeles, 22 in New York City, and nine patients in eight other North American cities. The Los Angeles Cluster Study, as it became known, offered powerful evidence that GRID not only was transmissible but *was the work of a single infectious agent*." Shilts would later explain that "infectious agent" was a reference to the human immunodeficiency virus and not Dugas. His explanation, however, suffered because Dugas continued to surface in his text—such as in explaining for readers issues such as the "asymptomatic carrier state" that some people infected with HIV experience. He wrote, "Gaëtan, for example, had infected at least one man before he had any symptoms of [gay-related immune deficiency, or GRID] himself. Another two had contracted it from Gaëtan while he showed signs only of lymphadenopathy. Gaëtan had his lesions when he spent Thanksgiving weekend with [an] Orange county hairdresser." It was clear Shilts had extensive access to Dugas's medical record and had, through interviews and other research, carefully reconstructed Dugas's activities, which he described as "truly remarkable." He had categorically declared Dugas's direct connection to infections of at least 40 of the 248 men diagnosed as early as 1982.[24]

Beyond using Dugas's experience as a means of explaining the complexities of communicable disease transmission, Shilts went further by creating an unflattering profile of the Canadian, who had succumbed to AIDS on March 30, 1984, at the age of thirty-two, three years before the publication of Shilts's book. Shilts offered bold, troubling quotes attributed to Dugas (while not revealing specifically where they came from), claiming that the young man had often declared himself "the prettiest one" upon entering a gay bar or bathhouse or had made postcoitus claims to his lovers that "I'm going to die and so are you."[25] Shilts's passage about who Dugas was or what he represented for gay men is noteworthy:

> Gaëtan was the man everyone wanted, the ideal for this community, at this time and in this place. His sandy hair fell boyishly over his forehead. His mouth easily curled into an inviting smile, and his laugh could flood color into a room of black and white. He bought his clothes in the trendiest shops in Paris and London. He vacationed in Mexico and on the Caribbean beaches. Americans tumbled for his soft Quebecois accent and his sexual magnetism. There was no place the 28-year-old airline steward would rather have the boys fall for him than in San Francisco.[26]

Shilts's research followed Dugas from New York City to Toronto and even into his first-ever visits to gay bathhouses in West Hollywood.

Perhaps Shilts's greatest leap, however, came as he reported that "as [Dugas] traveled between San Francisco, Los Angeles, Vancouver, Toronto, and New York, he realized that if he kept to bathhouses where the lights were turned down low, nobody would ask him about those embarrassing purple spots. He was still the prettiest one."[27] Without Dugas alive to tell his own story, how could a writer such as Shilts, who often promoted the value of journalistic practices that included extensive fact checking, make such a leap into Dugas's mind and thoughts? This posthumous treatment of Dugas angered many readers; it even cast Dugas as a victim of sorts. Dugas's position in the Shilts text as villain stood in contrast to the admittedly cooperative nature Dugas displayed at times in helping AIDS researchers who were trying to understand the nature of the disease and its spread. Researchers William Darrow, James Curran, Marcus Conant, and Selma Dritz all remarked that Dugas had fully cooperated with questionnaires and one-on-one interviews regarding his sex life and other personal aspects of his life and health. Shilts's reporting on Dugas seemed to miss the highly human perspective of what it must have been like for Dugas to live his life, growing ill from unusual diseases with no clear answers from doctors about why or how and perhaps slowly beginning to understand that he and others were carrying the label of "Typhoid Mary" actors in a terribly frightened gay community. Dugas had tried to do some medical research on his own, often as part of investigations undertaken by others, and he even traveled to the CDC headquarters in Atlanta and to various health clinics in San Francisco and New York, trying to find answers.

After moving to Vancouver, Dugas attended a prominent AIDS conference to learn more about the disease. He also spoke publicly at a 1983 meeting called by a community-based group known as AIDS Vancouver. Dugas joined other men in asking questions when a medical panel began taking questions, "very pushy questions," as described by Dr. Brian Willoughby, a founding board member of AIDS Vancouver. "By pushy, I mean to say he asked questions about all of the issues for which there were no answers and asked them in a way that sort of felt like pushing buttons." When it was his turn to ask a question, Dugas offered a statement as well as a question: "So you shouldn't fear someone who has AIDS or [has] symptoms of AIDS because there's no specific reason why you should get in contact with AIDS with an infectious agent like you mention," he said. "Like, if you have a lover who has AIDS and you don't have AIDS, what is the warning you give the people? It seems like there's kind of a fear toward those people here . . . but you should, you know, not necessarily fear those people." Panelists responded by saying that someone (such as Dugas) who knew he had AIDS owed it to his sexual partners to disclose his status.[28]

Dugas also wanted to know whether a vaccine developed from a Hepatitis B study undertaken years earlier involving gay men had ties to the spread of AIDS. "The hepatitis vaccine, the new vaccine, that is now offered to gay men has been developed with gay men with hepatitis," he said, "so therefore anyone who would have received such a vaccine could have been exposed to AIDS." Doctors on the panel were quick to shut down the assertion that there was a link between the hepatitis vaccine and the onset of AIDS. Concern began to grow that Dugas would continue to ask questions for which there currently weren't any answers and so "undo" the good intentions of the conference organizers. A clearly frustrated Dugas pushed panelists to discuss whether any sort of test to determine who was an "AIDS carrier" had been developed and flashed a frustration shared by many as he was told once again that no definitive test existed and that no full understanding of the disease's transmission existed at the time.[29]

"Whether Gaëtan Dugas actually was the person who brought AIDS to North America remains a question of debate and is ultimately unanswerable," Shilts wrote near the end of *Band*. Repeating the ties between Dugas and the first cases of AIDS in New York City and Los Angeles "gives weight to the theory," and "in any event, there's no doubt that Gaëtan played a key role in spreading the new virus from one end of the United States to the other. . . . At one time, Gaëtan had been what every man wanted from gay life; by the time he died, he had become what every man feared."[30]

In all his interviews promoting the book, Shilts played defense. On the one hand, he understood the success the "Patient Zero" story was bringing to his book, and on the other hand, he was trying to tamp down that one portion of his work. He was perhaps most revealing in an interview with his former colleagues at the *Advocate* for their December 1987 take on *Band*: "It's funny, [Dugas] was the one person in the book I wasn't looking for. He just appeared. Everywhere I turned in doing the research, his figure arose."[31]

Shilts's editor, Denneny, stands by the decision to go forward with the "Patient Zero" story in the promotion of the book. He insists that Shilts balked loudly at the salacious approach to getting his work noticed but eventually relented. "It was the only way the mainstream press was going to cover this book, through this salacious, melodramatic, yellow journalism sort of way," Denneny said.[32]

That Denneny pulls blame to himself for the exploitive approach to the "Patient Zero" idea, complete with a press kit focused on Gaëtan Dugas, is instructive to know, but it has spared Shilts little of the wrath that followed then and even today. The one major complaint and criticism gay activists, scientists, and even journalistic experts have always raised with Shilts's otherwise comprehensive work in *And the Band Played On* has been the appropriateness of the publicity granted to "Patient Zero." Today Denneny says: "I feel somewhat guilty because Randy has always taken abuse for this when in fact he was very reluctant, and I basically had to twist his arm like mad to get him to agree with this approach. He really shouldn't have to take the responsibility for this. I have tried any number of times to publicly say, 'Hey, if you're going to blame someone [for "Patient Zero"], blame me.'"[33] Some believe, however, that Shilts fully understood what was required to sell a book, his brother Gary assessing that "Randy was a salesman, ultimately," and he found a way to go along with the "Patient Zero" story pitch.[34]

Scholar Richard A. McKay said Shilts had cast Dugas "as a specific character type" that shaped the Canadian's public legacy "as one of the most demonized patients in history." The mistreatment of Dugas by Shilts, according to McKay, resulted from "the journalist's selective use of knowledge about HIV incubation rates, dramaturgic decisions, and the narrow timescale of his inquiry. The hardworking journalist was very effective in drawing on an international network of contacts to bypass the barriers that public health officials had erected to protect the identities of those men who had been linked through an earlier sexual network. Yet [Shilts] used the ample information gathered in a highly selective manner."[35]

Shilts's research notes for *Band* reveal that he talked with many people, trying to create a posthumous picture of Dugas. As part of his efforts, Shilts created an

elaborate timeline in an attempt to re-create the details of Gaëtan's life—a decidedly difficult task for someone already in his grave. The notes reveal that Shilts
collected a wide spectrum of information. He described Gaëtan as "flamboyant, dyed sandy hair—platinum—stood out in a crowd—one of a kind—life of
the party—infectious laughter—witty—had a rough childhood—very private
man." Other descriptions were that "he liked to go out every night" and "he
could party for 48 hours straight without sleep." Another source told Shilts that
Dugas struggled to reconcile his homosexuality with his Catholic faith. Shilts
revealed that Dugas longed to live in San Francisco—a gay mecca and refuge for
him—and that he loved the sexual interest gay American men showed toward
him, especially at the baths. The collection of basic biographical information was
also important—that he grew up in Quebec City, later moved to Vancouver, and
eventually learned to speak English (French was his native language). Family
friends reported that he came from a large, competitive brood of siblings, and
his slightly effeminate mannerisms and rather slight build earned him the label
of "sissy" as a young boy. Dugas began working as a flight attendant in 1974 after
a brief stint as a hairdresser, and although he was based out of Montreal, he traveled frequently to the United States, Europe, and other parts of the world.

Shilts's notes revealed more troubling elements to the Dugas story. Dugas
apparently became frightened when friends began to get sick in the early 1980s—
part of the earliest stages of the AIDS pandemic—particularly when his sarcoma
blotches started showing on parts of his skin that he could not conceal with clothing and as he suffered night sweats and pronounced hair loss. Friends told Shilts
that during these times Dugas fell back into worries, likely fueled by his Catholic
upbringing, that AIDS was a punishment for embracing a sexuality that he feared
was contrary to God's will. There was also a defiance that arose, Dugas arguing
with his doctors about whether his cancer was communicable or not. Given the
large number of unknowns about the spread of the disease at this early stage,
Dugas ignored his doctors' warnings about engaging in sexual activity with others. By 1982 Dugas was spending more than half his time living in San Francisco
with a series of lovers while maintaining an active career as a flight attendant for
Air Canada. Slowed by a bout of pneumocystis pneumonia, he eventually went
back to Quebec City in 1984 and sought a lower profile. Shilts learned that Dugas's
health status had degraded considerably by March 1984 and that immediate family members had gathered at his side as his life came to a painful close.

After Dugas died, his family and friends mourned his loss but also wanted to
remember his life in a positive way. A tree was planted in his honor, and family

and friends recalled that he could be considerate and generous, willing to share his money and good times with almost anyone. Perhaps because the human aspects of Gaëtan's life were lost in the "big" discussion of whether or not he was *the* first or one of the first men to have "gay cancer" (what became known as AIDS), Shilts's writing about him still stings and still invokes heated dispute. The human aspect of Dugas was something Shilts clearly explored, but those aspects of the story as reflected in the research notes for *And the Band Played On* became lost in the bigger story. The CDC's Dr. James Curran thinks Shilts missed an important aspect of Dugas's story—that he was "very cooperative with us" despite being a "playboy." Curran said, "He came to Atlanta, and we interviewed him, and he gave us a lot of information, and he had the disease, and he was like everyone who was interested in knowing more and hoping for a cure to be found. He was not, however, 'Patient Zero.'"[36]

In the years after *Band*'s release, Shilts rarely addressed the impact of the Dugas story directly, although it was then, and it still is, the strongest criticism offered of his work. In a 1992 essay, Shilts offered a somewhat cryptic, if not marginally sympathetic, assessment of Dugas. "When I wrote about 'Patient Zero,' Gaëtan Dugas, the guy who knowingly spread AIDS, my first thought was, 'He's a jerk, totally narcissistic.' Yet here's somebody who was an orphan, adopted by a strict Catholic family in Quebec City where they really knew how to be strict, and I can't help but wonder what happened to him when he was a kid. Somebody who was that callous to other human beings must have had some terrible darkness in his past."[37]

Despite Shilts's reservations—never stated publicly at the time of the release of *And the Band Played On*—"Patient Zero" was ubiquitous in the coverage *And the Band Played On* garnered and was a tough topic to shake. No less than *CBS News* correspondent Harry Reasoner, who referred to Shilts as "the scribe and historian of the epidemic," proclaimed to the millions of primetime viewers of *60 Minutes* that Shilts had offered "a startling new theory, a theory the epidemiologists, the medical detectives believe."[38] In his report, Reasoner noted that the *San Francisco Chronicle* had hired "Shilts, a gay himself," in part to report about the gay community. With Reasoner, Shilts hammered on the essential point from his reporting:

> AIDS did not just happen. AIDS was allowed to happen. This disease did not emerge full-grown on the biological landscape, and I don't think you can look to medicine in order to understand how AIDS was able to spread so quickly across

this country unimpeded. I think you have to look at the politics of AIDS. And when you get into the politics of AIDS, you're left with one very unfortunate timing factor about this epidemic. AIDS was detected five months into the first Reagan administration. And this administration had come in with one over-riding commitment. That commitment was to keep the lid on federal domes-tic spending. Consequently, during the first years of the epidemic, whenever there was a choice between do we go whole hog against this epidemic, or do we keep the lid on domestic spending, the Reagan administration invariably chose to keep the lid on health spending. The fact is that the files of the Reagan administration are redolent with the odor of smoking guns.[39]

Shilts's assertion to the nation was clear: "Politics was allowed to triumph over public health. In 1987 the political question is, should we let a certain politi-cal version of morality triumph over what is good public health and educating people? And again, politics is triumphing over public health."[40] Reasoner quickly focused on Dugas as "Patient Zero," running a clip with Shilts explaining with little apparent apprehension:

It was through Gaëtan Dugas that they realized that AIDS was an infectious disease. . . . By the time they were done with the study, which became known as the cluster study, they found that 40 of the first 248 gay men who got AIDS in the United States had either gone to bed with Gaëtan Dugas or had gone to bed with someone who had gone to bed with him. With Gaëtan, you get a horrible combination of circumstances. You get a guy who has unlimited sexual stamina, who is very attractive so he has unlimited opportunity to act out that sexual stamina, and he is a flight attendant for Air Canada, so he gets these flight passes so he can fly out all over and have his fun in any number of cities. I mean, it was just a horrible combination of factors that helped really speed this disease into every corner of America.[41]

Historian Phil Tiemeyer from Kansas State University noted that few in the media questioned Shilts's suggestion, however qualified it became over time, that one man was responsible for AIDS in America, with report after report simply "reinforcing the salacious drama surrounding 'Patient Zero.'"[42] Canadian media were an exception, driven perhaps by the fact that one of their own played the role of villain. While Dugas's employers at Air Canada stood mute, Canadian AIDS experts "questioned the likelihood of ever being able to track down the original North American carrier."[43] Tiemeyer concluded, "Clearly, rather than requiring Shilts to clarify his exaggerated claims about Gaetan Dugas, the vast media attention instead allowed Shilts to capitalize on the unfortunate, easily misrepresented way Gaetan was intertwined within the early AIDS crisis."[44] Tiemeyer believed that Shilts's narrative "may not have led directly to [antigay] laws, but it did tighten the perceived link between AIDS and queer sexual depravity, thereby allowing such legal changes to occur more easily." Shilts's construction of the "Patient Zero" story affirmed for heterosexuals, especially conservatives, that "men who engage in anal sex and cavort in bathhouses invite plague-like diseases on themselves and the rest of society. For the world to make this sensational myth about the origin of AIDS in America . . . demonstrates more than anything else society's revulsion with gays' post-Stonewall sexual freedom."[45]

Duke University scholar Priscilla Wald suggested that Shilts and the mainstream media engaged in an "outbreak narrative" to help explain the complexities of the rapid spread of a fatal and communicable disease. Wald said that Shilts recognized that "the epidemiological investigation drama [represented by Dugas] would make his analysis widely readable," as did casting the CDC and other health officials as heroic characters in the story. Wald also noted that because of the publicity the "Patient Zero" story raised, the focus and main points of Shilts's book had been lost. Wald found Shilts in retreat on the importance of Dugas to the overall story: "Here I've done 630 pages of serious AIDS policy reporting, with the premise that this disaster was allowed to happen because the media only focus on the glitzy and sensational aspects of the epidemic," Shilts remarked. "My book breaks, not because of the serious public policy stories, but because of the rather minor story of 'Patient Zero.'" Wald adds a measure of doubt to how sincerely one should take Shilts and his claims of concern about the focus on Dugas: "Shilts weaves [Dugas] throughout the story, tracking his movements as [Shilts] depicts [Dugas's] increasing recalcitrance and malevolence." Shilts appeared "dismayed" that the "Patient Zero" story overshadowed his comprehensive analysis of the AIDS crisis, but as Wald concluded, "What he did not seem to consider was the conceptual power of the outbreak narrative, which [Shilts] helped evolve, to shift the terms of the analysis."[46]

Bioethicist Timothy F. Murphy suggested that Shilts created Dugas as the "Aristotelian efficient cause of the AIDS epidemic, insofar as he appears as its mechanism of transmission in this country, and the gay ideals were the formal cause of the epidemic, insofar as they shaped the culture in which transmission could occur easily." Murphy further challenged Shilts's claim that he was merely reporting the epidemic as it occurred and noted that portions of Dugas's life were fictionalized by Shilts "as an emblem and symbol for gay life and especially the excesses imputed to it." He adds, "If Dugas is blameworthy in the origins of the epidemic, by extension so too is the sexual ethos of gay life itself because Shilts uses Dugas, and especially his willful sexuality, as a figure for all gay men." Carrying Shilts's thesis further, Murphy notes that Shilts inspired an anger among gay men for his narrow construction of gay male sexuality by representing Dugas in the beginning of his work as a gay ideal, what every gay man wanted in a sexual partner, to becoming what every gay man dreaded, a pathogen-carrying killer with no morality. Murphy posthumously defended Dugas against the characterization Shilts created: "In many ways, Dugas lived no different from many of the continent hopping, urban peers of his time. Why therefore should the hammer of judgment fall as heavily on Dugas as Shilts's narrative requires, especially since a judgment replicates the homophobia that equates homoeroticism with AIDS, especially since a large measure of Dugas's fault was not that he lived differently from others, but merely that he got it first?"[47]

Shilts's failure to consider or understand the impact of his words remains irrespective of whether he believed Dugas was *the* Patient Zero or just *a* Patient Zero at the center of one cluster of HIV transmissions. Shilts himself had led a fast and fun life exploring what it meant to be gay in his earliest days in San Francisco, not an altogether different experience from that of Dugas. It is not surprising, then, that others would call out Shilts for his words and question the motives behind them.

After the release of *And the Band Played On*, Shilts returned briefly to the *Chronicle* newsroom before setting off on an ambitious book promotion tour that included stops in every major media market across the United States and with later visits to London and Melbourne. Patricia Holt, a newsroom colleague of Shilts at the *San Francisco Chronicle,* offered *Band* a glowing review—she christened Shilts as the official "mini-biographer" of AIDS and "one of the few people who saw the AIDS crisis for what it was." She made special mention of the "news" Shilts's book had generated via the screaming headline in the *New York Post*. Holt also offered some of the first explanations Shilts would engage in while trying to tamp down the commotion created by the headline assertion that one person, Gaëtan Dugas, had single-handedly brought AIDS to America. Using words such as "probably," "maybe," and "likely" in regard to his confirmed promiscuity in the gay community, Holt offered the first line of Shilts's defense in the "Dugas as Patient Zero" debacle, which would follow him for years to come. Holt asked, "Did AIDS actually come into the United States because of a single person, someone Shilts has tracked down and identified, someone, therefore, we can all blame?

Yes, yes, and no, as Shilts contends." Shilts responded, "It's a shame that some headlines initially focused on Dugas[, who is] a minor player in the complicated drama. . . . What should have been emphasized . . . was the accusation that the AIDS epidemic 'did not just happen to America,' it was allowed to happen by an array of institutions, all of which failed to perform their appropriate tasks to safeguard the public health."[48]

While Shilts attempted to cast a wide net of blame for the AIDS crisis—the government, health officials, the gay community, and the media—the *Los Angeles Times* zeroed in on his use of Dugas as a potential scapegoat. "The one person Shilts will never have to face is also the person who has, so far, stirred the most media interest in the book: 'Patient Zero.'"[49] The "Patient Zero" character *has* continued to overshadow larger points Shilts intended to make with *And the Band Played On* and remained at the center of the Shilts critique.

One of the most vociferous Shilts critics in the months and years after *Band*'s October 1987 release was historian Douglas Crimp at the University of Rochester. Crimp wrote that Shilts's book was "pernicious" and that proof of its worthlessness to the actual history of AIDS was its best-seller status, positive reviews from mainstream or straight media, and the fact that HBO used it to create a made-for-TV movie. Taking up a familiar review that Shilts's work relied heavily on creating heroes and villains in the story of AIDS, Crimp chastised Shilts for employing "imprecise, callous and moralizing" techniques in his reporting without apology, all while casting himself as one of the few heroes in the story. Crimp believed that Shilts "possessed contempt for gay political leaders, AIDS activists, and people with AIDS, and his delusions about their power to influence public health policy is deeply revealing of his own politics. But to Shilts, politics is something alien, something others have. . . . Shilts has no politics, only common sense; he speaks only the truth."[50] Crimp raised the troubling and provocative motive some gay leaders had asserted might exist for Shilts's approach:

> The criticism most often leveled against Shilts's book by its gay critics is that it is a product of internalized homophobia. In this view, Shilts is seen to identify with the heterosexist society that loathes him for his homosexuality and through that identification to project his loathing onto the gay community. Thus, "Patient Zero" . . . is Shilts's homophobic nightmare of himself, a nightmare that he must constantly deny by making it true only of others. Shilts therefore offers up the scapegoat for his heterosexual colleagues in order to prove that he, like them, is horrified by such creatures.[51]

Another strong Shilts critic to emerge in the decades since the publication of *And the Band Played On* is scholar Richard A. McKay, author of a 2017 book titled *Patient Zero and the Making of the AIDS Epidemic*. McKay declared Shilts's use of "Patient Zero" as one of the worst myths perpetrated via the AIDS crisis and asserted that its creation may have even contributed to subsequent efforts in the United States and elsewhere to criminalize alleged activities by people with AIDS infecting others. McKay has taken special effort to explore the views and reactions of Gaëtan Dugas's family and friends. McKay reported that they wondered about the breach in his medical confidentiality and how Shilts, the journalist advancing these claims, discovered his identity. McKay concluded, "They almost certainly could not have imagined the scale of the networks of sexual contact and information sharing at work in the construction of this persistent story of a man forever linked to the story of AIDS."[52]

McKay believes that Shilts engaged in a flawed analysis of William Darrow's original CDC cluster study by placing a "Patient Zero" at the center of a group of infections and that the study was already outdated when Shilts was writing *Band*. Shilts left the information in the book anyway because the "story-telling potential" of the concept was too good to resist. McKay said: "I argue that in the course of writing his popular history—and in spite of his stated aim of 'humanizing this disease'—Shilts became seduced with discovering and revealing the identity of the man he would call 'Patient Zero' . . . [and that Shilts] drew upon an extensive international network of informants and contacts to bypass the barriers of confidentiality erected by public health professionals. . . . Shilts's dark characterization of Dugas drew its intensity from—and indeed combined with—the journalist's intention to cast the disease itself as a character in history."[53] Further, McKay suggested that Shilts's use of Dugas as the centerpiece for the "Patient Zero" concept may simply have been an artifact of the fact that Dugas maintained a rather complete address book and was, at least initially, quite cooperative with epidemiologists and others attempting to learn more about what was then labeled GRID. "Shilts himself had written about the fact that scientists had discovered that the incubation period was actually much longer than previously thought," McKay pointed out. He believes Shilts's less-than-forthright reporting on this matter "created many unintended consequences and really starts to arise and really takes off from a very driven, ambitious, angry and upset journalist—Randy Shilts. Shilts seems to harness this idea and he and his publisher would eventually help to drive it to international dissemination."[54]

McKay assigned a sinister intent to Shilts's writing about Dugas. Noting that as a reporter Shilts possessed "a deep and pressing drive for professional success and career advancement" and had learned to "moderate the permissive attitude he had developed toward drinking, taking drugs, and sexual contacts in his youth," McKay concluded: "These experiences foreshadowed the blame [Shilts] would later attribute to Dugas and others whose infections were passed sexually. They also shaped [Shilts's] emerging sense of self as a moderate-acting, straight-talking reporter, who had survived what he viewed as the excesses of life in the gay fast lane and lived to write about them."[55]

Tiemeyer also noticed this theme, saying Shilts used Dugas as "the scape-goat extraordinaire of the AIDS crisis" and that Shilts and his publishers at St. Martin's Press "rode the wave of revulsion" created with "Patient Zero" to the best-seller list. Shilts succeeded, Tiemeyer believes, in creating a perfectly cast "promiscuous gay male flight attendant with an alluring Quebecois accent—a man who refused to give up sex even after learning of the infections and deadly nature of his ailment"—in fact, "a world-wide villain." Tiemeyer has suggested that "complex motives" existed for Shilts and his publishers to slander Dugas, but they conveniently filled in existing discourse about suspected unchecked sexual excess among gays, and Shilts's book made the case for these "tropes" with noteworthy "succinctness and psychological impact." He added, "The fact that so many people still believe Gaetan Dugas brought AIDS to North America is testament to the impact of Randy Shilts's 'Patient Zero' myth. The myth's power owes far more to the operation of stereotypes about male flight attendants and gay men, coupled with Shilts's own skillfully articulated rendition of the story, than it does to medical facts."[56]

Tiemeyer believes that Shilts unwittingly played into the hands of 1980s conservatives and their efforts to "foreclose normalization of people with AIDS" and that he even fueled highly charged suggestions that people living with AIDS should be quarantined. Tiemeyer's indictment is based on "a close reading of Shilts's text[, and] I conclude that Shilts crafted the 'Patient Zero' myth to more broadly demonize what I call 'recalcitrant queers,' those who preached a safe-sex, positive, non-monogamous vision of homosexuality even in the face of the AIDS crisis. The end result was to broadly stigmatize a queer lifestyle amidst the larger public, while politically jeopardizing the civil rights of only a more concentrated group of People with AIDS (PWAs)." The result was that Shilts successfully raised Dugas from the grave and created a "fantastical myth" of the AIDS crisis that placed Dugas as a central character in linking the mysterious, heretofore "African disease" to the American heartland. Tiemeyer reclaimed McKay's theme that Shilts kept "Patient Zero" alive because of the irresistible narrative it allowed: Shilts's vilification of Dugas in *And the Band Played On* "seems anachronistic, belonging more to the hysteria of summer 1983 than to fall 1987." Tiemeyer openly accused Shilts of "artful writing," "outright misrepresentations," "omission of key facts, misconstrued CDC data, and colorful embellishments" of Darrow's CDC cluster study to bolster the idea of the evil promiscuous gay man at the center of all AIDS in North America.[57]

As predicted, the publicity surrounding "Patient Zero" worked brilliantly: the *New York Times* not only quickly featured Shilts's book prominently in its Sunday book review section but also published additional news stories about the claims in the story, including the controversy stirred by the naming of "Patient Zero." Other national media picked up the story as well, and Shilts's book was in reprint within weeks and eventually landed—and stayed for weeks—on the *Times'* best-seller list for nonfiction books. The *Times* avoided most of the hoopla about the "Patient Zero" angle of the story for its book review by Richard Reinhold. Published in the October 31, 1987, edition, Reinhold's take focused on profiling Shilts, with Gaëtan Dugas and the concept of "Patient Zero" not mentioned in the review. Reinhold did mention that some gay leaders were critical of Shilts's work, saying that it lacked emphasis on the positive aspects of how the gay community had responded to the AIDS crisis. Reinhold's reporting also carried a questionable passage tucked in at the end of the profile, with Shilts saying that his own health was "just fine" and that he "had not taken the AIDS antibody test because there is no medical treatment available if the test is positive and because he engages in no activity believed to spread the virus that causes AIDS."[58] Reinhold's statement, likely something Shilts told him directly, conflicts with later disclosures by Shilts that he learned that he had tested positive for HIV antibodies on the day he turned in his final draft of the manuscript for *Band*—almost a year before its release and the time of the Reinhold interview.

Contrasting reactions to Shilts's work continued to emerge. As mainstream and generally heterosexual sources heaped praise on Shilts, criticism from the homosexual community continued to grow. The criticism Shilts felt from the gay community was highlighted in a *Los Angeles Times* preview of *And the Band Played On* in which the annual Castro Street Fair served as backdrop, an event where Shilts "figured his chances were equally good of getting slugged or hugged." *Band* had just arrived in San Francisco bookstores and was a popular item. Regardless, Shilts began the first of many efforts to explain or at least downplay the publicity that had surrounded "Patient Zero" following the screaming headlines offered by the *New York Post* in its gratuitous preview of Shilts's work, blaming the *Post* and other headline writers for "blown out of proportion" accounts of his book. As in other instances, however, the discussion of *Band* and its writing style (which Shilts referred to as "pure Michener") was secondary to the requisite description of Shilts as "an openly gay reporter." The *Times* focused on Shilts's claims of "personal integrity": "To me, being open about being gay is solely a statement of personal integrity. I'd met a lot of older gay professionals who lived their lives in terror that they were going to be discovered. I decided I was never going to be in a position in my life where I had to cover up who I was."[59]

Shifting back to Shilts's groundbreaking book, the *Times* noted Shilts's frustration that his news articles on the emerging "gay cancer" created little ripple among fellow journalists. "I'm not God's gift to journalism," Shilts said. "The people who gave me memos [about government inaction on AIDS] would have done anything to get them into the papers," but other investigative reporters "who were real men didn't want to cover AIDS-related anything. It was trivial. . . . There was lots of sob sister reporting. There was great, eloquent science reporting, but nobody was doing behind-the-scenes political stuff." Shilts acknowledged that he based his approach to the AIDS story—which he happily distinguished from the approach used by other journalists—on his sexual identity. "I wasn't just an author doing a story," he said. "I live in the gay community and AIDS is a part of my life. The people who have died because of institutional neglect aren't just 'those people out there,' they're people I care about." Despite such altruism undergirding his reporting, Shilts could not escape the wrath of many in the gay community, allowing, "The gay community didn't want me to write about things like bathhouses that made gays look bad. But to me, that was like going to one side of a burning building and covering the firemen trying to put out the fire, and then ignoring the guy on the other side who's dumping gas on it."[60]

"It's been a helluva time to be a reporter," Shilts wrote in a *New York Native* article about the AIDS crisis, all the while privately coming to the growing conclusion that the power of journalism to impact or change the world had its limitations. He openly bemoaned the pressure he routinely received to "write more upbeat stories about AIDS" and "inspiring stories about gay men dying serenely at 34 and the good deeds of their lesbian sisters." For Shilts that held no value. "As far as I'm concerned, writing upbeat stories about the AIDS epidemic would be like writing about the party favors on the Titanic."[61]

While in Melbourne, Australia, promoting his book in August 1988, Shilts admitted that the criticism leveled at him from many in the gay community had taken its toll. "In the Castro Street area where I live, the center of the city's gay community, for a long time people shouted abuse at me on the streets. I couldn't go to restaurants, friends wouldn't be seen with me in public. I spent a lot of time at home. It was something the gay community just could not accept. I approached the issue with the objective criteria of a reporter, rather than with their prejudice," he said.[62] Although the *Bay Area Reporter*, the gay weekly back home in San Francisco, had written a generally favorable review of *Band*, it also noted that Shilts's book signing at the Love That Dares Bookstore in the city had included a security guard posted nearby because of reported death threats on Shilts's life.[63]

After *And the Band Played On* came out, Shilts visited college campuses across the nation, packing in overflow audiences of students and others interested in the growing AIDS menace and commanding speaking fees of $10,000. He found his mailbox filled with queries from almost every corner of the world written by people wanting to know more about AIDS.

Not surprisingly, the rough-and-tumble treatment controversial and pioneering AIDS researcher Dr. Robert Gallo received in Shilts's *Band* (Gallo was later immortalized in a dark performance by Alan Alda in the film version of the book) prompted heavy criticism for Shilts's work from the noted scientist. Gallo, most noted for his role in helping discover the human immunodeficiency virus as the infectious agent responsible for AIDS and his leadership in developing the HIV-antibody test, took immediate issue with many of Shilts's assertions in *Band*. He eagerly told reporters that he had talked directly to Shilts about needed corrections. "He told me he would correct every single thing that I told him about, but the damage is done," Dr. Gallo told the *Los Angeles Times* in the weeks following the book's release in 1987.[64] Book editor Michael Denneny said both he and Shilts talked repeatedly by phone and through letters with Dr. Gallo about his concerns in sometimes-contentious discussions. Shilts memorialized one of those discussions in an October 16, 1987, letter to Dr. Gallo, just as *And the Band Played On* was released. In it, Shilts confirmed that subsequent versions of the book would include more "implicit" references to the work Gallo and his team had done in isolating HIV along with scientists from the Pasteur Institute in France. "I think this point is implicit in other parts of the book," Shilts wrote, "but, in fairness, I want to make sure it is utterly clear to the reader."[65]

*Rolling Stone* writer Jon Katz, in writing about the release of *And the Band Played On*, noted that "no other mainstream journalist had sounded the alarm so dramatically, caught the dimensions of the AIDS tragedy so poignantly" as had Shilts and added: "But Shilts's work matters not only because it's about gays or AIDS but because he has broken journalism's hoary tradition of viewing conviction as anti-journalistic, even unethical. He has fused strong belief with the gathering of factual information and the marshaling of arguments, the way the founders of the modern press did. In doing so, he has exposed the notion of objectivity as bankrupt, ineffective, even lethal."[66] Katz rejoined Shilts's lament about the lack of meaningful response to his work, discussed at length by Shilts in a first-person account for a March 1989 *Esquire* magazine article called "Talking AIDS to Death." Katz asked:

> If *And the Band Played On* was so great, why hadn't newspapers already done it? The answer goes to the heart of the way journalism works, or doesn't. By any definition, the advent of AIDS was one of the most compelling stories of modern times. It met every criterion for a story the media would ordinarily rush to cover: intrigue, celebrity, politics, medical mystery, sex, unspeakable tragedy, pathos and death. . . . Yet at least five years went by before Rock Hudson's death in 1985 forced the spreading epidemic onto front pages and evening newscasts.[67]

Shilts critic Richard McKay also referenced the growing frustration Shilts demonstrated via the stories he wrote first about homosexuals and their struggles in society and later about people with HIV/AIDS—both stories that directly impacted his own life. "Randy Shilts very passionately, very ardently tried to explain homosexuality to the straight world," McKay believes. "When he came out of the closet, he was part of the gay liberation movement of the 1970s, and was convinced that much of the homophobia that he was witnessing was a result of a lack of understanding of what it meant to be homosexual. He believed that if only he could do a really good job of explaining homosexuality to straight people, some of this prejudice might go away."[68]

McKay's discourse on the idea that Shilts believed his journalism could change the world is borne out by comments Shilts made later in his life. As journalist John Weir suggested, a political ideology buttresses Shilts's journalism: "He believes the way to justice is to replace lies with facts."[69] The argument that some, particularly those on the left, have with Shilts and his commitment to facts is that facts can be interpreted, manipulated, omitted, emphasized in particular ways, or even purposefully misstated. Some of Shilts's "facts"—such as those about "Patient Zero" and his role in the advent of HIV and AIDS in America—are presented as truth and have the impact of truth, whether they are based on a shaky factual basis or not. Similarly, McKay believes that Shilts's prolific schedule of writing about HIV and AIDS convinced him that the inaction he perceived occurring on the national and local levels was the result of deep-seated homophobia and anger.[70]

# CHAPTER 12

# Conduct Unbecoming

Anyone paying attention could have predicted the subject of Shilts's last book: whether gay individuals could or should serve openly in the US military. Once again, news events had good timing for Shilts's new interest: a 1990 battle by Edward Modesto, a decorated colonel in the US Army, to avoid court-martial fell into Shilts's lap. It wasn't the first such battle the military had engaged against a gay soldier, Air Force Technical Sergeant Leonard Matlovich's protracted battle starting in 1974 perhaps being the best known. Colonel Modesto, an Indiana native and an army dentist for eighteen years (just two years shy of receiving his full military pension), faced a sixty-five-year prison term "largely stemming from the fact that he is gay or bisexual" and was being made an example of because of his rank, Shilts believed. Another half-dozen soldiers faced charges and discharges from the military in connection with the Modesto inquiry, an investigation that was responsible for the alleged suicide of an air force major implicated as well.

The army suspected Modesto of violating the military's rules against homosexual conduct or against any "conduct unbecoming an officer," so army investigators raided Modesto's home, which he shared with his male lover. The investigators promptly reported that they had discovered a large collection of wigs and women's clothing. Modesto said that they belonged to his lover, who worked part-time as a female impersonator at a local gay bar. Modesto, a father of three, had begun the process of coming out after he reached the age of forty and was estranged from his wife at the time of his arrest. Wire stories by the Associated Press appeared in newspapers across the country under unflattering headlines such as "Dancing Colonel Gets the Boot," "Army Not Amused by Drag-Loving Dentist," and "Transvestite Army Colonel Is Facing Court-Martial."[1]

According to Shilts, military officials were forthcoming about the results of their search of Modesto's home but refused to talk about his pending court-martial: "It is the Department of Defense policy that homosexuality is incompatible with military service. Homosexual acts by a soldier are a criminal offense under military law," Fort Carson's public affairs officer, Sergeant Mike Howard, told Shilts. Beyond that, the military clammed up to an outside and civilian source such as Shilts; "We're not going to be able to give our perspective on this," Howard concluded.[2] Multiple offers to get Modesto to resign and forfeit his rank and pension failed. The military conducted a trial and found Modesto guilty on charges of violating the military's ban on homosexuality. His sentence was nine months at the military prison at Fort Leavenworth, Kansas, a $27,000 fine, and a dishonorable discharge. Lack of evidence provided grounds for the dismissal of additional drug-related charges. Modesto served his time, paid his fine, and came out to tell Shilts about how the military he loved and had dedicated his life to had treated him like a criminal. The ugly and unfair process that the military used to get Modesto out served as appropriate inspiration for Shilts to proceed with digging deeper on the issue of gays serving in the military.

As preparations for the 1991 Persian Gulf War commenced, Shilts continued his focus on gays in the military, offering an opinion column that predicted troubles for the military in recruiting and assigning ground troops for the battle to push Saddam Hussein's Iraqi forces out of neighboring Libya. "Some experts believe that if a shooting war lasted longer than a few months, the military may need more troops than are now available among both active duty and reserve personnel," Shilts opined, meaning a draft might be necessary, which would run head-on into the emerging reality of an openly gay segment of society virtually unknown during earlier military conflicts.[3] Two days later, Shilts reported as a news story "an abrupt policy shift in the event of possible war in the Persian Gulf" that "may allow openly gay personnel to serve in the military based on the services' 'operational needs.'"[4] Shilts followed this hopeful news with a report based on interviews he did with sixty closeted gay men, lesbians, and bisexuals categorized as active duty and their understanding that coming out meant facing a dishonorable discharge.[5] Despite that reality, Shilts found a lesbian woman serving as a support specialist in the 129th Army Evacuation Hospital who was openly challenging the ban on gay service. She had grown weary of suggestions that she wear her hair longer and embarrassing moments when she had to avoid having her photo taken with friends at a women's music festival. Reservist Donna Lynn Jackson was originally designated to go to the Persian Gulf and serve in a military hospital unit within fifty to one hundred miles of the combat zone, but her assignment abruptly changed after her coming out. Moves to eliminate personnel like Jackson continued despite internal documents uncovered by Shilts that indicated a stop-loss effort was underway to keep personnel levels high for key positions such as translators, technically skilled positions, and hospital and medical services, particularly in a ground war with Iraqi forces expected to produce significant casualties for both sides.[6]

Sensing the growing sentiment for a change in the military's gay ban policy, first adopted in 1942–43, Shilts wrote that forty members of Congress had written to President George H. W. Bush asking the Defense Department to suspend discharges under the policy—a letter Bush ignored.[7] Shilts further upped the ante with an exclusive story published on June 25, 1991, that revealed he had obtained a copy of a confidential army memo sent to Pentagon officials that urged reversal of the gay ban policy. The military quickly dismissed the memo as having come from an army officer "acting on his own initiative" and stated that there would be no change in policy forthcoming.[8]

Shilts would keep attention focused on the issue throughout 1991, including the pending discharge of Army Colonel Margarethe Cammermeyer for being a lesbian. Cammermeyer had answered yes when asked whether she was gay during a 1989 investigative interview, setting in motion the military's discharge process. A nurse and veteran with six years of active duty (including a Bronze Star, won in the Vietnam War), she had once been selected the army's Nurse of the Year, honors that meant nothing once she disclosed that she was gay, Shilts reported.[9] In the weeks that followed, Shilts was contacted by a number of gay members of the military expressing disgust and anger about the treatment of Cammermeyer. They legitimately worried that if a decorated colonel was no longer safe from being drummed out of the military because she was gay, what chance did they stand? Shilts produced dozens of articles telling their stories, including one in which he quoted then defense secretary Dick Cheney as referring to the gay military ban as "a bit of an old chestnut," years before Cheney revealed that one of his two daughters was gay. During this period, Pentagon spokesman Pete Williams was outed as a closeted gay man by activist/author Michelangelo Signorile.[10] Shilts took exception to Williams's outing in a "Pro/Con" feature the *Chronicle* ran on its editorial pages on August 8, 1991. Shilts wrote, "Partisans on both sides of the outing debate are claiming the moral high ground in the inevitable rush of news stories surrounding the revelation" and highlighted that Cheney advocated the need for private lives to remain private when it came to Williams and others in military command. Cheney did nothing, however, to stop the active process of identifying and discharging enlisted personnel suspected of or confirmed as being gay. "What's clear from both sides of this debate is there's plenty of hypocrisy to go around." Shilts joined those who declared Williams's outing as unnecessary and unfair to him professionally and personally but also took issue with Cheney's "awesome institutional hypocrisy." Cheney told reporters of his intent to keep Williams (who later became an NBC legal correspondent covering the US Supreme Court) in place as the Pentagon's front man with the media while widespread discharges of active duty personnel went forward. "He has said, in effect, that while he believes homosexuality should be no barrier to serving in the Defense Department's most privileged echelons, he still backs the ban on allowing gays to serve as lowly boatswain's mates and staff sergeants. To the hundreds of thousands of lesbians and gay men in uniform, the contradiction is nothing short of cruel," Shilts wrote.[11]

The column gave Shilts the opportunity to highlight the manner in which the military rooted out gay soldiers, including harsh interrogations, harassment, and threats of prison terms if they didn't disclose the sexual identities of other service members. He spotlighted new legislation introduced by twenty-nine members of Congress, all Democrats, that would end the exclusion of gays in the military, a bill that ultimately gained little to no traction in the House or Senate.

As he had done before while writing *And the Band Played On*, Shilts drew from the growing catalog of stories he was writing on the subject for his daily news writing for the *Chronicle* for the content for his new book, *Conduct Unbecoming*. Getting *Conduct Unbecoming* off the ground presented some problems that Shilts initially worried would kill the project. To help, he talked his friend Linda Alband into moving back to San Francisco from Seattle to be his personal assistant; he paid her with funds derived from the skyrocketing sales of *Band*. Alband thinks Shilts wanted her around because of her work in the 1970s with Vietnam Veterans Against the War and her knowledge of both active duty and veteran service members. Alband showed up at Shilts's new apartment on Saturn Street in San Francisco; it included an extra bedroom converted into an office. As money continued to come in from book sales and film rights for *Band*, Shilts decided to splurge a bit. He bought a new car (one he proudly showed off to everyone he knew), a computer to replace the typewriter he used to write his first book, and a condominium on Duncan Street in the city's tony Diamond Heights neighborhood. Shilts took in more than $1 million in royalties and film rights fees for his work but still struggled financially at times, forever shackled by a lack of fiscal discipline and knowledge.[12]

As he started working on *Conduct Unbecoming*, Shilts confided to friends about his fear that no one would care enough about the plight of homosexuals trying to serve in the military. This included heterosexuals who supported banning gays from the military but also gays themselves who wondered why any of their kin would even *want* to serve in the military. A final complication was the highly closeted nature of gays serving in any of the nation's armed forces. It seemed initially that only those who faced dishonorable discharges or other military charges were willing to talk with Shilts as he wrestled with a demanding timeline for completing the book amid emerging personal health struggles related to his HIV (and subsequent AIDS) diagnosis. Shilts's sometimes-neglected health and treatment plan for his HIV infection meant his diagnosis eventually progressed to what most called full-blown AIDS. "Randy was always pretty positive about his health until the very end when he started getting these opportunistic infections," Alband said. "He got on AZT very early, a lot earlier than many other people." The AZT treatments, however, came in massive doses, what some considered "toxic," and Alband estimated, "I am sure it probably helped keep some people alive a lot longer, but it also took an incredible toll. I don't know anyone who received AZT in those early days in the heavy doses like Randy received who survived."[13]

As Shilts started the research and writing for *Conduct Unbecoming*, he did so in a sober world, one in which the booze and pot that had played such a prominent role in his younger life were no longer present. Added to that pressure was the secret about his HIV status and movement toward an AIDS diagnosis. He worked so hard, in fact, that he sometimes missed appointments for subsequent treatments featuring aerosolized pentamidine mists. The mist treatments, which are no longer recommended for people suffering recurring bouts of pneumocystis pneumonia, were one of the only known treatments at the time. The forty-five-minute treatments, which required Shilts to sit attached to a nebulizer machine every four weeks, were not something he enjoyed. Shilts viewed sitting huffing on a mister as wasted time—there was work to do.

That work included nationwide searches via classified ads, networks of contacts, and mountains of Freedom of Information Act requests to uncover active military or veterans willing to talk about the issue of gays in the military. "I guess I was operating on my own stereotypes of military people," Shilts noted about the reluctance he expected to find among active duty and retired veterans. "I figured they wouldn't want to rock the boat and that they wouldn't want to be named, they were more conservative, even people who are out," he said. "But it was actually very easy."[14] The search to find willing interview subjects started with classified ads placed in gay newspapers across the nation, which resulted in about three hundred replies ranging from veterans who had served in Vietnam to currently serving enlisted personnel. The work was painstaking because it required Shilts to not only sort out who would make appropriate interview subjects but also read through their life stories in order to help set a context or understanding of their desire to serve in the military (for those who had enlisted voluntarily).

The original publication date of *Conduct Unbecoming* was in late 1991 as a lead-up to the upcoming Democratic and Republican presidential primaries in 1992. The deadline was pushed back when the scope of the work indicated it would be impossible to finish the book before the election. Shilts wrote from more than eleven hundred in-person interviews conducted by him or his associates, and he collected more than fifteen thousand government documents, mostly via the federal Freedom of Information Act. Among the leads Shilts pursued in completing the work was a personal letter he wrote to the son of General Douglas MacArthur in an attempt to confirm repeated claims made to Shilts that alleged General MacArthur had ignored military demands that homosexuals stop serving in active units. It was a "fact" Shilts could never confirm.

The life of Dr. Thomas A. Dooley III, a navy lieutenant and physician who focused much of his work on combating illness and Communism in isolated areas of Southeast Asia, including Vietnam and Laos, was another undertaking for *Conduct Unbecoming*. Dooley's best-selling 1956 book, *Deliver Us from Evil,* put a spotlight on the heartbreaking needs of the still-developing region. It was during Dooley's book tour, Shilts uncovered, that allegations stating that Dooley participated in homosexual encounters emerged, and he was subsequently kicked out of the military (and officially untethered from the Catholic Church as well). Shilts wrote to one source close to Dooley, "I see Dooley's life as being a wonderfully dramatic historic backdrop" for *Conduct Unbecoming*.[15]

Shilts said it was painful telling Dooley's story, that of a man utterly committed and convinced of the value of American democracy and a Legion of Merit winner. "[Tom Dooley] was indisputably a shining example of everything the military considered good," Shilts said. "Tom Dooley is the personification of what's bad about the [no gays policy of the military]. His story says everything about it." Shilts offered on the pages of *Conduct Unbecoming* that Dooley's life was a great contradiction. "He had believed that America was the land of the free and had defended her against totalitarianism; yet Tom Dooley's own life was evidence that this promise of freedom was a sham."[16]

The lion's share of the writing on *Conduct Unbecoming* was completed by the early fall of 1992, but Shilts's rate of work was slowing, and his growing (but still not publicly disclosed) medical issues were creating problems. A friend and former professional colleague introduced Shilts to ideas posited by researchers Robert Ben Mitchell, Harris L. Coulter, and others who suggested AIDS might actually be a manifestation of late-stage or chronic syphilis and should be treated as such. These new ideas found more acceptance among French and German doctors who were also more optimistic than their American counterparts about the possible survival and treatment of AIDS-related illnesses. At his friend's behest, Shilts scheduled a week-long trip to Germany in the late summer of 1992 to do what many others had done: seek out new answers and new hope amid the grim reality of an AIDS diagnosis. The German trip was expensive, Alband noted, and didn't provide any miracle answers. It also left Shilts physically depleted for weeks after he returned to California.[17]

Deadlines set by the book's publisher, St. Martin's Press, had frequent modifications. Shilts's editor, Michael Denneny, kept "buying time" with his bosses at St. Martin's, who continued to push for a completed manuscript. Unknown to most, as 1992 ended, Shilts was dangerously close to death, with his book unfinished. On Christmas Eve, as he stuffed stockings with small gifts, he experienced an "episode" of shortness of breath and terrible chest pain, and he heard a small pop in his lungs. Shilts had suffered a collapsed lung (officially known as a pneumothorax episode), an artifact of earlier bouts with pneumocystis pneumonia. Alband was at Shilts's home in Guerneville, near the Russian River in Sonoma County, California, when the incident occurred, and since his breathing stabilized and he said he felt better, no one called for an ambulance. In fact, the next day Shilts drove to San Francisco to begin a house- and dog-sitting favor for his partner Barry Barbieri, who was going out of town for family commitments. Another friend stopped in to check on Shilts a day later, found him lifeless on a sofa, and called 911. "If they hadn't called 911, Randy would probably have died," Alband said. "Randy was in the hospital then for more than two months and was very, very ill."[18]

Alband notified Denneny, who decided to keep the news of Shilts's collapse secret. Instead, Denneny packed a bag and headed to San Francisco, where he found his author unable to speak, breathing through a ventilator at Davies Medical Center under an assumed name and in and out of consciousness. Beyond the primary concern of Shilts's survival, there remained the issue of his unfinished book. Based off the success of *And the Band Played On*, St. Martin's had advance orders for more than 250,000 copies of *Conduct Unbecoming* but no completed manuscript and an author in and out of a coma.

In the days that followed, Alband and Denneny ran a covert operation to break into Shilts's files and records and try to do what they could to save the book. Alband recalled that Shilts "was jealously sitting on his boxes of materials, sources and information in the hospital like it was his security blanket. I would try and get into his boxes of information in the hospital room when he would fall asleep, but he woke up and found me rummaging through them and grabbed it back and held it to his chest."[19] Denneny needed to convince a clearly depleted Shilts that he must accept help, or the book would never be complete. Denneny said, "By flying out to San Francisco and being on the spot I was able to handle things out there without the home office. They would simply have to accept whatever I was doing."[20] When he was conscious, Shilts was sometimes lucid and sometimes not, but he was clear on one thing: if news of his AIDS-related illness got out, no one would pay attention to his latest effort on gays in the military and instead would focus on the pending death of its author. Denneny and Alband both believe that literally hundreds of people in San Francisco probably knew of Shilts's hospitalization but out of respect kept the secret until Shilts was ready to disclose it himself.[21]

Finally able to communicate with Shilts, Denneny laid it on the line: the completion of the book's last three hundred pages was imperative as Arkansas governor Bill Clinton prepared to become the nation's forty-second president. The integration of gays into the military would be a very hot issue for the new administration, given repeated promises Clinton had personally delivered to gay leaders and donors about how he would address the policy. Denneny recalls:

I said to Randy, "If we were going to have any chance whatsoever, we have to get this moving. I can finish this for you, but I gotta make sure you understand that situation that we're in and that I get a clear answer from you." Well, he said, "OK, I trust you, you do it." ... I am a great believer in authors having the final cut on their book. I was very reluctant to do this, but it was the only way that we were ever going to get the book done. Randy was in a semi-coma a lot of the time. He would be in a coma for four or five hours, and then he would float into consciousness for ten or fifteen minutes, and you could talk to him, he would brighten up again.[22]

Denneny said one of the things that pleases him is that most readers are unable to pinpoint where Shilts's writing stopped and Denneny's started. After he regained his health, Shilts said *he* knew exactly where his writing stopped and Denneny's began, and he intended to rewrite the ending to his own satisfaction (a task he was not able to complete). Deadlines and Shilts's questionable medical and mental condition forced a major decision to cut a large section of the book regarding the just-ending Gulf War. Added to later drafts were details from that part of Shilts's research.

Word was beginning to spread that the nation's anointed "openly gay journalist" and now author was about to release his newest book, *Conduct Unbecoming: Gays and Lesbians in the U.S. Military*, as Shilts's reporting and books now routinely gained significant notice, particularly among straight media sources. In this period, a normally positive honor—obtaining the title "Person of the Week" from Peter Jennings on *ABC World News Tonight*—served to annoy Shilts, as Jennings referred to him as "an angry man" in the profile piece. Shilts said he hated controversy, "but I do what I think is right. And I'm not going to change a story so that people will like me."[23] Another problem arose while Shilts struggled to recuperate as the editors of *Newsweek* (who had paid Shilts an $8,000 advance for a cover story on the gays in the military issue) tried to avoid an embarrassing screw-up. The *Newsweek* fact-checker was unable to reach Shilts, who, unknown to the fact-checker, was unconscious during most of the period when the fact-checking process was underway. In desperation, Alband stepped up and provided the information *Newsweek* editors were requesting.

The cover article offer from *Newsweek* reflected Shilts's growing prominence on the issue of gay men and lesbian women being drummed out of the military. Most Americans knew nothing about the gays in the military issue, meaning it fit perfectly into Shilts's view of the purpose or meaning for his journalism. Obscure cases of gay men or lesbian women trying to stay in the military had come and gone before, but Shilts successfully unearthed and highlighted the often-draconian efforts the military engaged in to root out homosexuals.

The gays in the military issue quickly moved to the top of most LGBTQ activists' agendas for the 1992 presidential election, and in a tight three-way race against incumbent President Bush and Reform Party gadfly Ross Perot, Clinton couldn't resist promising gay supporters via fund-raising events that he would end the ban. The Clinton campaign may have thought the promise was just one of those made during the heat of a campaign and one to make donors happy, but gay men and lesbian women were listening and expected Clinton to fulfill his promise. The battle over whether gay men and lesbian women could serve openly or at all in the nation's armed forces continued to grow in intensity.

Clinton was elected the nation's forty-second president, but history would show that opposition Republicans in Washington, DC, were happy to let the new Clinton Democrats, the outsider "Arkansas Clintonians," take a run at a controversial issue about the role of gays in one of society's most honored and respected organizations, the military. The record would show that the Clinton team ran their own train off the tracks, getting sidetracked onto the gays in the military issue in their first few weeks in office, away from their "It's the economy, stupid" mantra, which had served them so well in winning the White House. One of Clinton's top aides, George Stephanopoulos, reported that as president-elect, Clinton was earnest in his desire to keep his word to end the ban. High-level gay advisors to Clinton, including David Mixner, urged him to act as boldly as President Truman had once done in ordering the full racial integration of the military forces. Stephanopoulos said the role of gays in the military was the top issue on the minds of General Colin Powell and other members of the Joint Chiefs of Staff who met with Clinton in the weeks between the November 1992 election and when he took office on January 20, 1993. Clinton met an immediate roadblock. The Joint Chiefs were adamant—the reality of changing the policy was nonexistent. Stephanopoulos, in a moment of rare directness about the limitations of the presidency, noted that "Clinton's formal powers [on the issue] were bound by the fact that he was a new president, elected with only 43 percent of the vote, who had never served in the military and stood accused of dodging the draft." As a result, the Joint Chiefs of Staff could not be persuaded of the value and feasibility of a policy change. The Joint Chiefs' message to Clinton, Stephanopoulos reported, was that "keeping this promise will cost you the military. Fight us, and you'll lose—and it won't be pretty."[24]

A protracted and ultimately unsuccessful effort to end the ban played out throughout the first months of the Clinton administration—much to the chagrin of other Clinton advisors who were livid the issue had essentially derailed Clinton's primary agenda based on righting the nation's economic path. The battle would rage on during 1993 and 1994 and resulted in a compromise, the unartfully named "Don't Ask, Don't Tell" policy, finally installed in February 1994.[25]

As the congressional battle over gays in the military raged on, Shilts's health was improving, and the final work on *Conduct Unbecoming* was complete. As it was released, Denneny tried to grab headlines (as he had done before with *Band*) by highlighting a claim in *Conduct Unbecoming* that asserted that Persian Gulf War general Norman Schwarzkopf privately did not oppose allowing lesbians and gays to serve as military personnel, a claim Schwarzkopf publicly denied repeatedly.

For his part, Shilts stuck to his main thesis: "The military ban is the most dramatic example of the fact that lesbians and gay men in America are not truly free, that this is not a free country," he asserted, and that examination of the military's ban on gays served as a "wonderful microcosm of prejudice against gays and lesbians in the country as a whole." Shilts seemed pleased and excited about the attention the book was receiving, acknowledging, "My great fear was that this would be an issue nobody would care about."[26]

With *Conduct Unbecoming,* Shilts attempted to take up the issue of how the military exiled gay members who had been out for decades and the rather inhumane manner in which it did it. Shilts found that the military had passed through various eras since the 1940s with the official banning of gays, periods that reflected a view that gays were criminals or sick individuals; that gays were a security risk; or, more recently, that gays would be disruptive to unit cohesion and military order.[27] Beyond these themes, Shilts's research had strong implications for the role of women in the military, particularly the ongoing struggle with sexual harassment of female enlistees and officers, the military's and society's application of sodomy rules and laws applied to homo- and heterosexuals, as well as how the military handled HIV and other sexually transmitted diseases among its ranks (the latter of which Shilts referred to as "an admirable effort").[28]

Shilts said his research revealed to him a "pandemic" of sexual harassment and abuse of women in the ranks of the military. "I had always known intellectually that there was a relationship between the women's movement and the gay movement, but I'd never seen the mechanics of how it works out in people's lives," he said. "This book allowed me to figure it out: Both of the movements reflect a threat to the ideology of masculinity, which remains the central cultural imperative in America."[29] Shilts's text offered a thoughtful critique of the long-term supposition that the military was good at "making men out of boys," with the ban setting the context for the ongoing American debate about the roles of men and women. Shilts said, "The military is an institution that guarantees to do one thing beyond all else, and that is to take boys and make men out of them. The reason the military did not want women . . . has been the same reason the military does not want gay people. The presence of women and gay people in the military is a threat to those individuals who sought out this institution as a way to reinforce their own sense of manhood."[30]

## CHAPTER 13

# Disclosing HIV

S hilts knew from past experience that getting his new book, *Conduct Unbecoming*, mentioned in media interviews was key to getting it sold to readers. He also knew that he would finally have to come to terms with public disclosure of his HIV status, something he could no longer conceal. The groundbreaking research Shilts had undertaken to chronicle the fight for inclusion of openly gay women and men in the US armed forces coincided, unfortunately, with Shilts's diagnosis of what was to become a series of HIV-related ailments, this time Kaposi's sarcoma and its hard-to-hide accompanying skin lesions.

Shilts's health issues came up immediately. *Los Angeles Times* reporter Bettijane Levine wrote, "There are two reasons why Randy Shilts says he shouldn't be talking. First, he must conserve his strength while recovering from a collapsed lung, a complication of AIDS. Second, the publishers of his book . . . threatened that 'there will be no book' if the author doesn't close his mouth until late April when the volume hits the stores."[1] Whether he would admit to understanding it or not, the fact that America's most celebrated author on the AIDS crisis was now living with AIDS was news to reporters near and far. His health bouncing from decline to brief periods of rebound, Shilts undertook the requisite media interviews but now via satellite and telephone or by hosting reporters in his San Francisco condo. His fragile health would not withstand any national book tour. The details or descriptions of his health struggles seemed to depend on his mood. In some interviews, Shilts would openly discuss the lung collapse he had suffered: "They cut you open, staple it back together again, and then sort of glue it to the inside of your chest. And so now my breathing problems are almost entirely related to having had open-chest surgery."[2] Later, in another interview, Shilts would grow angry that a reporter was asking about his health status.

"I often said this book was going to kill me, but I meant it figuratively, not literally," Shilts told his *San Francisco Chronicle* colleague Patricia Holt for a profile accompanying the release of *Conduct Unbecoming*. Shilts expressed gratitude to his book editors and research assistants for "finishing" the book while he remained hospitalized. Showing the growing distance between his own coming out in 1972 and his rise to gay and literary "stardom" in 1993, he expressed surprise "to see how open a lot of the younger people in the military today are about being gay. Most of them are ordinary people who happen to be gay and don't mind who knows it."[3]

The dissonance facing Shilts was real—he had struggled terribly but privately with how to handle disclosure of his HIV status. It was an interesting contrast to how he had handled as a younger man the level of openness he expressed about his sexuality and open questions about whether his coming out at such an early point in his young life had left irreparable scars. Shilts said privately to friends and later publicly that his principal concern was that coverage of his HIV status would overshadow the meaning and impact of his other work. "I had been out of the hospital for six, seven weeks, but there were a lot of rumors," Shilts told *Rolling Stone*'s Garry Wills. "I was not ashamed [of my HIV status] or anything, it just added another element of complexity in terms of dealing with people. . . . I would have preferred to do it after my book [*Conduct Unbecoming*] was released because it is frustrating being on TV and having a very limited amount of time and being asked about my health rather than this book I spent four years on." Publicly disclosing his HIV status would be decidedly different from coming out as a college student long ago. Randy Shilts was no longer an anonymous college student—he was a known and respected journalist and emerging "gay celebrity."[4]

The juxtaposition of Shilts's work with his own personal HIV status was one that reporters and their readers would naturally focus upon. By the time *People* magazine came around to writing up its first-ever profile of Shilts, writer David Ellis spent considerable time discussing Shilts's HIV status in a précis meant to highlight his new book and how it arrived at a key time in Washington as the nation began to address inclusion of openly gay men and women in the military. The article emphasized Shilts's battle with a collapsed lung, mentioned the oxygen tank at his side, and questioned whether he had become a "professional AIDS victim." Shilts declared that his HIV status "was no different than having high blood pressure or some other life-threatening illness" and accused others of applying a "melodramatic veneer" to AIDS. Photos accompanying the story are in classic *People* magazine style but show an obviously frail Shilts in poorly fitted clothes walking in the yard of his Guerneville, California, home with his dog, Dash. Also included is a rare photo of Shilts with his partner Barry Barbieri above the quote: "You can be too serious about [AIDS]; you can't let it wreck your life." To close the article, Ellis quoted Shilts as saying he had perhaps written on his last gay-themed subjects, Shilts offering, "I think I've sort of said it all."[5]

This open portrayal of Shilts with AIDS caused some to go back in their minds—or in their news stories—to review what Shilts had said during the release of *And the Band Played On* about his own HIV status. The "stay-at-home book tour" for *Conduct Unbecoming* included even more pointed and personal questions from reporters than before. Gone were his more generalized and subject-changing responses from years earlier. "No, I don't," he told the *Chicago Tribune* when its reporter inquired in 1987 about whether he had AIDS. "That has come up in several interviews. I think it is an irrelevant and smarmy question. It assumes that any gay man has AIDS. But no, I do not have AIDS." Shilts successfully changed the subject then, focusing on his claim that as a gay reporter he had an advantage, because gay leaders could not mislead him about gay sexual practices: "I knew what was going on. And although any good reporter could have gotten the information that I did, I was the only one who cared enough to devote my career to it."[6]

Even his hometown newspaper, the *Aurora Beacon-News*, had inquired about his HIV status in an 1987 story. To the "Do you have AIDS question?" Shilts said he did not and that he had not taken the antibody test for HIV, contradicting claims he made elsewhere that he learned his HIV-positive status as the manuscript for *And the Band Played On* was completed.[7]

The AIDS question came up again in a lengthy 1987 author's profile of Shilts for the *Charlotte Observer* in which Shilts summed up his feelings about being tested for AIDS: "It's one thing for a heterosexual to go for an AIDS test. That person is going for reassurance. It's very scary to go for an AIDS test if you're gay, especially if you are in a high risk group. You have to be prepared to face a death sentence. I am not prepared for that."[8] When Shilts spoke these words, he knew his test result was positive for HIV.

Throughout all the interviews and questions in the months following the release of *Band*, Shilts's candor in answering "the AIDS question" is an issue in doubt, even if the question was a highly personal one and one that he was not obligated to answer. The truth is, however, that during the time he made some of the statements reported in late 1987 as he toured the nation promoting *And the Band Played On*, Shilts already knew his HIV status, based on his later accounts that he learned of his status on the day he turned in the manuscript for the book earlier in 1987. At the time, however, he made no such disclosures about his HIV status—and perhaps made a distinction between having AIDS (which he did not have at *Band*'s release) and being aware that he had tested positive for HIV. No one challenged how forthcoming—or honest—Shilts was being on the issue of his personal HIV status. In an October 1987 article by Robert Reinhold of the *Los Angeles Times*, Shilts said his health was "just fine" and said he had not taken the AIDS antibody test because no medical treatment was available if the test was positive and because he currently engaged in no sexual activity believed to spread the virus that causes AIDS.[9] Again, this was inconsistent with what he would eventually disclose about learning he was HIV positive. A careful parsing of that passage reveals that at least part of it is a lie (or at least a misinterpretation) of what Shilts knew regarding the results of an HIV antibody test taken weeks before.[10]

Further examination of his statement reveals that he spoke in the present tense when describing his sexual activities and whether they placed him at risk of HIV infection. He carefully avoided specific or detailed disclosure or discussion of his past sexual activities, which clearly had placed him at risk of HIV infection, including a first-person account for an early gay health report in the *Advocate* of having battled hepatitis.[11]

The release of *Conduct Unbecoming* and the nearly simultaneous release of the film version of *And the Band Played On* added to the ongoing commentary on Shilts's HIV status, including a report by one of Shilts's youthful (but since discarded) political heroes, conservative pundit William F. Buckley Jr. The cerebral Buckley unapologetically posed a pointed, personal question about Shilts: "Why did Randy Shilts contract AIDS? It has been a long time since we discovered what brings on that terrible disease. That he should have exposed himself suggests an obsessive appetite alien to common sense. Do such appetites argue against totally felicitous relations between gay and non-gay?"[12] The irony of Buckley's criticism on such a personal issue, especially from someone Shilts had admired as a youth, was a lot to take. Shilts challenged Buckley's presumption that the "fact that I knew so much about AIDS and how it indicates that I had compulsions that were alien to common sense": "People getting diagnosed today are still likely to have gotten the virus before anybody knew that AIDS was going to be a threat or that it even existed."[13]

Regardless of how and/or when Shilts contracted the virus that causes AIDS, by 1993 the realness and openness of his HIV status and subsequent full-blown AIDS infection were at hand. In August and again in December 1992, he had suffered major setbacks after being diagnosed with *Pneumocystis carinii* pneumonia. His December bout required hospitalization, lung surgery, respiratory therapy, and heavy sedation. Shilts's lengthy hospital stay had fueled the growing rumor that he had AIDS and the obvious need by February 1993 to make a formal announcement about his health. Three years of AZT drug treatments, the only approved treatment for people with AIDS at the time, had slowed but not stopped the advance of the disease. Shilts met with family, friends, his book editor, and his agent and was convinced of the need to make a public disclosure of his status. The story that the man who had chronicled the earliest days of the AIDS pandemic was now one of its victims was big news, and Shilts wanted to control his own story. He attempted to do so via a one-page, unsigned letter on *San Francisco Chronicle* letterhead dated February 16, 1993. Shilts said he learned of his HIV status in March 1987, and "the disclosure raised a number of questions. Should I continue to cover AIDS?" Shilts said he told his editors of his situation, and "we decided that my health status should not prevent me covering AIDS any more than a reporter with a bad heart should avoid covering cardiology. So I continued writing about AIDS."[14]

Cleve Jones was among a small number of friends who eventually learned of Shilts's HIV status before he went public, but it wasn't until August 1993 that Jones learned that Shilts's HIV status had transitioned to what was then referred to as "full-blown AIDS." Jones confirmed as much during a visit to Shilts's home in Guerneville, where his dog, Dash, rushed out to greet Jones, but Randy remained inside, tethered to an oxygen tank and a sofa. "The front door was open, and we were calling out his name, and then we went in, and Randy was sitting there on the sofa with oxygen," Jones said. "That's how I found out. He hadn't told anyone really, and I think I said to him, 'Randy, what the fuck? After all the stuff we've been through, after all the ways we've been there for each other, and you have kept this a secret? Why?'" Jones said. Shilts told Jones and all his other confidants that he wanted to keep covering stories that mattered to him at the *Chronicle* and finish his book about gays in the military.[15]

*Chronicle* staff writer Leah Garchik interviewed Shilts about his HIV status for a February 16, 1993, page 2 story titled "Reporter, Author Randy Shilts Reveals That He Has AIDS." The use of the word "reveals" in the *Chronicle's* headline reflected the noteworthy nature of the disclosure and its repetition in newspapers across the nation and on network television news. Garchik reported that Shilts "decided to disclose his condition because he had been besieged by inquiring telephone calls from members of the gay community and the national press. It seems the open secret surrounding his HIV status began to collapse, and Shilts had to make a decision about disclosure. 'I want to talk about it myself rather than have somebody else talk.'" Repeating his dramatic version that he learned of his HIV status on March 16, 1987, the day he finished writing *And the Band Played On*, Shilts said he instantly made the decision not to discuss his personal HIV status. He also said that *Chronicle* editors agreed with his proposal to move him from daily news reporting as a national correspondent to writing a weekly column for the paper's editorial pages because he was preoccupied with coming to terms with his diagnosis. "I was afraid I couldn't do any project that lasted longer than a week," he said. He ultimately settled on the idea that it was time to move on from full-time reporting on AIDS and turn his attentions to other issues.[16] Shilts's self-assessment was that learning he was HIV positive was no one's business and should not affect his professional work. Optimistically, Shilts said in his disclosure statement, "I do not plan on giving any further interviews on my health status." The subject came up in every subsequent story written about Shilts.[17]

Public discussion of his health status always seemed to irritate Shilts. "I didn't want to become an AIDS poster boy," he told *Rolling Stone*. "I didn't want to be doing interviews on TV about substantive issues and then have it overwhelmed by personal questions about me. I still don't think I'm that interesting, you know, as opposed to the information I have."[18] During an April 1993 appearance on *The Charlie Rose Show*, Shilts's irritation continued to rise as Rose asked questions about the effectiveness of AZT as a treatment for AIDS, the drug approval process in the United States, and whether there was a need for an "AIDS czar" to address the issue. Shilts's irritation boiled nearest to the surface when Rose queried him about his own HIV status and asked him why he waited so long to disclose that he had AIDS. "Well, this interview is one of the reasons why," Shilts said. "Here I have spent the last four years researching and writing about gays and lesbians in the military and yet here we sit discussing issues related to my own personal health status, which I don't think is all that interesting." Rose retorted that he had opened the interview with more than fifteen minutes of questions about Shilts's research for *Conduct Unbecoming*. Still annoyed, Shilts replied, "Well, yes, but I was really worried that stuff about me personally would overshadow my work, and I consider, I am a professional journalist, not a professional AIDS activist, and I don't want to get pulled into this role of professional AIDS activist."[19]

Clearly, Shilts was concerned with controlling the news story about him, landing in an unusual spot for a journalist used to writing stories about others rather than being the subject of the story. Interestingly, despite years as a newspaper journalist who would have resisted similar treatment from a source, he wanted to keep particular aspects of his story out of the hands of his interviewers. Returning to his ubiquitous claim that "I am not an activist, and I don't feel comfortable being an activist. I am a journalist," Shilts again revealed the transformative nature he believed his journalism could have: "I think I make my contribution to the world as a journalist. There are plenty of AIDS activists out there, but not so many journalists out there who have been able to do what I have been trying to for the last few years."[20]

Shilts told Rose that information could overcome homophobia and antigay prejudice. "The main reason I did the book was that, as I traveled around, I believed that a major point of *And the Band Played On* was to show how antigay prejudice interfered with our society's ability to deal with AIDS," Shilts said. "I realized that with a lot of heterosexuals, they could be very well meaning people, but they were in some sort of denial when it comes to the existence and devastating effects that antigay prejudice has."[21]

Shilts particularly took on what he termed "juvenile-level testimony" before congressional committees considering Clinton's edict to integrate gays into the military. He noted how quickly those discussions fell into fearful explanations of how gay men in a military setting would just use their access to gain sexual partners or overwrought discussions of how gay and nongay men and women would utilize restrooms and showers. "That reflects an overall social attitude that gay men are sex-obsessed animals who do nothing but ponder how to seduce heterosexuals," Shilts said, noting that the argument was a red herring and that existing military policy covering fraternization could deal with any such problems, however rare or common they might be.[22]

Shilts appropriately linked the importance of breaking down the military's ban on homosexuals to that of its earlier struggles to integrate racial minorities and women into its ranks and the military's reluctance to change. Shilts attributed the struggles to integrate women into the armed forces as more closely aligned to efforts to preserve masculinity—much like what was behind banning gays from openly serving. Shilts told Rose: "The issue of women in the military was never about women. It was about men and their desire to define their masculinity. . . . And this issue has very little to do with gay people. It's all about heterosexuals, particularly heterosexual men, . . . [who are] using an institution to define their manhood, and then if you let these people in who define you being less than a man, less than a human, then it takes away from the ability of that institution to give one their own self-definition."[23]

The subject of Shilts's AIDS diagnosis came up during another national interview, this one on the critically acclaimed National Public Radio program *Fresh Air*, hosted by journalist Terry Gross from WHYY in Philadelphia. While spending most of her interview with Shilts examining the key points of his book on gays in the military, Gross did wrap up the interview with a rather direct question: "Randy, you developed AIDS when you were writing this book about gays in the military. I wonder whether having written such an important book about AIDS and whether your diagnosis and condition has affected your outlook and perspectives on the topics that you research?" Shilts said he "unfortunately knew a great deal about AIDS" but had purposefully decided to stop writing about it as a reporter because it was just too stressful. He told Gross, "I live in the gay community in San Francisco, and so most gay men here are HIV positive. . . . I was dealing with it professionally, and then I was dealing with it in my own life, and so it became just too much, so I gave up writing about it. I was starting to get psychosomatic symptoms because of the press."[24]

Gross clarified with Shilts by recalling the 1987 interview she conducted with him for the release of his book *And the Band Played On* and how she had inquired about his status at that time. She noted that Shilts did not disclose his status at that point. Shilts replied, "Well, heterosexuals don't have a lot of etiquette around that issue because it is intensely private, and it is not necessarily something I wanted to discuss on national TV. I could not believe it when people asked me about my HIV status, just like they were asking about whether it was a nice day, as if they had a right to know."[25]

Shilts may have had a point—interviews granted for articles intended to be about the release of *Conduct Unbecoming* invariably were required to make often-lengthy mention of Shilts's struggle with AIDS. But his struggle with AIDS *was* in the forefront of his life in 1993. Shilts was too weak physically to go to New York for interviews booked with ABC's *Good Morning America*, NBC's *Today Show*, CBS *This Morning*, PBS's *Charlie Rose Show*, CNN's *Larry King Live,* and Ted Koppel's ABC franchise *Nightline,* all of whom agreed to satellite interviews with Shilts from his San Francisco condo. Stories in the *Los Angeles Times* and the *Boston Globe* both seemed particularly focused on Shilts's HIV status. The *Boston Globe* noted that the book was released as he was "traveling in the twin worlds of rapidly growing celebrity and slowly failing health."[26]

After his HIV status became public knowledge, Shilts would occasionally let go with small details about how he believed he became infected: "I was probably infected in 1980 or '81, before anyone knew about AIDS," adding, "I am a recovering alcoholic and didn't quit drinking until '84. It happened somewhere in that fog, some forgotten moment."[27] Shilts's lover in the era before he quit drinking and smoking marijuana, Steve Newman, believes he became infected probably during raucous parties the couple hosted at their fashionable high-rise condo on Gough Street.[28]

Despite the difficulty of even speaking at length with interviewers because of his regular need for oxygen following the collapsed lung episode, Shilts worked hard promoting the key messages of *Conduct Unbecoming*, which had won widespread interest as the gays in the military issue continued to simmer in Washington. In a story that irritated Shilts significantly, Jeffrey Schmalz of the *New York Times* put Shilts's health status front and center for a gravely titled April 22, 1993, piece, "Randy Shilts: Writing Against Time, Valiantly." It was not an unexpected move, as Schmalz, who openly disclosed his own HIV status before Shilts did, wrote about related issues for the *Times* prior to his death in November 1993. As a result, it was clear Schmalz was not going to leave Shilts's HIV status as a sidebar. Schmalz crafted sentences that highlighted the painful reality of Shilts's life: "These should be the best of times for Randy Shilts. His new book is hitting stores now. . . . A movie based on his first book . . . is about to go into production. An HBO film of his second book . . . is about to go into production. He has a 23-year-old boyfriend, a 10-acre retreat in the country, even a trusty dog." The contrast Schmalz painted included mentioning that Shilts was tied to an oxygen tank in order to breathe and slowly shuffled to answer the door: "One minute he is the old Randy Shilts, a blur of energy and issues and passion. . . . The next, he isn't Randy Shilts at all. He's just another gay man with AIDS, scared and tired."[29]

"I have to take care of myself," Shilts told Schmalz, "Another thing could knock me out. I can't get pneumonia again. I have a good life . . . [but] I'd be happier if I didn't have to worry about dying." Despite his health challenges, Shilts's wit was on full display as Schmalz pulled a noteworthy quote from him about his situation: "HIV is certainly character-building. It's made me see all of the shallow things we cling to, like ego and vanity. Of course, I'd rather have a few more T-cells and a little less character."[30]

For those who missed the persistent melancholy reporting about Shilts's health struggles, it was made clear to all as an emaciated Shilts visited the set for production of the HBO Pictures adaptation of *And the Band Played On*, based on a screenplay written by Arnold Schulman. Director Robert Spottiswoode invited Shilts to the set. Shilts took photos with actors Lily Tomlin and Sir Ian McKellen. He was also able to attend the nonbroadcast premiere of the film on August 31, 1993, at the Samuel Goldwyn Theater at the Academy of Motion Picture Arts and Sciences pavilion in Beverly Hills, California, but public appearances away from his home base in Guerneville were becoming rare. He dispatched his brother Reed and his wife, Dawn, to attend the film's screening at the Kennedy Center in Washington, DC, on his behalf. Dawn Shilts recalled the surreal feeling of sitting in an audience with a mix of powerful politicians and agitated AIDS advocates and organizers. The options, rights, and proposed film treatment for the book went through several iterations before finally getting life from megaproducer Aaron Spelling and an $8 million budget. An all-star ensemble cast gathered for the production, including Tomlin, McKellen, Matthew Modine, Alan Alda, Richard Gere, Phil Collins, Anjelica Huston, and Steve Martin. Its broadcast premiere on HBO on September 11, 1993, produced high ratings and solid reviews, and the film eventually won three primetime Emmy Awards. In the United States, distribution of the film was limited to HBO and its subscribers but was a theatrical release in twenty nations across the globe. The film was one of Shilts's biggest financial windfalls, adding handsomely to the more than $1 million he had taken in via advances, royalties, and rights for *And the Band Played On* and *Conduct Unbecoming.*

A parade of national reporters continued to make their way to Shilts's door to seek his views—perhaps in response to Schmalz having portrayed him as near death and labeling him "a star, treated as a pre-eminent chronicler of gay life and spokesman on gay issues."[31]

# CHAPTER 14

# Journalist versus Advocate

Interestingly, the content of *Conduct Unbecoming* allowed Shilts to break at least partially free of the criticism that his writing lacked proper representation or consideration of lesbian women as part of the story. Given that his first two books were a biography of an openly gay politician and an exposé of the advent of a communicable disease pandemic mostly among gay men, the absence of women from his work was understandable or at least explainable. Shilts had well armed his critics, as many pointed to hysterical news stories by Shilts on the pages of the *Chronicle* and later as part of *And the Band Played On* about a working female prostitute still soliciting customers despite having swollen lymph nodes and night sweats—early signs of AIDS. The prostitute, whom Shilts identified as Silvana Strangis, represented about the only woman in the AIDS story for Shilts, contended critics. Shilts's editors played a role as well, since the *Chronicle* story about Strangis ran under the headline "A 'Monster' Dilemma on AIDS: Working Prostitute Waits for Test," emphasizing Shilts's reporting that a clinic offering AIDS testing wasn't open on Fridays so Strangis could confirm if she was, in fact, ill. Shilts later told author James Kinsella, "I knew the clinic had closed [on Fridays]. My point was that this was a working prostitute"; nonetheless, "I shouldn't have let the city editor do the lead saying she was turned away [for an HIV test]. It wasn't fair."[1]

With *Conduct Unbecoming*, Shilts did not waste the opportunity to explore issues of misogyny exclusively experienced by gay women. "Especially for lesbians," Shilts wrote, "the issues are more complex than simple homophobia because they also involve significant features of sex-based discrimination. There are many men who never wanted women in *their* Army or *their* Navy in the first place, and the military regulations regarding homosexuality have been the way to keep them out for the past decade."[2] He acknowledged the stereotypes that surrounded the feminist movement in general and that its critics successfully scared off some women by noting the existence of gay women in the ranks of those seeking to advance the rights of women. As a result,

> although the vast majority of women accepted the central tenets of women's liberation, such as the demand for pay equity, the right to abortion, and expanded job opportunities, most amended the allied opinions with the proviso, "I'm not one of *those* women's libbers, but ..." What was meant was, "I'm not a lesbian, but ..." The enemy of the women's movement would always be homophobia, as much as male chauvinism, although there were some who argued that you could never be quite sure where anti-gay prejudice ended and misogyny began.[3]

Shilts wrote compassionately about the ceaseless preoccupation of the military in rooting out lesbians. "As the presence of women became more pronounced in every [branch of the service], an entire mythology evolved, imbuing lesbians with menacing qualities—far darker, in fact, than anything that had been attributed to gay men in recent years."[4]

Beyond allowing him to explore the experiences of gay women, the topics of *Conduct Unbecoming* also offered themselves as helpful content to explain and understand homosexuality in American culture. Shilts said the manner in which the military had dealt with homosexuals throughout history closely reflected society's dealing with the "unwanted other." Heterosexuals "define the limits of freedom for the homosexual minority. The story of homosexual America is therefore the story of heterosexual America." Shilts's work accurately traced the advent of the issue of "national security," which grew out of the post–World War II era and was punctuated by an obsessive fear of Communist infiltration (aided by closeted homosexuals who may have been subject to blackmail by foreign spies). He openly acknowledged that "networks of homosexuals" had, in fact, existed in the US military as far back as World War I. "The military's gay members were connecting with one another not just for sexual reasons, but because they understood they shared a common bond and common dangers," Shilts wrote. "The creation of gay communities at military bases throughout the world only mirrored what was happening to gay people in civilian society. . . . The big difference between civilian gays and their military brethren was that gays in the armed forces still needed code words to conceal themselves."[5] The preserved historic role played by personnel such as Edward Modesto, Perry Watkins, Leonard Matlovich, Margarethe Cammermeyer, Jim Foster, Michael Hardwick, Roberto Reyes-Colon, Miriam Ben-Shalom, and others in fighting for survival in the US military is in great measure because of Shilts's commitment to their stories.

*Conduct Unbecoming* provided a previously unexplored look at the other issues at hand, including ambivalence on the part of many gay leaders (and even civil libertarians) about standing up for gay men and/or lesbian women who wanted to serve in the military. Shilts noted that few gay activists "could muster much enthusiasm for helping anybody associated with the armed forces. Efforts for equal rights for gays would not extend to gays in uniform. The discrimination against them would, in effect, have the sanction of the gay movement for many years to come." His work also revealed the military's earliest efforts to deal with servicemembers testing positive for HIV, explaining that "most of the military, like most of civilian society, was refusing to come to grips with the threat posed by this mysterious new disease." The AIDS epidemic presented a great challenge to military leaders in acknowledging not only that gay men were a part of every branch of the military but also that "the appearance of the baffling new disease [in the military], whose cause had yet to be discovered, added to all the nagging uncertainties about homosexuality." In October 1985 the Defense Department announced a formal program to screen active military members and potential recruits for AIDS and quickly learned the disease was more widespread amid its ranks than ever suspected, Shilts reported, including among "a substantial number of high-ranking officers, including many in remarkably responsible and sensitive jobs."[6]

The reviews for *Conduct Unbecoming* were again as generally favorable as they had been for *And the Band Played On*. *Time* magazine writer R. Z. Sheppard offered that the book "has the heft and urgency of a journalistic milestone."[7] John D'Emilio, writing for the *Nation*, asserted, "Randy Shilts's hard-hitting exposé, *Conduct Unbecoming*, should become a formidable weapon in the hands of those committed to overturning the military's exclusion policy. Rarely has a book's publication been better timed to achieve maximum impact." D'Emilio labeled Shilts's narrative as "shocking" but remarked that the book was lacking balance "not between good guys and bad guys, but between oppression and resistance or even oppression and ordinary life and survival." Ultimately, "Shilts has written a book about the abuse of power, about totalitarian practices and a totalitarian ethic in the midst of a democratic society. Everything about the stories he recounts is offensive—deeply so—and their implications are dangerous," D'Emilio concluded.[8] The military's own Sunday segment, an insert to *Stars and Stripes* magazine, reported on and excerpted a portion of Shilts's book but offered no actual review. *Stars and Stripes* writer Timothy Cahill wrote that Shilts had told the story "not just [of] homosexuals, but necessarily, of heterosexuals; not just of exceptional courage by gay servicemembers on battlefields and in courtrooms, but also of repeated injustice by their straight comrades. He describes how, in the effort to rid the ranks of homosexuals, those in command have not violated only military and civilian laws, but also, by extension, the Bill of Rights, the Golden Rule and the Ten Commandments."[9]

Michael Denneny believes *Conduct Unbecoming* was an even more important work of nonfiction and literary journalism than *And the Band Played On*, although *Band* sold many more copies and had a much larger critical success. Denneny said, "From a purely technical point of view, *Conduct Unbecoming* is an even bigger writing accomplishment than *Band* in terms of the sheer difficulty of weaving all of those different stories and getting a narrative continuity out of it."[10]

With Shilts's third book taking up a critical gay issue in the greater heterosexual American culture, scholar Jessea Greenman made a distinction about Shilts and how people and the media cast him as both a journalist and a representative of the gay community. Greenman noted that most mainstream media referred to him as "the *first* openly gay reporter hired for a major mainstream newspaper" when in reality "Shilts became the *only* openly gay reporter writing on lesbian and gay issues for a major mainstream newspaper, and was to remain the only such reporter for some time after 1981." The distinction is important, Greenman noted, given that a great deal of responsibility and respect flows toward the first person to reach any status. "As a consequence," she observed, "Randy Shilts was regarded by mainstream media and the public as the only voice for lesbian and gay America. There were no other sources known to the media against which to compare Randy's perceptions and perspective," causing a level of authority and weight to be applied to Shilts's words. "This made his role highly problematic for the lesbian and gay community," Greenman believes.[11]

The "take me to your leader" approach of the mainstream media cast Shilts as a gay advocate or activist leader when he held no official leadership role or responsibility in any gay organization or community. "The question remains: did Randy Shilts represent anyone and, if so, whom?" Greenman asked. She adds, "What makes Randy Shilts unique is that, for a longish and crucial period in history, he was accepted by the mainstream as an expert, not only on AIDS, but also on the gay community," resulting from his role as a gay man writing about gay issues, which gave him an exclusive "insider status."[12]

Author and activist Michelangelo Signorile added to the premise, noting that by the time Shilts's second book, *And the Band Played On*, came out in 1987, Shilts was well received as a gay media spokesperson, in part because he placed partial blame for the AIDS crisis on gay men. Signorile contends Shilts was "seen less as an activist attacking the powers that be than a critical commentator on the gay movement itself," and "he was just the kind of television talk show spokesperson the media liked at the time. . . . [A]s long as he also attacked the gay community for this disease that straights were afraid of getting, editors and publishers would be sure to invite him back. In their bias-tinged perceptions, Shilts was 'fair' and provided 'balance' rather than behaving like what they called a pure 'advocate.'" This "balanced" (or objective) role for Shilts became problematic, Signorile believed, because it played effortlessly into the expectations and norms of "a virulently anti-gay society [where] messages that resonated most were the ones faulting the gay community for the AIDS pandemic."[13]

Casting of Shilts or any journalist as an expert has a long tradition in journalism via what Marianna Patrona, a journalism scholar from Greece, deemed a "participation framework," where "journalists are shown to possess insider knowledge of political activity" but, perhaps more importantly, "are positioned to express personalized, albeit expert, views on the motives of political actors, and the far-reaching ramifications of their actions for government, the economy and the people." Patrona noted that the journalistic function of gathering and constructing information in specific creates a "professional" or "authoritative" role for journalists and that "this role epistemologically positions the journalist as superior to the general public."[14]

Shilts considered the basic journalistic struggle when the journalist himself is the source or subject of the story. Shilts walked straight into the description of himself as just what he claimed he was not: activist. Shilts said, "I feel like I'm part of the solution. So I am not just stepping in on the problem."[15] His use of the phrase "stepping in on the problem" is an interesting choice of words, one that is often used in describing the role of reporters who observe and report but don't openly seek or claim a role as change agent. To the contrary, Shilts was forthrightly claiming an activist role, "I feel like I'm part of the solution," an unshielded role as a person who wants things to change—in this case, for homosexuals wishing to serve in the armed forces of the United States.

It wasn't just the mainstream media, however, that sought Shilts as "the gay expert." As early as 1980 he appeared on a popular San Francisco radio program, *The Gay Life with Randy Alfred,* and attempted to give voice to fears about mainstream journalists reporting on the gay movement. Shilts readily took up a discourse offered most vocally in later days by his critics that "mainstream media reports about homosexual issues bring out every dirty sexual thing" and that "in the long run, it creates perception. . . . [T]here is going to be a hangover, so to speak, for some time . . . [that will just] further alienate gay people from the media, which is a real shame, but I don't think you can blame gay people when the media lies like it does."[16]

Shilts also discussed what he termed "open and defacto discrimination" against openly gay journalists who, like him, struggled to find or keep employment in mainstream media and who, at the same time, had to do battle with gay media consumers. "Openly gay people in the media have to be or appear to be even more fair [in covering gay subjects]," Shilts said while discussing with Alfred a *CBS News* documentary titled *Gay Power, Gay Politics,* which aired nationally on April 26, 1980.[17] Alfred, Shilts's host, went beyond simply commenting on the hour-long telecast. He spent weeks documenting forty-four separate distortions or misstatements he found in the report and filed an official complaint against CBS with the National News Council, a voluntary, nonprofit media watchdog group that existed between 1973 and 1984 and was funded by private foundations. Alfred said CBS had based its report on "a systematic use of hearsay, oversights, exaggerations, distortions, inflammatory buzzwords, leading questions, and misleading and deceitful editing" and had engaged in "patterned distortion." In September 1980 the National News Council, after having dismissed some of Alfred's original complaints, supported a resolution that CBS had presented a biased report: "By concentrating on certain flamboyant examples of homosexual behavior the program tended to reinforce stereotypes. . . . The program exaggerated political concessions to gays and made them appear as threats to public morals and decency."[18] For his part in commenting on the damaging CBS report, Shilts said, "I think all of us in our roles as reporters have suffered tremendously at the hands of the gay community itself because when we do a gay story, we do both sides, because that is our professional obligation. I think a lot of gay people would prefer that we do not do both sides, but of course, that is our job to do that."[19]

Signorile often regarded Shilts with begrudging respect and noted that any success Shilts enjoyed as an "official gay spokesman" flowed from his ability to infiltrate what Signorile called "the Trinity of the Closet," including the New York print, broadcasting, and publishing media; the Washington, DC, political landscape; and Hollywood's entertainment industry.[20]

To his credit, Shilts both acknowledged and expressed aversion for his anointed role as gay community spokesperson. He believed being one of the first openly gay reporters anywhere granted him national prominence as a spokesperson, "and so some people in the gay community believe that when I'm on *Nightline* or *Donahue* or when I'm writing, my job is to be the spokesman for the community. My role is to present information and present both sides of the information."[21] Shilts took an incongruent position, on the one hand expressing dismay at the inherited role of gay spokesman and on the other ticking off news shows and interviews he readily accepted. The television appearance that seemed to generate the most criticism of Shilts involved the sleazy syndicated daytime shock-TV show of the late 1980s, *The Morton Downey Jr. Show*. On the Downey show, which aired in June 1988, Shilts and other panelists were reduced to shouting down audience members and the host about their advocacy for quarantining people with HIV and AIDS. The loud Donnybrook that was standard fare on Downey's show clearly forced Shilts into the gay spokesman role—whether he wanted it or not.

Shilts seemed to understand that his new position as a gay spokesman was based on where he worked, adding, "I am perceived now as part of a power structure. I work for *The Chronicle*. It's a major institution, and since some of my point of views have run counter to the community, especially around the bathhouse stuff . . . people don't like me, that's basically why they're mad at me. . . . It's like I became wrapped up as some kind of authority power figure."[22]

Shilts openly suggested that criticism he received from the Left about his granted and/or assumed role as a gay spokesman was born, at least partially, out of what he perceived as professional and literary jealousy. Shilts's suggestion that jealousy had reared its head in LGBTQ consideration of his life and work gains credibility as an argument when one considers how the mainstream media have seemingly only "allowed" a certain number of homosexuals to "cross over" into mainstream participation. Shilts had done so (as Signorile suggested) in many important aspects of American life: journalism, publishing, politics, and entertainment. "The fear that the straight community will listen only to a limited number of homosexual voices may be endemic among gay and lesbian writers," journalist John Weir noted. "But what is remarkable about Shilts's career is that his dedication to replacing prejudice with fact is both his singular innovation in gay and lesbian journalism and the source of his alienation from homosexual activists, writers, and politicos."[23]

Shilts's designated (and embraced) role as a journalistic expert was fully engaged in 1991, when NBA All-Star Earvin "Magic" Johnson became the biggest celebrity since the now-deceased Rock Hudson to announce he had contracted HIV. Shilts was back on the AIDS beat, declaring that Johnson's disclosure came at a "crucial time" and created hope among AIDS advocates that "renewed attention will mobilize badly needed action against the epidemic." Shilts continued, "The past year has been the worst of times for those organizing to fight the disease. The media have grown bored with covering AIDS; new government actions against the epidemic have ground to a halt, and the public has grown apathetic." Shilts declared that Johnson's disclosure "could prove to be an even more compelling development" than Hudson's deathbed disclosure because Johnson was viewed as young, healthy, in the prime of his NBA career, "and not rumored to be or perceived to be gay."[24]

Shortly after the Johnson HIV disclosures made news, attention quickly focused on the case of a twenty-three-year-old Florida woman named Kimberly Bergalis who was believed to be the first known case of AIDS transmission via a doctor or other clinician. Shilts, again invited to offer commentary on the case, quickly drew scorn *and* praise—familiar territory by now. Bergalis and her grief-stricken parents testified before a congressional committee about her experience in contracting AIDS, likely from her infected dentist. Writing a guest editorial in the *New York Times*, Shilts expressed sympathy for the Bergalis family but sought to put the family's anger and sense of injustice into perspective. "I'm angry too that I've had to watch half my friends waste away and die miserable deaths from this disease," he wrote. "What is so troubling about the Bergalises' anger is that they do not seem to acknowledge the suffering of others," highlighting that Kimberly had complained that she had to suffer from AIDS even though "she didn't do anything wrong." Shilts wrote, "With those words she seemed to be separating those who don't deserve AIDS from those who do. These were troubling words. Gay men express their love differently from the majority, it's true, but those who contracted AIDS didn't do anything 'wrong.'" He bluntly suggested that the Bergalis family should turn their anger toward the Reagan and Bush administrations and other leaders in Washington who had yet to act in ways Shilts thought could hamper or end the spread of AIDS, which was affecting about one million Americans as he wrote the editorial. "The lesson from the sad story of Kimberly Bergalis is that we will not fight AIDS by fighting each other," he wrote. "The answer for AIDS will come only when Americans extend to all people dying of AIDS the same compassion Kimberly Bergalis received."[25] Angry letters came in, some containing the expected vitriol, doubling down on Kimberly Bergalis's claim that she was an "innocent victim" of AIDS but that gays and intravenous drug users were getting what they deserved. Bergalis succumbed to complications of AIDS on December 8, 1991, at the age of twenty-three.

Publicity efforts continued for Shilts's new book, *Conduct Unbecoming*, but promoting the book was competing for space in his mind with the growing reality that his physical health was dramatically diminished and that his life might be ending.

# CHAPTER 15

# Unfinished Work

One of the last national interviews Shilts gave was on *60 Minutes*, the same show that a half decade earlier had helped propel Shilts and his writing about AIDS to international acclaim. Reporter Steve Kroft noted as he introduced the story that was originally broadcast on CBS on February 20, 1994, just three days after Shilts's death, "It's not often that we do stories about reporters, but Randy Shilts was more than a reporter." Explaining that producers at *60 Minutes* had begun work on its profile of Shilts weeks before, Kroft described him as "a pioneer of sorts" and "a witness to 20 years of social change that allowed him to express, far better than most—at least to straight people—what it's like to be gay in America." Reflecting the ever-authoritative and assured manner in which Shilts seemed to discuss anything in the waning days of his life, he told Kroft that even as a college journalist he knew his professors were wrong and that "it was so obvious that [gay issues] were going to be a huge story," because "you can't hurt as many people as get hurt under the status quo, you can't disrupt that many people's lives without it ending up causing a kind of reaction that breeds news stories."[1]

Shilts enjoyed some tremendous luck or great vision, after all, in being in the right place at the right time for emerging news waves. He was front and center for the political rise of gay icon Harvey Milk; he was at ground zero in San Francisco for the AIDS pandemic in America; and his last years were spent exploring the integration of gays into the armed services—an issue that played out in Washington over the following two decades. Shilts's confidants, like Linda Alband, noted that even his planned future projects (such as an examination of sexual abuse inside the Catholic Church) seemed to be at the center of the news spotlight. Shilts specifically entertained ideas of launching a national column fashioned off the success of conservative George Will but with a progressive perspective. "He thought a national column would allow him to explore a variety of other issues," Alband said. "In many respects, he thought he had said all he could on gay issues. I know he gets some criticism for this from the gay community, but his audience was really straight people, because he wanted them to understand what it was like to be gay in America. He was not interested in writing for an insular audience or group of gay people. He thought that was what other gay writers did. He wanted to write in the mainstream media."[2]

Shilts shared with Kroft, as he had with many other reporters, thoughts about the backlash he experienced from both gay and straight sources. He said he began a practice many people undertake as they become aware their lives are drawing to a close: he reflected on what his life had meant, even though a reporter asking him to do the same for the record had hurt his feelings in earlier days. "A lot of times people sit down and they want to ask you these soul-searching questions, almost as if you have some sort of sustaining wisdom now that you know, pre- sumably, that you're coming closer to God or something like that," Shilts said. "It's a real drag." A gaunt and drawn-looking Shilts added that he was not going happily unto his death: "I have never felt it was evitable. I can't say I feel bitter. You go through your 'why me?' stage and it's very frustrating."[3]

Less than a month before he died, Shilts dashed off one final letter to the editor to his old bosses at the *Advocate* regarding their coverage of the Clinton administration's compromise on gays in the military with the new "Don't Ask, Don't Tell" policy. He noted that President Clinton had fallen short of sealing the deal on an important gay civil rights issue and wandered into the familiar role of politicians as liars. Shilts attempted to prognosticate the future by declaring, "The [gay rights] movement is growing, and many people recognize the justness of the cause. But final social consensus remains decades off, and our adversaries remain far more powerful than the gay side. . . . This does not mean that the gay movement's goals will not be achieved. They will. But that will come not in years but in decades." Never shy about self-promotion (and seemingly answering a question no one had asked), Shilts ended his letter asserting that his new book, *Conduct Unbecoming*, "is the best thing I've ever done" and that it bothered him that it resided on the best-seller list for only six weeks. "I truly believe that in years to come it will be seen as being far more significant than *And the Band Played On*. Along with its impact on the particulars of the issue, I believe it is the first book to merge lesbian, gay, and women's themes in a way that will make sense to the average reader. These aspects got overlooked because reviewers focused so much on the military reportage." He also announced that he was at work on "a new ending" for the paperback version of the book, and it would finally "conclude the way I always wanted it to." It was an ending he would not live to write—but he didn't let that stop him from getting in a last word. Shilts closed his letter with a read-between-the-lines reference to his pending mortality: "And while we're talking conclusions, hopefully, history will record that I was a hell of a nice guy and that people who have criticized me are a bunch of fools and bimbos."[4]

Shilts's personality, mixed with strong waves of stubbornness and contrarian ideas, caused him to rail against the undeniable compromises present in his physical health, though as 1993 gave way to 1994 there was every indication that he was in rapid decline. In December 1993 Alband wrote up notes from a conversation with Shilts concerning his wishes for a funeral or a memorial service and titled it "Ongoing Considerations." Alband wrote that the top concern was "getting Randy better" and that he worried about the continuation of his health care benefits from the *Chronicle*, which were set to run out in October 1994. Shilts focused on "getting better" and visualized some sort of future that met his health care needs. He planned to continue with his work, demonstrating an overly optimistic outlook, something that Shilts and many other people facing death far too early in life embraced.

Alband wrote, "[Randy] wants to be buried at Guerneville Cemetery" after a funeral with a closed casket. His preferred location for a public funeral was the rotunda of the San Francisco City Hall (a ceremony that never occurred, although a memorial service at Glide Memorial Church did) and a smaller, private ceremony somewhere outdoors near his Guerneville home (a brief graveside service occurred). Shilts said he wanted his funeral to be "political" and not religious. "He would love to have his body taken to the steps of the Federal Building to agitate for more AIDS funding," Alband wrote in her notes.[5]

*Chronicle* newsroom colleague Susan Sward, who still copes with the grief of his death decades later, recalled visiting him in the final weeks of his life. "He was a wasted man full of tubes," she said, "but he would not say good-bye."[6]

The last time Alband saw Shilts was in early January 1994, when she drove seventy-five miles from San Francisco to his home in Guerneville to personally deliver a prescription from a San Francisco doctor. She found Shilts struggling to remember appointments or other obligations, including regular transfusions for his growing anemia. It was during these days that Alband learned the depth of

Shilts's confusion and declining ability to keep track of details. A routine phone call from editors at Bantam Books (a subsidiary of Random House Books, which purchased the paperback rights for *And the Band Played On*) revealed that Shilts had failed to tell them about edits and updates needed before the new edition was printed. The edits were just one of the details falling through the cracks as life diminished.

Death finally silenced the brilliantly verbose Randy Shilts just after 2:00 a.m. on February 17, 1994, inside his Guerneville home with only Barry Barbieri at his side. News of his death spread quickly—the *San Francisco Chronicle* devoted a banner headline on page 1 of its February 18, 1994, edition to report the news: "Writer Randy Shilts Dies at 42—Pioneer in Coverage of AIDS." Staff writers Lori Olszewski and David Tuller included the expected information about Shilts's life but also found a wide array of sources to quote about the meaning and impact of his life and writing, including former *Washington Post* reporter Carl Bernstein; Dr. Marcus Conant, a pioneering physician in the fight against AIDS; editor Michael Denneny; and literary agent Fred Hill. *Chronicle* editor Bill German said, "*The Chronicle* has much reason to be grateful to Randy Shilts. Randy brought us a wonderful mix of professionalism, honesty and openness that pointed the natural way for a newspaper to cover gay issues, AIDS issues and related community concerns." He said members of the *Chronicle* newsroom were grieved over the loss of their friend. "To say we shall miss him is a vast understatement," German said.[7]

Former *Chronicle* reporter and editor Keith Power offered a first-person reflection on Shilts's death and noted that when he first arrived at the newspaper, "we did not anticipate the sheer productivity of the young man. . . . [But] I was captivated by Randy's enthusiasm, energy and—I had to admit—keen sense of what a news story was and how to land it in time for the first edition." Power wrote personally of Shilts also, noting that he had "courage" amid sometimes bitter criticism from the gay community. He also had the tenacity to push the *San Francisco Chronicle* and its editors to move the newspaper into the national forefront of coverage of the growing AIDS crisis. Power said he perceived "a shadow over Randy" during the increasingly less frequent times when he was in the newsroom. "In this peak year of working closely together, spending hours peering into the computer screen shoulder by shoulder, the subject of his own health never came up," Power said. He also said that the two shared an open, knowing laugh when Power took a swig from Shilts's coffee cup, defying the irrational fear that one could get AIDS from drinking from the same cup as an HIV-positive person.[8]

Accolades and notice for Shilts's death poured in. The prominent *New York Times* obituary was something he likely would have reveled in seeing, with *Times* reporters Jennifer Warren and Richard C. Paddock referring to Shilts as "tenacious" and "the nation's foremost chronicler of gay life and the AIDS epidemic."[9] San Francisco mayor Frank Jordan ordered flags on all city buildings to fly at half mast for one day. Movie producer/director Oliver Stone, who had signed up for an ultimately never produced film version of Shilts's book *The Mayor of Castro Street* and a coproducer on a never produced HBO option for *Conduct Unbecoming*, said, "Randy Shilts was a warm, gentle and compassionate man. He did much to lift the human spirit." One of Shilts's earliest and most reliable sources of information, Dr. Selma Dritz, who had retired from her post as the assistant director of the San Francisco Health Department by the time Shilts died, noted, "If more people had listened to Randy, far fewer people would have died. The people who blocked the research in those days have a lot to answer for, including [Randy's] death."[10]

US Secretary of Health and Human Services Donna Shalala was in San Francisco two days after Shilts's death promoting President Clinton's plans to extend universal health care access to all Americans, and she used the occasion to eulogize Shilts. Speaking on the president's behalf, she said, "This past week the whole country lost one of our strongest and best fighters in the fight against AIDS. His tireless work as a reporter and advocate made sure that the band simply didn't play on and on and on. He worked to mobilize all of us. And so, as he is laid to rest, we all must remain restless until we reach out to everyone in the country who is HIV positive or has AIDS. It's time the government does that too."[11]

The speakers who took to the pulpit during a lively memorial service for Shilts at Glide Memorial United Methodist Church on February 22, 1994, were an interesting cross section of the professional and personal friendships Shilts developed over the course of his life, including Denneny; Conant; Dritz; David Perlman, *San Francisco Chronicle* science editor; Frank M. Robinson, a former Harvey Milk speechwriter turned novelist; Howard Wallace, founder of the Lesbian/ Gay Labor Alliance of the San Francisco AFL-CIO; Dr. Donald Francis, a former CDC official and clinical AIDS researcher; Perry Watkins, retired US Army staff sergeant; Leroy Aarons, president of the National Lesbian and Gay Journalists Association; and the Reverend Cecil Williams, pastor of Glide Memorial United Methodist Church. Shilts's wooden casket was front and center, decked with a huge floral spray and a copy of his *San Francisco Chronicle* press pass pasted on one end.

In his remarks, Perlman recounted his newsroom interactions with Shilts and how the two of them had negotiated their own "spheres" related to covering the AIDS story. "Randy made friends, and many of you know, he made some enemies too because he called the shots the way they were," Perlman said. "He was not afraid to report things truthfully and did so during his every waking moment." Perlman drew a chuckle when he recalled attending the 1989 International AIDS Conference with Shilts and how they parceled out stories pouring from the event. "At the very end of the conference we were wrapping up our reporting, and we were gathered in this incredibly tiny reporting space," Perlman said. "We sat side-by-side writing on these ancient laptops, and the hubbub was unbelievable. There were all these people around us making all sorts of noise, and I turned around to tell them to shut up, and then I realized they were all there as Randy's supporters . . . Randy's fan club. I said to Randy, 'For God's sake, will you shut these guys up! I'm trying to write a story, and you're trying to write a story!' and he said, '*I* can write a story under any circumstances.'" Robinson recalled some of Shilts's earliest days of reporting covering his former boss, the late Harvey Milk, and his dedication to writing his first book, *The Mayor of Castro Street*. Robinson and Denneny both made a special point to praise Shilts as a journalist, not an activist. "Randy considered himself a journalist first, last, and always," Robinson said. Robinson also recalled that among Shilts's detractors were many in the gay community itself: "I sometimes wonder if they understood how much he loved the gay community and how hard he fought the injustices it faced."[12]

Outside the stately Glide Memorial Church along Ellis Street in the Tenderloin District, a small handful of protestors from the Westboro Baptist Church of Topeka, Kansas, attempted to have their voices heard. The group was comprised entirely of family members of the vitriolic "pastor" of the church, the Reverend Fred W. Phelps, who said they had come to San Francisco to picket Shilts's funeral. Phelps described Shilts as "a famous fag" and added, "The fag-dominated entertainment and media worlds are making a hero of this gerbil mongering moron, and touting his anal copulating lifestyle as a glorious thing to be emulated by American youth."[13] The "protest" lasted less than sixty seconds. The overflow crowd of more than twelve hundred Shilts supporters who could not fit into the church and who listened to the service over loud speakers installed outside were separated from the protestors along Ellis Street by barricades and a large phalanx of helmeted riot officers from the San Francisco Police Department. Westboro members, arriving fifteen minutes after the memorial service had begun, briefly unfurled their increasingly "famous" "God Hates Fags" posters and trotted up to the corner of Ellis and Taylor Streets. They "dodged eggs and pieces of fruit thrown by counter demonstrators," the *San Francisco Chronicle* reported. "Phelps' followers ducked and ran, and retreated to vans that had brought them from the airport. As they left, the crowd roared victoriously."[14] Inside, the Reverend Cecil Williams announced to the audience's delight, "The Reverend Fred Phelps has come, and the Reverend Fred Phelps has gone."[15]

Later, away from the noise and crowds of the city, a smaller group of Shilts's family and friends gathered at the cemetery in Guerneville for a brief memorial, led by his brother Gary Shilts. The words Gary said that day are lost to memory, but many years later he was again called on to eulogize his brother back home in Illinois as West Aurora High School inducted Randy Shilts into its Hall of Fame. Gary spoke lovingly of his brother and told the students, parents, and community members gathered: "To those of you who don't fit in; to those of you who feel like outsiders; to those of you who are geeks, nerds, goths, queers, lames, preppies, whatever, Randy would say, 'Remember this: You will be out of here soon. And, when you leave, you can go anywhere you want to go. And when you get there, you will find a big, beautiful world that is anxiously waiting to meet you. It is waiting for your ideas, your thoughts, your music, and your dreams.'"[16]

A few weeks after Shilts's burial, *Chronicle* colleague Susan Sward offered a thoughtful remembrance under the title "The Price of Freedom" and noted, "Looking back, it seems almost as if history handed Randy his moment: With a passion I have rarely seen equaled in the business, Randy pushed, wheedled and cajoled until his AIDS stories made their way from the back pages of *The Chronicle* to the front page." But Sward said her record of Shilts's life was more personal. "Bit by bit, Randy and I struck up one of those city room friendships that happen in the business—intense in the pursuit of the news with little or no contact outside the job. As we grew close—he laughingly called me his 'Big Sister'—he talked to me about the attacks on him from the gay community and its press." He also took Sward into his trust and told her of his HIV-positive status not too long after learning of it himself. "I don't remember him expressing any irony about contracting the virus he had done so much to tell the nation about," she wrote. "I do recall that our conversation turned quickly to treatment possibilities and how he could fight on." As he grew more ill throughout 1993 and his death became something even he was willing to consider, Sward would join others for quick lunches at his city condo and later longer visits at his Russian River home, chairs pulled up next to the sofa where he lay attached to an oxygen tank so he could keep his end of the conversation going. "Those who accompanied me were men,"

Sward said, "and I often would be the one to pull the conversation with Randy as close as it ever got to the effect of the disease on his soul. . . . Not that Randy wanted a lot of disease-and-darkness talk anyway. He didn't. Randy wanted to live[, and] several months ago he complained to me that some people would cling to his words as if they carried special weight because he was so ill. Randy wanted to talk about the future." Sward's last visit was at Shilts's Guerneville home. "By this time, he was hooked up to some machine that helped him breathe, and his room felt like a hospital room. Standing by the big window in his living room, looking out at a creek cascading down a hillside, I felt Randy was slipping away. That was a difficult thought because Randy could get me thinking that AIDS and death might make an exception in his case."[17]

Consistent with the sometimes complicated and even controversial nature of Shilts's life, his final will also caused a fight. In the months following his death, attorney Paul Newman of the San Francisco law firm of Keil & Connolly wrote to Shilts's beneficiaries that getting the will into probate was proving difficult. Shilts had left a will that provided for two executors who would not serve as coexecutors, an attempt to split his assets as broadly as he could among family and friends.[18] The executor problem was not the only issue at hand: in November 1993 Shilts had signed an updated will, amending his original 1992 document. In the 1993 will (executed just four months before he died), Shilts donated all his research materials and completed writings to the gay and lesbian archives at the San Francisco Public Library but did not grant the library the copyright to his published books, which were designated for Denneny as a "literary" asset. Denneny's primary role, envisioned by Shilts, was to protect and maximize the funds represented in the copyright so that his three successful books could assist Barbieri with his living expenses. The titles and deeds to his handsome Guerneville refuge and a San Francisco condominium also went to Barbieri. Other designations included $10,000 for a special needs trust for his brother David Shilts, who lived at a group home in Michigan; funds to establish a Randy Shilts journalism scholarship at the University of Oregon; and donations to the Gay and Lesbian Alliance Against Defamation, the National Gay and Lesbian Task Force, the Human Rights Campaign, and a local AIDS service provider in San Francisco, Eighteenth Street Services. Another series of smaller gifts went to other family and friends. History has clouded what actually occurred with whatever assets remained, and some family and friends named in the will claimed they never received any funds after Shilts's death. The University of Oregon journalism program has honored Shilts posthumously, but not with funds received from his estate. Shilts took special pains to ensure Barbieri would be taken care of, directing the trustees of the will to distribute funds for Barbieri's "health, education, support, and maintenance, for as long as he shall live."[19]

Barry Barbieri sat for only one interview following Shilts's death, a front-page story written by Betsy Bourbon, a staff writer at the *Russian River News* in Guerneville, California. Bourbon's focus was what life is like for the gay men left after their partners died, and she provided the then-twenty-four-year-old Barbieri a platform to tell his story. Barbieri recalled the night the two men met inside the popular Rainbow Cattle Company, a gay bar on Guerneville's Main Street, in October 1991. Shilts was immediately attracted to the younger and darkly handsome Barbieri, then a student at Santa Rosa Junior College. When Shilts met Barbieri, he ended a relationship with another man just after acquiring his new Guerneville home. Shilts engaged his new, younger mate in discussions about what major Barbieri should pursue in college. The relationship grew quickly, and within a year the two were splitting their time between Shilts's San Francisco condo and his Guerneville home. The two men "married" in a private ceremony inside a Buddhist shrine on their property over Memorial Day weekend in 1993, less than a year before Shilts died and more than a decade before gay marriage would finally be legal in the United States.[20]

"This book did him in," Barbieri said, referring to *Conduct Unbecoming*, completed in the closing months of Shilts's life. "He was a total workaholic. He got up at 5:30 in the morning and worked until one in the afternoon. The rest of the time he was on the phone. . . . He loved every minute of it. He finished the book . . . [but] he never admitted the book sped up anything [related to his HIV status]. The timing was perfect for the book. He was just thrilled. He knew the ultimate impact would come after he died." In addition to his worry that writing the book had undermined Shilts's health, Barbieri reported that although Shilts remained asymptomatic of AIDS for many years, he contracted pneumonia more than once, and "he had a lot of denial and delayed care for the pneumonia."[21]

# Conclusion

For the nearly forty-three years he was alive, timing always seemed to be an incredibly important aspect of Randy Shilts's life. He came of age in the heart of the "baby boom" in the middle of six boys born to the Shilts family in as quintessential an American town as there is, Aurora, Illinois. His recognition and eventual acceptance of his homosexuality coincided with an incredible period of growth and change in American culture as gay liberation slowly inched forward. One of the major centers where that liberation was taking place was San Francisco, where an ambitious and driven Shilts arrived just in time in the mid-1970s. Likewise, his journalism career corresponded with the rise of one of the most important—and tragic—figures of the movement, Harvey Milk. Shilts was there for Milk's political ascension and for the ugly hate that cut down his life. Likewise, Shilts was pioneering a role as an openly gay reporter in the newsroom of one of the nation's major dailies, the *San Francisco Chronicle*, just as the most important public health issue in a century commenced in the form of HIV and AIDS. Finally, as the nation struggled to accept and integrate lesbians, gays, bisexuals, and transgender persons into American culture, Shilts was one of the first to see the battle lines forming as the nation's military wrestled with how to handle the new gay reality.

His timing had been impeccable, in part perhaps as a result of just chance or good luck amid the march of time but also because of his incredible journalistic instincts. Few were the journalists who could beat Shilts on finding and expanding a good news story when he saw one. He was, in the end, the consummate journalist, occupying an elevated role in both straight and homosexual society, as difficult a balancing act as one might expect.

Beyond timing, irony played a cruel role in the story of Randy Shilts. As his HIV status gave way to a diagnosis of full-blown AIDS, Shilts's almost manic drive slowed to a crawl. Tethered to an oxygen tank for the last months of his life, he would have to leave to others his plans to take up long-standing and widespread allegations of child sexual abuse in the Catholic Church. Death took Shilts before he could explore the topic of church-based abuse, but history records that he was there to consider it before it exploded into an international issue that could no longer be ignored.

His work and life, therefore, are best considered incomplete and interrupted. Time has left Shilts vulnerable to a critique that is deficient. Critics have taken posthumous aim at Shilts from many directions, and the once ferocious fighter who could give as good as he got is silent. There are many questions—personal and professional—left unanswered about Shilts that even the passage of time cannot adequately address. Personally, did he lie or choose to mislead the world about his HIV status (assuming he owed the world any explanation of it)? Professionally, did he adhere to strict rules of so-called objective journalism as a reporter and later an author, or did he cave in to the irresistible charm of good storytelling? Was his approach to journalism—or new journalism—one that withstands the test of time, or does it reflect a problematic approach that perhaps alters or distorts history? Did he understand at the time that his words would, whether intentionally or not, cruelly victimize one gay man, Gaëtan Dugas, with conflicting evidence to seal the indictment against Shilts—his "Patient Zero" theory was woefully wrong?

It seems likely Shilts could not have avoided revisiting the issue of "Patient Zero" and could not have ignored the clear evidence that emerged in 2016 that officially exonerated Dugas. In 2016 Michael Worobey, an environmental biologist at the University of Arizona in Tucson, and a team of researchers published a groundbreaking article in *Nature*, a scientific journal, about the origins of HIV in North America. In it, they detailed work that confirms that HIV genomes found in the samples of gay men tested during the earliest days of the pandemic in the United States could be traced back to strains spread from Zaire to Haiti in about 1967. Those genomes then spread to New York City in 1970 or 1971, years before Dugas was even of age, let alone before he had become the globe-trotting flight attendant Shilts had outlined in his book. The study also took pains to underline the mistake Shilts had made in creating a "Patient Zero" when the original cluster study of which Dugas was a part actually labeled him "Patient O" for "Outside of California." Worobey and his colleagues wrote, "We also recovered the HIV-1 genome from the individual known as 'Patient O' and found neither biological nor historical evidence that he was the primary case in the U.S."[1]

*New York Times* reporter Donald C. McNeil Jr. linked the "Patient Zero" mythology directly to Shilts's book, noting, "Although Mr. Shilts did not accuse Mr. Dugas of starting the American epidemic, he demonized him as a deliberate spreader of the virus who ignored a doctor's demand that he stop having unprotected sex, and cold-bloodedly told some sex partners that he had 'gay cancer' and now they might get it." McNeil quoted Howard W. Jaffe, one of the original Dugas cluster study authors, as noting that he was unsure who first used the term "Patient Zero," but "after Randy Shilts did, we started saying it ourselves."[2]

One of Shilts's critics, Dr. Richard McKay, while repeating his belief that Shilts may have intentionally ignored information that contradicted his original "Patient Zero" thesis, nonetheless finds agreement with what Shilts believed was his major point. McKay, noting that the "Patient Zero" concept served as a barrier to more fully grasping the economic, legal, and cultural barriers to health care and education, called these "structural factors" "important determinants" that helped further the panic and hysteria surrounding AIDS. McKay's latter point affirms Shilts's stated objectives in *And the Band Played On* and in his news reporting that AIDS progressed to an incredibly deadly state because experts among mainstream medical, political, media, and even straight and gay cultural circles in America simply ignored the music the band was playing.[3]

Shilts *had* accurately captured that Dugas was at the center of a particular cluster of HIV infection among gay men studied by Dr. William Darrow and others. Worobey suggested that Shilts drifted into a "kind of ascertainment bias," focusing on Dugas because he had been so helpful to researchers in sharing personal contact information. Worobey's research showed that nearly 7 percent of gay men in New York City and 4 percent of gay men in San Francisco had HIV at the time Dugas was participating in the study.

Beyond the reconsideration of Shilts's "Patient Zero" that new facts and evidence required, Shilts's early work on exposing the ugly realities of drumming gays and lesbians out of the US military proved historic. In 2008, as the House Armed Services Committee took up the first review in fifteen years of the compromise "Don't Ask, Don't Tell" policy, Shilts's name figured prominently. An article in *Time* magazine during the 2008 presidential election between Senator Barack Obama of Illinois and Senator John McCain of Arizona referred back to Shilts's research on the issue. It documented that 5,951 service members were discharged in a four-year period prior to 1990—a figure barely unchanged, with 5,327 gays discharged between 1996 and 2000. Obama promised voters legislation to end the DADT policy, while McCain opposed the move. In 2010 Congress approved the repeal of DADT with now-president Obama, affirming the importance of Shilts's record of gay servicemembers:

> While today marks the end of a particular struggle that has lasted almost two decades, this is a moment more than two centuries in the making. There will never be a full accounting of the heroism demonstrated by gay Americans in service to this country; their service has been obscured in history. It's been lost to prejudices that have waned in our own lifetimes. But at every turn, every crossroads in our past, we know gay Americans fought just as hard, gave just as much to protect this nation and the ideals for which it stands.[4]

As the "Don't Ask, Don't Tell" and "Patient Zero" stories required a revisiting of Shilts's work, his voice silenced by death, he was unavailable to elaborate upon or defend his work. Posthumously, he was demonized by some for getting part of the story of the emergence of gay America in the twentieth century wrong. As a journalist and author dedicated to precise detail, he undoubtedly would have revisited both issues in the years that followed—and perhaps offered valuable context and clarification.

It is tempting to ponder how Shilts would conduct his journalism and book writing in today's more democratized means of journalism, where information is a commodity held by many and broadcast as quickly as hitting the post or send button and the reading of books has dropped. Would his assumed or earned role of informed journalistic expert have a continued place? Perhaps in the world of cable television, where such "panelist experts" still thrive, Shilts would be front and center as a frequent contributor.

This understanding or placement of Shilts and his journalism is important to a fuller and fair analysis of his work. Posthumous treatment of Shilts by critics is harsh, but a copious, more inclusive consideration of Shilts and his work is in order. In the larger view of Shilts, serious questions about "Patient Zero" or other issues of objectivity notwithstanding, there is no diminishment of Shilts's contribution to journalism and advancement of knowledge and understanding of gay people—an ever-onward movement toward more liberation of homosexuals in the United States and across the globe. In both the categories of journalism and gay liberation, Shilts's work contributes greatly to enhancing these components of society and is remarkable from beginning to end. There is direct evidence that his journalism changed the world in which it existed. Gay bathhouses closed, and San Francisco and the larger gay community finally tackled, however painfully, issues related to the limits of sexual freedom amid the fledgling gay liberation movement—nothing less than Shilts advocated for in his writing. Shilts's effort to shine a light on the painful and unethical efforts to ban openly gay or lesbian people from serving in the military helped bring an end to the discriminatory practices of the US military, although it would take more than a decade to achieve this goal. These cultural and political shifts would likely have occurred with or without Shilts, but his reportage on them in their earliest days assures him an important place in the history of journalism and of gay liberation.

If he were alive today, Shilts would likely be surprised to find the issues of gay marriage, child adoption, and even nondiscrimination in housing, employment, and public accommodations still listed on the "gay agenda" in the twenty-first century. He likely would have remained in the forefront in hammering away for progress on issues that could bring homosexuals into the fullness of liberty in American life.

But as time ran short, not too long before he died, Randy Shilts seemed to understand that he wouldn't get to write or even read the last chapter on his life. He told a reporter that he grimaced at the prospect of having to offer some sort of great philosophical statement about life—it came too close to the painful reality that his own life was drawing to an end. He captured the sadness that his short-ened life still invokes when he said he was "left with the strange feeling that your life is somehow finished without being completed."[5]

# Notes

Preface

1. Craig Kridel, ed., *Writing Educational Biography: Explorations in Qualitative Research* (New York: Garland Publishing, 1998).

Introduction

1. K. E. Bliss, *The International AIDS Conference Returns to the United States: Lessons from the Past and Opportunities for July 2012,* report of the CSIS Global Health Policy Center (Washington, DC: Center for Strategic & International Studies, March 2012).

2. Randy Shilts, "Talking AIDS to Death," *Esquire*, March 1, 1989, 124, 133.

3. Nilanjana R. Bardhan, "Transnational AIDS-HIV Narratives: A Critical Exploration of Overarching Frames," *Mass Communication & Society* 4, no. 3 (2001): 283–309, 283.

4. M. Brodie, E. Hamel, L. A. Brady, J. Kates, and D. E. Altmaneds, *AIDS at 21: Media Coverage of the HIV Epidemic 1981–2002,* printed as a supplement to the *Columbia Journalism Review*, March/April 2004 (Menlo Park, CA: Henry J. Kaiser Family Foundation, 2002).

5. Thomas W. Netter, "The Media and AIDS: A Global Perspective," in *AIDS: Prevention through Education: A World View*, ed. Jaime Sepulveda Amor, Harvey Fineberg, and Jonathan M. Mann (New York: Oxford University Press, 1992), 241–53, 242.

6. Sally Lehrman, "AIDS Coverage Has Been Lost in Recent Years," *Quill*, March 2004, 24–25.

7. David Colby and Timothy Cook, "Epidemics and Agendas: The Politics of Nightly News Coverage of AIDS," *Journal of Health Politics, Policy & Law* 61, no. 2 (1991): 215–49, 219.

8. Brodie et al., *AIDS at 21*, 3.

9. Ibid., 1.

10. Ibid., 5.

## Chapter 1. Aurora Dawn

1. Mike Myers interview with Raphael "Ralph" Benmergui, *Midday*, Canadian Broadcasting Corporation, originally aired February 20, 1990, https://www.youtube.com/watch?v=2ymTmBPoJCE.

2. Gary Shilts, interview, July 31, 2014, Aurora, Illinois.

3. Gary Shilts, email, October 11, 2011.

4. Reed Shilts, interview, October 18, 2014, Kalamazoo, Michigan.

5. Betty Friedan, *The Feminine Mystique* (New York: Norton, 1963), 1.

6. Reed Shilts, interview, October 18, 2014, Kalamazoo, Michigan.

7. Gary Shilts, interview, July 31, 2014, Aurora, Illinois.

8. Dennis Shilts to Randy Shilts, January 14, 1980, James C. Hormel LGBTQ Center.

9. Dennis Shilts to Shilts family members, June 5, 1992, Hormel Center.

10. Reed Shilts, interview, October 18, 2014, Kalamazoo, Michigan.

11. Gary Shilts, interview, July 31, 2014, Aurora, Illinois.

12. Reed Shilts, interview, October 18, 2014, Kalamazoo, Michigan.

13. Garry Wills, "Randy Shilts: The *Rolling Stone* Interview," *Rolling Stone*, September 30, 1993, 50.

14. Reed Shilts, interview, October 18, 2014, Kalamazoo, Michigan.

15. W. J. Thorburn, *A Generation Awakes: Young Americans for Freedom and the Creation of the Conservative Movement* (Erie, PA: Jameson Publishing, 2010).

16. Randy Shilts Papers, Hormel Center.

17. Reed Shilts, interview, October 18, 2014, Kalamazoo, Michigan.

18. Wills, "Randy Shilts," 50.

19. *Muses* (Aurora West High School student literary magazine), May 1969.

20. *Red & Blue* (Aurora West High School student newspaper), December 6, 1968.

21. Randy Shilts Papers, Hormel Center.

22. Ibid.

23. *Aurora (IL) Beacon-News*, June 17, 2012.

24. Reed Shilts, interview, October 18, 2014, Kalamazoo, Michigan.

25. Randy Shilts, Aurora College grade report, 1970, Hormel Center.

26. Reed Shilts, interview, October 18, 2014, Kalamazoo, Michigan.

27. Linda Alband, email, January 4, 2013.

28. Randy Shilts to Gary Shilts, February 15, 1976, Hormel Center.

29. Ibid.

30. K. Kelley, "Randy Shilts: The Interview," *San Francisco Focus*, June 1989, 65–66, 94–113.

31. Ibid.

32. Linda Alband, email, January 4, 2013.

33. Randy Shilts diary entry, January 9, 1978, Hormel Center.

34. Randy Shilts diary entry, July 19, 1973, Hormel Center.

35. Randy Shilts diary entry, August 27, 1973, Hormel Center.

36. Randy Shilts diary entry, August 25, 1973, Hormel Center.

37. Ibid.

38. L. Udesky, "An Interview with Randy Shilts, Author of *And the Band Played On*," in *Democracy in Print: The Best of "Progressive" Magazine 1909–2009*, ed. Matthew Rothschild (Madison: University of Wisconsin Press, 1991), 133–35, 133.

39. Randy Shilts, interview by Eric Marcus, March 1989, transcript, in Marcus's research materials.

40. Paul Welch, "Homosexuality in America: The 'Gay' World Takes to the City Streets," *Life*, June 26, 1964, 66–74.

41. Lorraine Prince to Linda Alband, October 17, 1994, Hormel Center.

42. Shilts, interview.

43. Udesky, "An Interview," 134.

## Chapter 2. Eugene Days

1. Ben Agger, *Sixties at 40: Leaders and Activists Remember and Look Forward* (New York: Routledge, 2015).

2. Randy Shilts, interview by E. Marcus, March 1989, transcript.

3. Ibid.

4. Ibid.

5. Terry Gross, producer and interviewer, transcript of interview with Randy Shilts, *Fresh Air*, April 23, 1993, American Public Radio via WHYY.

6. S. A. Callister, "Shilts: 'Incredible Programs We Can Do,'" *Oregon Daily Emerald*, March 30, 1973, 6.

7. "Emerald Endorsement Interviews," *Oregon Daily Emerald*, March 6, 1973, 5.

8. "Shilts: Incredible Things We Could Do," *Oregon Daily Emerald*, March 30, 1973, 6.

9. Shilts-Gonzalez campaign flyer, University of Oregon, undated, Hormel Center.

10. "Twenty Seek Student Posts," *Eugene Register-Guard*, April 17, 1973, 6.

11. Shilts-Gonzalez campaign flyer.

12. Shilts, interview.

13. Ibid.

14. George T. Nicola, "Oregon LGBTQ History since 1970," July 2, 2015, http://www.glapn.org/6007historyLGBTQrights.html.

15. Randy Shilts, excerpts from undated and untitled student essay, Hormel Center.

16. Michael Dotten, email, March 8, 2013.

17. Greg Leo, email, April 2, 2013.

18. Gail Hoffnagle, email, April 22, 2013.

19. Greg Leo, email, April 2, 2013.

20. Joshua Marquis, email, March 8, 2013.

21. Drex Heikes, email, March 10, 2013.

22. Robert Liberty, email, April 2, 2013.

23. Jerry Harris, email, March 11, 2013.

24. Randy Shilts to Jennifer King, University of Oregon Associate Dean, September 22, 1992, Hormel Center.

25. Shilts, interview.

26. Garry Wills, "Randy Shilts: The *Rolling Stone* Interview," *Rolling Stone*, September 30, 1993, 49.

27. Randy Shilts, "Support Needed for Gay Rights Bill," *Oregon Daily Emerald*, May 18, 1973, 4.

28. Wills, "Randy Shilts," 50, 49.

29. J. Weir, "Reading Randy," *Out*, August–September 1993, 45–49.

30. Duncan McDonald, telephone interview, September 1, 2011.

31. Ibid.

32. Ibid.

33. Ibid.

34. "Shilts Places in Hearst Contest," *Oregon Daily Emerald*, April 1, 1975, 4.

35. Patrick O'Driscoll, *Denver Post*, February 18, 1994.

36. Patty Hearst and J. Reeves, *The Trial of Patty Hearst* (San Francisco: Great Fidelity Press, 1976).

37. Duncan McDonald, telephone interview, September 1, 2011.

38. John W. Crawford to Randolph A. Hearst III and Ira P. Walsh, William Randolph Hearst Foundation, May 30, 1975, Hormel Center.

39. Ira P. Walsh to John W. Crawford, University of Oregon, Department of Journalism, June 2, 1975, Hormel Center.

40. Randy Shilts, "Pot Lookout Tied to Ex-assessor," *Oregon Daily Emerald*, January 30, 1975, 1.

41. Shilts, interview.

42. Randy Shilts, unpublished and untitled typed manuscript, 1974, Hormel Center.

43. Ibid.

44. Ibid.

45. Ibid.

## Chapter 3. Living Out

1. Randy Shilts, diary entry, July 1, 1974, Hormel Center.

2. Reed Shilts, interview, October 18, 2014, Kalamazoo, Michigan.

3. Ibid.

4. Randy Shilts, diary entry, July 10, 1971, Hormel Center.

5. Randy Shilts, diary entry, July 27, 1971, Hormel Center.

6. Reed Shilts, interview, October 18, 2014, Kalamazoo, Michigan.

7. Gary Shilts, interview, July 31, 2014, Aurora, Illinois.

8. Duncan McDonald, personal communication, September 1, 2011.

9. Randy Shilts to Linda Alband, July 29, 1975, Hormel Center.

10. Randy Shilts, "Secret Identity Troubles Homosexuals," *Willamette Valley Observer*, February 21, 1975, 5, 23.

11. Dudley Clendinen and Adam Nagourney, *Out for Good: The Struggle to Build a Gay Rights Movement in America* (New York: St. Martin's Press, 1999), 12.

12. Ibid., 13, emphasis added.

13. Randy Shilts, "Candy Jar Politics: The Oregon Gay Rights Story," *Advocate*, August 13, 1975, 11.

14. Randy Shilts, "Future of Gay Rights? The Emerging Gay Middle Class," *Advocate*, October 22, 1975, 12.

15. Randy Shilts, "Hepatitis Doesn't Come from Needles: The Decade's Best Kept Medical Secret," *Advocate*, January 12, 1977, 6.

16. "David Goodstein Dies at 53; Advocate for Homosexuals," *New York Times*, June 26, 1985, https://www.nytimes.com/1985/06/26/us/david-goodstein-dies-at-53-advocate-for -homosexuals.html.

17. Charles Kaiser, *The Gay Metropolis, 1940–1996* (New York: Houghton Mifflin Company, 1997).

18. Untitled report in the *Advocate*, May 1, 1976, 8.

19. Clendinen and Nagourney, *Out for Good*, 252.

20. Randy Shilts to Gary Shilts, February 15, 1976, Hormel Center.

21. Randy Shilts, interview by Eric Marcus, March 1989.

22. Ibid.

23. Randy Shilts, "A Most Conventional Convention," *Advocate*, August 11, 1976, 7.

24. Ibid., 8.

25. D. Battle, "What New York Is Doing to Ensure a Safe Convention," *U.S. News & World Report*, July 5, 1976, 15; D. E. Rosenbaum, "No 'Purple Planks,' Democrats' Platform Geared to Unity as Carter Faces a Smooth Road Ahead," *New York Times*, June 16, 1976, A13.

26. Shilts, "A Most Conventional Convention," 9.

27. Randy Shilts, "Sodomy Repeal Signed by Washington Governor," *Advocate*, July 30, 1975, 5–6.

28. *Advocate*, September 1976, 8.

29. Randy Shilts to Robert McQueen and Sasha Gregory-Lewis, editors of the *Advocate*, memorandum, January 16, 1976, Hormel Center.

30. Randy Shilts, "Gay Youth: The Lonely Young," *Advocate*, June 1, 1977, 32–34, 44.

31. Rodger Streitmatter, *Unspeakable: The Rise of the Gay and Lesbian Press in America* (Boston: Faber and Faber, 1995).

32. Randy Shilts, "VD," *Advocate*, April 21, 1976, 4.

33. Shilts, "The Decade's Best-Kept Medical Secret."

34. Ibid., 24.

35. Randy Shilts, *And the Band Played On* (New York: Penguin Books, 1987), 89.

36. Rodger Streitmatter, "Gay Community News," in *Encyclopedia of Gay Histories and Cultures*, ed. George E. Haggerty (New York: Garland Publishing, 2013), 369–70.

37. Randy Shilts, "The Gay Voice of *The Village Voice*: Arthur Bell," *Advocate*, March 23, 1977, 15–16.

38. Shilts, "A New Plague," 26.

39. Ibid., 16.

40. Randy Shilts to Robert McQueen, editor of the *Advocate*, December 14, 1977, Hormel Center.

41. Randy Shilts, diary entry, December 31, 1977, Hormel Center.

42. Linda Alband, personal communication, January 4, 2013.

43. Randy Shilts, diary entry, December 31, 1977, Hormel Center.

44. Randy Shilts, diary entry, June 11, 1978, Hormel Center.

45. Randy Shilts, diary entry, June 24, 1978, Hormel Center.

46. Linda Alband, personal communication, January 4, 2013.

47. Shilts, "The Gay Voice," 15.

48. Garry Wills, "Randy Shilts: The *Rolling Stone* Interview," *Rolling Stone*, September 30, 1993, 50, 48.

49. Anita Bryant, *The Anita Bryant Story: The Survival of Our Nation's Families and the Threat of Militant Homosexuality* (Old Tappan, NJ: Revell Publishing Company, 1977).

50. W. Strub, "The New Right's Anti-Gay Backlash," in *Understanding and Teaching U.S. Lesbian, Gay, Bisexual, and Transgender History*, ed. Leila J. Rupp and Susan K. Freeman (Madison: University of Wisconsin Press, 2014).

51. Robert McQueen and Randy Shilts, "The Movements Born Again," *Advocate*, July 27, 1977, 7.

52. Ibid.

53. Randy Shilts, "The President's Nephew," *Christopher Street*, June 1979, 29–34.

## Chapter 4. Finding a Voice

1. Randy Shilts, *And the Band Played On* (New York: Penguin Books, 1987), 205–6.

2. Randy Shilts, "Thanks: Letter to the Editor," *New York Native*, April 11–24, 1983, 4.

3. John-Manuel Andriote, *Victory Deferred: How AIDS Changed Gay Life in America* (Chicago: University of Chicago Press, 1999), 17–18.

4. Dudley Clendinen and Adam Nagourney, *Out for Good: The Struggle to Build the Gay Rights Movement in America* (New York: Touchstone, 1999), 249, 252.

5. Cleve Jones, telephone interview, October 4, 2011.

6. Randy Shilts to "Jim," February 13, 1976, Hormel Center.

7. Cleve Jones, telephone interview, October 4, 2011.

8. Harvey Milk to Randy Shilts, handwritten card, undated, Hormel Center.

9. Cleve Jones, telephone interview, October 4, 2011.

10. Clendinen and Nagourney, *Out for Good*, 252.

11. Randy Shilts, diary entry, February 8, 1978, Hormel Center.

12. Randy Shilts, diary entry, January 29, 1978, Hormel Center.

13. Clendinen and Nagourney, *Out for Good*, 373.

14. Rodger Streitmatter, *Unspeakable: The Rise of the Gay and Lesbian Press in America* (Boston: Faber and Faber, 1995), 242.

15. *Ayer Directory of Publications* (1972–82); *IMS Ayer Directory of Publications* (1983–85). The *Advocate* printed the "Statement of Ownership, Management, and Circulation," November 2000–November 2005.

16. Shilts, *The Mayor of Castro Street: The Life and Times of Harvey Milk* (New York: St. Martin's Press, 1982), 102.

17. George Osterkamp, personal communication, February 15, 2013.

18. P. Hardman, "Randy Shilts Goes to KQED," *Bay Area Reporter*, March 3, 1977, 6.

19. Tony Ledwell, "Gay Reporter Covers Beat for TV Station," *Baltimore Evening Sun*, March 7, 1977, 18.

20. Hardman, "Randy Shilts Goes to KQED."

21. Tony Ledwell, "Gay Newsman Covers Familiar Beat," *Abilene (TX) Reporter-News*, March 3, 1977, 26.

22. K. A. Nishikawa, T. L. Towner, R. A. Clawson, and E. N. Waltenburg, "Interviewing the Interviewers: Journalistic Norms and Racial Diversity in the Newsroom," *Howard Journal of Communications* 20, no. 2 (2009): 251.

23. Edward Alwood, *Straight News: Gays, Lesbians and the News Media* (New York: Columbia University Press, 1996).

24. Randy Shilts, diary entry, January 9, 1978, Hormel Center.

25. R. Epstein and R. Schmiechen, producers, *The Times of Harvey Milk* (documentary, 1984).

26. Randy Shilts, KQED-TV news report, July 5, 1977, San Francisco Bay Area Television Archive, J. Paul Leonard Library, San Francisco State University.

27. Shilts, *The Mayor of Castro Street*, 163–68.

28. Randy Shilts, diary entry, January 9, 1978, Hormel Center.

29. George Osterkamp, personal communication, February 15, 2013.

30. Ibid.

31. Randy Shilts, diary entry, March 22, 1978, Hormel Center.

32. Randy Shilts, diary entry, March 31, 1978, Hormel Center.

33. David Israels, personal communication, October 8, 2012.

34. Belva Davis, personal communication, February 8, 2013.

35. Belva Davis and V. Haddock, *Never in My Wildest Dreams* (Sausalito, CA: Poli Point Press, 2011), 205.

36. Randy Shilts, KQED-TV news report, October 9, 1978, Bay Area Television Archive.

37. Ibid.

38. 1978 general election results, California secretary of state, Sacramento.

39. Randy Shilts, KQED-TV news report, October 9, 1978, Bay Area Television Archive.

40. Jerry Carroll, "Gay Happy Days Are Here Again," *San Francisco Chronicle*, November 28, 1978, 3.

41. Randy Shilts, KQED-TV news report, November 8, 1978, Hormel Center.

42. Clendinen and Nagourney, *Out for Good,* 377.

43. Ibid., 379.

44. Ibid., 379–80.

45. Randy Shilts, "The Private vs. the Public Senator John V. Briggs," October 27, 1978, unpublished typewritten draft, 10, Hormel Center.

46. Randy Shilts to the editor of the *Sacramento Bee*, October 30, 1978, Hormel Center.

47. Shilts, "The Private," 10.

48. Bill Bucy to Randy Shilts, August 30, 1978, Hormel Center.

49. Clendinen and Nagourney, *Out for Good,* 380–81.

50. Shilts, "The Private," 8.

51. John Briggs, undated newsletter article, http://www.anthemvoice.org/resources/John+Briggs+Responds.pdf (accessed October 17, 2018).

52. Gore Vidal, *Point to Point Navigation: A Memoir* (New York: Random House, 2007), 67.

53. M. Kilduff, "Supervisor Dan White Resigns from Board," *San Francisco Chronicle*, November 10, 1978, 1.

54. M. Kilduff, "White Wants Supervisor's Job Back," *San Francisco Chronicle*, November 16, 1978, 1.

55. KQED-TV, unedited tape, Randy Shilts interview with Mayor George Moscone, June 25, 1977, San Francisco Bay Area Television Archive.

56. KQED-TV, unedited tape, Randy Shilts interview with Mayor George Moscone, June 21, 1977, San Francisco Bay Area Television Archive.

57. Maitland Zane, "Mayor Balks at Reappointing White," *San Francisco Chronicle*, November 21, 1978, 10.

58. Maitland Zane, "Women's Advocate May Be Moscone's Choice for Board," *San Francisco Chronicle*, November 23, 1978, 10.

## Chapter 5. The Life and Times

1. George Osterkamp, telephone interview, February 15, 2013.

2. Rita Williams, telephone interview, June 6, 2012.

3. Ibid.

4. Randy Alfred, host/producer, *The Gay Life*, February 28, 1982, KSAN-AM Radio, San Francisco, www.glbthistory.org/gaybackmachine/randyalfred.html (accessed September 2, 2011).

5. Randy Shilts, typewritten manuscript, "The Other Story," December 1978, Hormel Center.

6. Randy Shilts, diary entry, April 6, 1986, Hormel Center.

7. Randy Shilts, interview by Eric Marcus, March 1989.

8. Randy Shilts, diary entry, March 31, 1978, Hormel Center.

9. Randy Shilts, diary entry, April 19, 1978, Hormel Center.

10. Randy Shilts, diary entry, June 9, 1978, Hormel Center.

11. Edward Alwood, *Straight News: Gays, Lesbians and the News Media* (New York: Columbia University Press, 1996), 176.

12. Rejection letter, KRON-TV, April 1980, Hormel Center.

13. Shilts, interview.

14. Michael Denneny, telephone interview, August 11, 2016.

15. M. Meenan, "A Rare and Worthy Life: Michael Denneny Looks Back on a Life Dedicated to Important Books," *Gay City News*, June 24–30, 2004.

16. Michael Denneny, personal communication, November 23, 2011.

17. Ibid.

18. Randy Shilts, *The Mayor of Castro Street: The Life and Times of Harvey Milk* (New York: St. Martin's Press, 1982), xiv, xv.

19. Ibid., xv.

20. Ibid., xvi.

21. Ibid., 3.

22. Ibid., 4–6.

23. Ibid., 29.

24. Ibid., 160.

25. Ibid., 88, 113.

26. Ibid., 244.

27. Ibid., 128.

28. Ibid., 134, 136.

29. E. Mehren, "Gay Author in Straight Mainstream," *Los Angeles Times*, March 25, 1982.

30. Ibid.

31. St. Martin's Press undated news release, "Advance Critical Acclaim for *The Mayor of Castro Street*" by Randy Shilts, Hormel Center.

32. James Kinsella, *Covering the Plague: AIDS and the American Media* (New Brunswick, NJ: Rutgers University Press, 1989), 162–64.

33. Michael H. Price, "Let Us Be Gay in the Bay Area," *Fort Worth Star-Telegram*, April 18, 1982.

34. Alfred, *The Gay Life*.

35. Garry Wills, "Randy Shilts: The *Rolling Stone* Interview," *Rolling Stone*, September 30, 1993.

36. Alfred, *The Gay Life*.

37. Shilts, *The Mayor of Castro Street*, xiv.

38. Ibid.

39. Ibid.

40. Ibid., 74, 103.

41. Randy Shilts reporting on the White Night riots, May 22, 1979, KQED-TV unedited tape, San Francisco Bay Area Television Archive, J. Paul Leonard Library, San Francisco State University.

42. Alfred, *The Gay Life*.

43. Ibid.

44. David Israels, telephone interview, October 8, 2012.

45. Ibid.

46. Randy Shilts, "Tense, Torn City Braces for White's Release," *San Francisco Chronicle*, January 5, 1984, A1.

47. Ibid.

48. James Clifford, "White's Release Scheduled for Today," *DeKalb (IL) Daily Chronicle*, January 6, 1984, 5.

49. Wills, "Randy Shilts."

## Chapter 6. Becoming the AIDS Scribe

1. D. Romine, "About the Author: Gay Reporter Randy Shilts Finds Fame by Exposing Fear and Ignorance," *Charlotte Observer*, November 8, 1987, 1E.

2. R. Reinhold, "AIDS Book Brings Fame to a Gay San Franciscan," *New York Times*, October 31, 1987, 7.

3. Randy Shilts, interview by Eric Marcus, March 1989.

4. Edward Alwood, *Straight News: Gays, Lesbians and the News Media* (New York: Columbia University Press, 1996), 204.

5. S. Sward, "The Price of Freedom," *San Francisco Chronicle*, March 6, 1994, A12.

6. C. Lozano, director, "Reporter Zero" (television episode), February 12, 2006, KTVU-TV, San Francisco.

7. Sward, "The Price of Freedom."

8. Wes Haley, interview, January 9, 2012, San Francisco.

9. Marcus Conant, telephone interview, September 6, 2011; Randy Shilts to Dr. Marcus Conant, August 8, 1981, Marcus Conant Papers, University of California Digital Library, https://calisphere.org/item/58ac2046–5fe0–4739–9cad-ecac0392dc0e/.

10. David Perlman, "A Pneumonia That Strikes Gay Men," *San Francisco Chronicle*, June 6, 1981, A4.

11. David Perlman, interview by M. Weiss, "AIDS at 25: Reflections on Reporter Randy Shilts," 1994, http://blog.sfgate.com/chroncast/2006/06/03/aids-at-25-reflections-on -reporter-randy-shilts/ (accessed January 4, 2013).

12. Randy Shilts, "The Strange Diseases That Strike Gay Men," *San Francisco Chronicle*, May 13, 1982, A6.

13. P. Monahan O'Malley, interview by S. Smith Hughes, 1996, "The AIDS Epidemic in San Francisco," San Francisco AIDS Oral History Project, University of California, San Francisco.

14. Randy Shilts to Dr. Selma Dritz, handwritten note, May 13, 1983, Dr. Selma Dritz Papers, University of California, Digital Library, https://calisphere.org/item/881577bf-47b2-4ef2 -a7bc-4e7c8ddba6c0/.

15. Randy Shilts to Dr. Selma Dritz, typed letter, February 25, 1986, Dritz Papers, https://calisphere.org/item/59ec5224-0925-450c-afff-1c7bf20a6792/.

16. Shilts, "The Strange Diseases."

17. Monahan O'Malley, interview.

18. Alwood, *Straight News*.

19. James Kinsella, *Covering the Plague: AIDS and the American Media* (New Brunswick, NJ: Rutgers University Press, 1989), 168–69.

20. Ibid., 170–71.

21. Keith Power, "Reporter Driven by His Mission," *San Francisco Chronicle*, February 18, 1994, D6.

22. Shilts, interview.

23. Marcus Conant, personal communication, September 6, 2011.

24. A. J. Ammann, interview by S. Smith Hughes, 1996, "The AIDS Epidemic in San Francisco," San Francisco AIDS Oral History Project, University of California, San Francisco.

25. United Press International, "Saliva Hinted AIDS Transmitter," March 8, 1985.

26. Associated Press, "Husband of Woman Who Died of AIDS Shows Signs of the Disease," March 7, 1985.

27. Kinsella, *Covering the Plague*, 158–59.

28. Randy Shilts, "The Story in the Closet," *San Francisco Chronicle*, August 3, 1985, A7. The "demarcation point" quote is from Randy Shilts, *And the Band Played On: Politics, People and the AIDS Epidemic* (New York: St. Martin's Press, 1987), xxi.

29. K. Kelley, "Randy Shilts: The Interview," *San Francisco Focus*, June 1989, 65–66, 94–113.

30. Randy Shilts and Herb Caen, *The Quake of '89: As Seen by the News Staff of the "San Francisco Chronicle"* (San Francisco: Chronicle Books, 1989), xi.

31. David Israels, personal communication, October 8, 2012.

32. Alwood, *Straight News*, 204, 234.

33. K. Power, "Reporter Driven by His Mission," *San Francisco Chronicle*, February 18, 1994, D6.

34. Randy Shilts to Richard Thieriot and William Randolph Hearst III, May 2, 1990, Hormel Center.

35. Power, "Reporter Driven," D6.

36. M. Weiss, "Randy Shilts Was Gutsy, Brash and Unforgettable," *San Francisco Chronicle*, February 17, 2004, A1.

37. Randy Shilts, "March of AIDS through Society Hasn't Abated," *San Francisco Chronicle*, July 16, 1989, A1.

38. Ibid., A4.

39. Steve Newman, telephone interview, November 30, 2012.

40. Ibid.

41. Shilts, "March of AIDS," A4.

42. Phillip Matier, "Prop S Defeat a Setback for Gays," *San Francisco Examiner*, November 8, 1989, A1.

43. R. Shilts, "Deadly Parallels of Earthquake Stress," *San Francisco Chronicle*, November 20, 1989, A11.

44. Randy Shilts and D. Tuller, "AIDS Conference in SF Urges Bigger Role by U.S.," *San Francisco Chronicle*, October 12, 1989, A10.

45. Randy Shilts, "Age of Intervention: Fewer AIDS Cases Expected," *San Francisco Chronicle*, October 13, 1989, A4.

46. Randy Shilts, "Health Official's Pledge on AIDS: Restrictions to Curb Drug Profiteering," *San Francisco Chronicle*, October 14, 1989, A4.

47. Ibid.

48. Randy Shilts, "The Real Answer Is Equal Health Care," *San Francisco Chronicle*, October 16, 1989, A1; Shilts, "The Complex Issue of Drug Pricing," *San Francisco Chronicle*, November 6, 1989, A11.

49. Shilts, "The Real Answer," A1.

50. Randy Shilts, "Patiently Tiptoeing through the World of Word Twisters," *San Francisco Chronicle*, December 11, 1989, A8.

51. Randy Shilts, "The Era of Bad Feelings," *Mother Jones* 14, no. 9 (November 1989): 34.

52. Ibid., 34, 35.

53. *San Francisco Chronicle*, May 2, 1988; *Editor & Publisher*, December 12, 1987.

54. Shilts, "The Story in the Closet."

55. P. Reynolds, "Writing the Book on AIDS," *Boston Globe*, November 6, 1987.

56. Belva Davis, personal communication, February 8, 2013.

57. Shilts, interview.

58. Alan Mutter, personal communication, January 2, 2012.

59. L. Udesky, "An Interview with Randy Shilts, Author of *And the Band Played On*," in *Democracy in Print: The Best of "Progressive" Magazine 1909–2009*, ed. Matthew Rothschild (Madison: University of Wisconsin Press, 2009), 133–35.

60. Randy Shilts, "Fear of Epidemic in the Mud Huts," *San Francisco Chronicle*, October 5, 1987, A1.

61. Belva Davis, telephone interview, February 8, 2013.

## Chapter 7. Bathhouse Daze

1. Ira Tattelman, "Speaking to the Gay Bathhouse: Communicating in Sexually Charged Spaces," in *Public Space, Gay Space*, ed. William L. Leap (New York: Columbia University Press, 1970), 71.

2. David Perlman, interview by M. Weiss, "AIDS at 25: Reflections on Reporter Randy Shilts," 1994.

3. S. Kroft, producer, "Randy Shilts," *60 Minutes*, February 20, 1994.

4. John-Manuel Andriote, *Victory Deferred: How AIDS Changed Gay Life in America* (Chicago: University of Chicago Press, 1999), 75–77.

5. Ibid., 78.

6. Randy Shilts, "Some AIDS Patients Still Going to the Baths," *San Francisco Chronicle*, November 15, 1983, A4.

7. Randy Shilts, "On Bathhouse Politics," *San Francisco Chronicle*, June 15, 1984, A6.

8. C. L. Morrison, interview by S. Smith Hughes, 1994, "The AIDS Epidemic in San Francisco," 111–12, San Francisco AIDS Oral History Project, University of California, San Francisco.

9. Alan Mutter, telephone interview, January 2, 2012.

10. Randy Shilts, "Feinstein Defends Use of Bathhouse 'Spies,'" *San Francisco Chronicle*, June 1, 1984, 3.

11. Ibid.

12. Mervin Silverman, interview, January 8, 2012, El Cerrito, California.

13. Ibid.

14. James W. Curran, telephone interview, July 13, 2016.

15. K. Kelley, "Randy Shilts: The Interview," *San Francisco Focus*, June 1989, 94.

16. Linda Alband, telephone interview, January 4, 2013.

17. Mervin Silverman, interview, January 8, 2012, El Cerrito, California.

18. Mervin Silverman, interview by S. Smith Hughes, 1993, "The AIDS Epidemic in San Francisco," San Francisco AIDS Oral History Project, University of California, San Francisco.

19. Marcus Conant, telephone interview, September 6, 2011.

20. Ibid.

21. James W. Curran, telephone interview, July 16, 2016.

22. G. Heymont, "Shilts Calls Gay Leaders 'Inept,' 'Bunch of Jerks': *Chronicle* Reporter Stirs Controversy in Candid Interview in Skin Magazine," *Bay Area Reporter*, November 21, 1984, 1–2.

23. Cleve Jones, telephone interview, October 4, 2011.

24. Dudley Clendinen and Adam Nagourney, *Out for Good: The Struggle to Build a Gay Rights Movement in America* (New York: St. Martin's Press, 1999), 501.

25. R. A. Worden, letter to the editor, *Bay Area Reporter*, June 7, 1984, 4.

26. D. Goodman, letter to the editor, *Bay Area Reporter*, June 13, 1984, 6.

27. Randy Shilts, "A Farewell 'Orgy' at Sutro Baths," *San Francisco Chronicle*, June 4, 1984, A7.

28. B. Folk, letter to the editor, *Bay Area Reporter*, June 14, 1984, 6.

29. Randy Shilts, "Traitors or Heroes: Notes from the Plague," *New York Native*, July 16–29, 1984.

30. George Mendenhall, "Bathhouse Closing Decided, Delayed, Debunked," *Bay Area Reporter*, April 5, 1984, 1.

31. Shilts, "Traitors or Heroes."

32. R. Nelson, letter to the editor, *Bay Area Reporter*, December 13, 1984, 2.

33. H. Lader, letter to the editor, *Bay Area Reporter*, December 13, 1984, 4, emphasis added.

34. Ibid.

35. George Mendenhall, "Bathhouse Closing Decided, Delayed, Debunked," *Bay Area Reporter*, April 5, 1984, 1.

36. B. Pettit, "Toklas Demos Reject Baths Sex Ban; Club Denounces *Chronicle*'s Randy Shilts," *Bay Area Reporter,* April 19, 1984, 1–2, 4.

37. Mendenhall, "Bathhouse Closing Decided," 8.

38. James Kinsella, *Covering the Plague: AIDS and the American Media* (New Brunswick, NJ: Rutgers University Press, 1989), 172.

39. Brian Jones, "VD Rate Drops for Gay Men," *Bay Area Reporter*, April 15, 1984, 4.

40. Randy Shilts, interview by Eric Marcus, March 1989.

41. Mendenhall, "Bathhouse Closing Decided," 2.

42. Dion B. Sanders, "*National Enquirer* Rips Hennessey's Night at Chaps," *Bay Area Reporter*, April 26, 1984, 2.

43. Gary Schweikhart, "Shilts Responds to Critics," *Sentinel*, March 29, 1984, 1.

44. H. Britt, *The Gay Life*, April 24, 1984, KSAN-AM podcast, GLBT Historical Society, http://www.glbthistory.org/gaybackmachine/randyalfred.html (accessed September 2, 2011).

45. Sal Accardi, remarks recorded at AIDS public forum, April 24, 1984, KSAN-AM podcast, GLBT Historical Society, http://www.glbthistory.org/gaybackmachine/randyalfred .html (accessed December 24, 2011).

46. Jones, "VD Rate Drops," 1.

47. H. Britt, *The Gay Life*, May 13, 1984, KSAN-AM podcast, GLBT Historical Society, http://www.glbthistory.org/gaybackmachine/randyalfred.html (accessed September 2, 2011).

48. Ibid.

49. Edward Alwood, telephone interview, March 28, 2018.

50. Heymont, "Shilts Calls Gay Leaders," 1, 2.

51. Randy Shilts, letter to the editor, *Bay Area Reporter*, November 29, 1984, 2.

52. Shilts, "Traitors or Heroes."

53. Shilts, interview.

54. Ibid.

## Chapter 8. A Balancing Act for Shilts

1. D. Hastings, "Noted AIDS Writer Wants Bathhouses Shut Down," *Los Angeles Herald Examiner*, January 21, 1988, A11.

2. David Israels, telephone interview, October 8, 2012.

3. Ibid.

4. Steve Newman, telephone interview, November 30, 2012.

5. James W. Curran, telephone interview, July 13, 2016.

6. James Kinsella, *Covering the Plague: AIDS and the American Media* (New Brunswick, NJ: Rutgers University Press, 1989), 179.

7. Michelangelo Signorile, e-mail interview, October 7, 2011.

8. Randy Shilts, "The Era of Bad Feelings," *Mother Jones Magazine* 14, no. 9 (November 1989): 60.

9. Randy Shilts, "Politics of AIDS: ACT-UP's Acting Up Gets Mixed Reviews," *San Francisco Chronicle*, December 15, 1989, A4.

10. Ibid.

11. John Stanley, "A Look at Ethical Challenges of an Epidemic," *San Francisco Chronicle*, December 17, 1989, A1.

12. Randy Shilts, G. Smith, and M. Schwarz, producers, *Wrestling with AIDS*, December 14, 1989, KQED-TV broadcast, https://diva.sfsu.edu/collections/sfbatv/bundles/190109 (accessed February 1, 2013).

13. Randy Shilts, "AIDS Meeting Has Its Own Star Circuit," *San Francisco Chronicle*, June 21, 1990, A9.

14. Katherine E. Bliss, "The International AIDS Conference Returns to the United States: Lessons from the Past and Opportunities for July 2012," report of the CSIS Global Health Policy Center, March 2012, Center for Strategic and International Studies, Washington, DC, 4–9.

15. Shilts, "AIDS Meeting," A9.

16. Jane Gross, "Gay Journalists Gather to Complain and to Celebrate Progress at Work," *New York Times*, June 29, 1992, B6.

17. Richard Reinhold, "AIDS History a Frightening One," *New York Times* News Service, article appeared in *Lawrence (KS) Journal-World*, November 8, 1987, 6D.

18. Edward Iwata, "Stepping Out: Gay Journalists Meet Openly to Debate Their Struggles and Roles in the Media," *Editor & Publisher*, August 22, 1992.

19. J. Weir, "Reading Randy," *Out*, August–September 1993, 46.

20. Edward Alwood, *Straight News: Gays, Lesbians and the News Media* (New York: Columbia University Press, 1996), 267, 278.

21. Randy Shilts, *The Mayor of Castro Street: The Life and Times of Harvey Milk* (New York: St. Martin's Press, 1982), 122.

22. Iwata, "Stepping Out."

23. Randy Shilts, "Is 'Outing' Gays Ethical?," *New York Times*, April 12, 1990.

24. P. B. Snyder, producer, *CBS This Morning*, May 1, 1990, New York.

25. Michelangelo Signorile, *Queer in America: Sex, the Media and the Closets of Power* (Madison: University of Wisconsin Press, 1993), 154, 155.

26. Weir, "Reading Randy."

27. Ibid., 47.

28. Randy Shilts, "Proposed Bill Would End Ban on Gays in Armed Services," *San Francisco Chronicle*, May 20, 1992, A8.

29. Ransdell Pierson, "Uptight on Gay News: Can the Straight Press Get the Gay Story Straight? Is Anyone Even Trying?," in *The Columbia Reader on Lesbians and Gay Men in Media, Society and Politics*, ed. Larry P. Gross and James D. Woods (New York: Columbia University Press, 1990).

30. Cynthia Tucker, "Can Militant Minority Reporters Be Objective?," *Nieman Reports*, Spring 1994, 83, http://nieman.harvard.edu/reports/article/102065/1994-A-New-Agenda -for-Journalism.aspx (accessed December 24, 2012).

31. K. A. Nishikawa, T. L. Towner, R. A. Clawson, and E. N. Waltenburg, "Interviewing the Interviewers: Journalistic Norms and Racial Diversity in the Newsroom," *Howard Journal of Communications* 20, no. 2 (2009): 243–45, 251.

32. Belva Davis, telephone interview, February 8, 2013.

33. Ibid.; Pierson, "Uptight on Gay News."

34. James Boylan, editor, *Columbia Journalism Review*, to Randy Shilts, December 1, 1978, Hormel Center.

35. Ibid.

36. Iwata, "Stepping Out."

37. Signorile, *Queer in America*, 155.

38. Michelangelo Signorile, e-mail interview, October 7, 2011.

39. Michelangelo Signorile, e-mail interview, October 7, 2011.

40. Michelangelo Signorile, e-mail interview, October 7, 2011.

41. Rich Grzesiak, "Rocking Our Sinking Boat: Randy Shilts Talks Tough on Our Problems and Press," *Au Courant*, October 1987, 6–7.

42. Michael Denneny, telephone interview, August 11, 2016.

43. Ibid.

44. Grzesiak, "Rocking Our Sinking Boat."

## Chapter 9. Clean and Sober

1. Randy Shilts, diary entry, March 22, 1984, Hormel Center.

2. Randy Shilts, diary entry, November 1984, Hormel Center.

3. Gary Shilts, interview, July 31, 2014, Aurora, Illinois.

4. Randy Shilts, diary entry, March 11, 1972, Hormel Center.

5. Randy Shilts, diary entry, April 6, 1986, Hormel Center.

6. Suzanne Somers, "Randy Shilts," in *Wednesday's Children: Adult Survivors of Abuse Speak Out*, ed. Suzanne Somers (New York: Putnam / Healing Vision Publishing, 1992), 160.

7. Ibid., 163.

8. Ibid., 164.

9. Ibid., 163.

10. Gary Shilts, e-mail interview notes, 2014.

11. Reed Shilts, interview, October 18, 2014, Kalamazoo, Michigan.

12. Norma Shilts to Randy Shilts, July 13, 1980, Hormel Center.

13. Gary Shilts, interview, July 31, 2014, Aurora, Illinois.

14. Shilts, "Randy Shilts," 168.

15. K. Kelley, "Randy Shilts: The Interview," *San Francisco Focus*, June 1989, 101.

16. Shilts, "Randy Shilts," 162.

17. D. Romine, "About the Author: Gay Reporter Randy Shilts Finds Fame by Exposing Fear and Ignorance," *Charlotte (NC) Observer*, November 8, 1997, 1-E.

18. David Israels, telephone interview, October 8, 2012.

19. Daniel Curzon, *Dropping Names: The Delicious Memoirs of Daniel Curzon* (San Francisco: IGNA Books, 2004), 89.

20. Randy Shilts, interview by Eric Marcus, March 1989.

21. Steve Newman, telephone interview, November 30, 2012.

22. Cleve Jones, telephone interview, October 4, 2011.

23. Jane Weir, "Reading Randy," *Out*, August–September 1993, 49.

24. L. Udesky, "An Interview with Randy Shilts, Author of *And the Band Played On*," in *Democracy in Print: The Best of "Progressive" Magazine 1909–2009*, ed. Matthew Rothschild (Madison: University of Wisconsin Press, 1991), 135.

25. Cleve Jones, telephone interview, October 4, 2011.

26. Don Francis, telephone interview, January 20, 2013.

27. David Israels, telephone interview, October 8, 2012.

28. Cleve Jones, telephone interview, October 4, 2011.

29. Cleve Jones, personal communication, October 4, 2011; Dustin Lance Black, speech, Colorado State University, April 29, 2011.

## Chapter 10. Strike Up the *Band*

1. Michael Denneny, telephone interview, November 23, 2011.

2. Garry Wills, "Randy Shilts: The *Rolling Stone* Interview," *Rolling Stone*, September 30, 1993.

3. Randy Shilts, *And the Band Played On: Politics, People, and the AIDS Epidemic* (New York: St. Martin's Press, 1987), xxii, emphasis added.

4. Michael Denneny, telephone interview, November 23, 2011.

5. Ibid.

6. Don Francis, telephone interview, January 10, 2013.

7. Shilts, *And the Band Played On*, 607.

8. Ibid., xii.

9. Ibid.

10. Don Francis, telephone interview, January 10, 2013.

11. Ibid.

12. Shilts, *And the Band Played On*, 395.

13. Carol Pogash, telephone interview, March 19, 2018.

14. Randy Shilts to Dr. Selma Dritz, typed letter, February 25, 1986, Dr. Selma Dritz Papers, University of California Digital Library, https://calisphere.org/item/59ec5224-0925-450c-afff-1c7bf20a6792/.

15. William Darrow, telephone interview, February 1, 2013.

16. Selma Dritz, interview by S. Smith Hughes, 1993, "The AIDS Epidemic in San Francisco," San Francisco AIDS Oral History Project, University of California, San Francisco, emphasis added.

17. J. W. Curran and H. W. Jaffee, "AIDS: The Early Years and the CDC's Response," *Supplements* 60, no. 4 (2011): 64–69.

18. D. M. Auerbach and W. W. Darrow, "CDC: A Cluster of Kaposi's Sarcoma and *Pneumocystis carinii* Pneumonia among Homosexual Male Residents of Los Angeles and Orange Counties, California," *Mortality & Morbidity Weekly Report* 31, no. 3 (1982): 305–7.

19. William Darrow, telephone interview, February 1, 2013.

20. D. M. Auerbach, W. H. Darrow, H. W. Jaffe, and J. W. Curran, "A Cluster of Cases of the Acquired Immune Deficiency Syndrome: Patients Linked by Sexual Contact," *American Journal of Medicine* 76, no. 3 (1984): 487–92.

21. William Darrow, telephone interview, February 1, 2013.

22. Ibid.

23. James W. Curran, telephone interview, July 16, 2016.

24. Isabella Awad, "Journalists and Their Sources: Lessons from Anthropology," *Journalism Studies* 7, no. 6 (2006): 992.

25. William Darrow, telephone interview, February 1, 2013.

26. Ibid.

27. Richard McKay, "'Patient Zero': The Absence of a Patient's View of the Early North American AIDS Epidemic," *Bulletin of the History of Medicine* 88, no. 1 (2014): 161–94.

28. James W. Curran, telephone interview, July 16, 2016.

29. Marcus Conant, telephone interview, September 6, 2011.

30. Cleve Jones, telephone interview, October 4, 2011.

31. Ibid.

## Chapter 11. The Sum of Zero

1. Michael Denneny, telephone interview, November 23, 2011.

2. Ibid.

3. "The Man Who Brought AIDS to America," *New York Post*, October 6, 1987, 3.

4. Douglas Crimp, *Melancholia and Moralism: Essays on AIDS and Queer Politics* (Boston: MIT Press, 2004), 481.

5. "Canadian Said to Have Key Role in Spread of AIDS," *New York Times*, October 7, 1997, B7.

6. M. Stinton and A. Eaton, "The Monster Who Gave Us AIDS," *Star*, October 27, 1987, 6–7.

7. W. A. Henry III, "The Appalling Saga of 'Patient Zero,'" *Time*, October 19, 1987, 40–41.

8. J. Miller and P. Abramson, "The Making of an Epidemic: A Reporter Pursues the Origins of the AIDS Crisis," *Newsweek*, October 19, 1987, 91–93.

9. A. Steacy and L. Van Dusen, "'Patient Zero' and the AIDS Virus," *Maclean's*, October 19, 1987, 53.

10. W. Hines, "The AIDS Epidemic: A Report from the Front Lines," *Washington Post*, October 11, 1987, X1.

11. Tempo, *Chicago Tribune*, November 1, 1987, 1.

12. M. Binyon, "Washington View: Telling Chapters on U.S. Failure to Combat AIDS," *Times* (London), October 17, 1987.

13. "AIDS: The Man They Blame," *Sunday Mail*, November 22, 1987.

14. *National Review*, November 6, 1987, 19.

15. *People*, December 28, 1987.

16. "MDs Doubt Claim Canadian Carried AIDS to Continent," *Toronto Star*, October 7, 1987, 1.

17. Randy Shilts, "Patient Zero: The Airline Steward Who Carried a Disease and a Grudge," *Toronto Star*, December 12, 1987, M1.

18. George S. Buse, "Advertisement Stirs Furor Anew over 'Patient Zero' Allegations," *Windy City Times*, September 8, 1988, 8.

19. *Time*, October 12, 1989.

20. Andrew Herrmann, "Victim Zero: Airline Steward Played Key Role in Spreading AIDS in America," *Chicago Sun-Times*, October 11, 1987, A17–18.

21. Randy Shilts, *And the Band Played On: Politics, People and the AIDS Epidemic* (New York: St. Martin's Press, 1987), 251.

22. Herrmann, "Victim Zero."

23. Buse, "Advertisement," 8.

24. Shilts, *And the Band Played On*, 147, emphasis added.

25. Ibid., 165.

26. Ibid., 21.

27. Ibid., 79.

28. Vancouver AIDS 30/30 Project, video retrieved at https://www.youtube.com/watch?v=f5wJXYxNu88.

29. Ibid.

30. Shilts, *And the Band Played On*, 439.

31. R. Bluestein, "Cries and Whispers of an Epidemic," *Advocate*, November 24, 1987, 65.

32. Michael Denneny, telephone interview, November 23, 2011.

33. Ibid.

34. Gary Shilts, e-mail interview notes, 2014.

35. Richard McKay, "'Patient Zero': The Absence of a Patient's View of the Early North American AIDS Epidemic," *Bulletin of the History of Medicine* 88, no. 1 (2014): 184.

36. James W. Curran, telephone interview, July 16, 2016.

37. Randy Shilts, "Randy Shilts," in *Wednesday's Children: Adult Survivors of Abuse Speak Out*, ed. Suzanne Somers (New York: Putnam / Healing Vision Publishing, 1992), 169.

38. L. Bergman, "Patient Zero," *60 Minutes*, November 1, 1987, https://www.youtube.com/watch?v=EsUMFPvZ6wo (accessed December 20, 2012).

39. Ibid.

40. Ibid.

41. Ibid.

42. Phil Tiemeyer, *Plane Queer: Labor, Sexuality and AIDS in the History of Male Flight Attendants* (Berkeley: University of California Press, 2013), 177.

43. Canadian Press, "Montreal man brought AIDS here: book," *Montreal Gazette*, October 7, 1987, 3.

44. Tiemeyer, *Plane Queer*, 178.

45. Ibid.; E. Damarest, "AIDS: 'Patient Zero' Discussed at History Association Panel," *Windy City Times*, January 18, 2013; "'Patient Zero' and the 'Recalcitrant' Queer," Committee on Lesbian, Gay, Bisexual and Transgender History 5, American Historical Association, http://aha.confex.com/aha/2012/webprogram/Session6545.html.

46. Priscilla Wald, *Contagious: Cultures, Carriers, and the Outbreak Narrative* (Durham, NC: Duke University Press, 2008), 231, 254.

47. Timothy F. Murphy, *Ethics in an Epidemic: AIDS, Morality, and Culture* (Berkeley: University of California Press, 1994), 13–14, 17–18.

48. Patricia Holt, "Behind the Tragedy of AIDS," *San Francisco Chronicle*, October 18, 1987, B1.

49. B. Siphen, "The AIDS Chronicles: Randy Shilts Writes the Biography of an Epidemic and Finds More Bunglers Than Heroes," *Los Angeles Times*, October 9, 1987.

50. Crimp, *Melancholia and Moralism*, 315.

51. Ibid., 481.

52. Richard A. McKay, "Communicative Contacts: Randy Shilts, Gaëtan Dugas, and the Construction of the 'Patient Zero' Myth," January 7, 2012, Committee on Lesbian, Gay, Bisexual and Transgender History 5, American Historical Association, http://aha.confex.com/aha/2012/webprogram/Session6545.html.

53. Ibid.

54. Richard McKay, "Patient Zero: The Legacy of a Powerful Origin Story," October 27, 2011, AIDS@30: Three Decades of HIV/AIDS, King's College, London, retrieved July 2, 2012, http://www.kcl.ac.uk/innovation/groups/chh/events/aids@30.aspx (no longer available).

55. Ibid.

56. Tiemeyer, *Plane Queer*, 138, 139.

57. Ibid., 140, 168, 171–74.

58. Richard Reinhold, "AIDS Book Brings Fame to Gay San Franciscan," *New York Times*, October 31, 1987.

59. Siphen, "The AIDS Chronicles."

60. Ibid.

61. Randy Shilts, "Traitors or Heroes: Notes from the Plague," *New York Native*, July 16–29, 1984.

62. E. Sterel, "A Reporter's Sad Vigil," *Melbourne Herald*, August 19, 1988.

63. *Bay Area Reporter*, December 3, 1987.

64. Siphen, "The AIDS Chronicles."

65. Randy Shilts to Dr. Robert Gallo, National Institutes of Health, October 16, 1987, Hormel Center.

66. Jon Katz, "AIDS and the Media Shifting out of Neutral: How Randy Shilts Chucked the Notion of Objectivity and Got the Story," *Rolling Stone*, May 27, 1993, 31–32.

67. Ibid.

68. Richard McKay, *Patient Zero and the Making of the AIDS Epidemic* (Chicago: University of Chicago Press, 2017).

69. John Weir, "Reading Randy," *Out* 47 (August–September 1993).

70. McKay, *Patient Zero*.

## Chapter 12. Conduct Unbecoming

1. Randy Shilts, *Conduct Unbecoming: Gays and Lesbians in the U.S. Military* (New York: St. Martin's Press, 1992), 711–12.

2. Randy Shilts, "Army Colonel Could Be Jailed on Gay-Related Charges," *San Francisco Chronicle*, October 18, 1990, A6.

3. Randy Shilts, "Say You're Gay, Avoid the Draft," *San Francisco Chronicle*, January 9, 1991, A21.

4. Randy Shilts, "Military May Defer Discharge of Gays," *San Francisco Chronicle*, January 11, 1991, A19.

5. Randy Shilts, "Gay Troops in Gulf War Can't Come Out," *San Francisco Chronicle*, February 18, 1991, A1.

6. Randy Shilts, "Army Discharges Lesbian Who Challenged Ban," *San Francisco Chronicle*, January 19, 1991, A6.

7. Randy Shilts, "Bush Asked to OK Gays in Military," *San Francisco Chronicle*, March 18, 1991, A1.

8. Randy Shilts, "Pentagon Memo Urged Reversing Ban on Gays in Military," *San Francisco Chronicle*, June 25, 1991, A1.

9. Randy Shilts, "Ambition to Lead Derailed Career," *San Francisco Chronicle*, August 5, 1991, A12.

10. Michelangelo Signorile, *Queer in America: Sex, the Media and the Closets of Power* (Madison: University of Wisconsin Press, 1993).

11. Shilts, "Say You're Gay," A19.

12. Linda Alband, email to the author, January 4, 2013.

13. Ibid.

14. Garry Wills, "Randy Shilts: The *Rolling Stone* Interview," *Rolling Stone*, September 30, 1993, 32.

15. Randy Shilts to Gary Allison, July 16, 1991, Hormel Center.

16. T. Cahill, "On the March for Gay GIs," *Stars & Stripes Sunday*, May 30, 1993, 1, 4–5.

17. Linda Alband, email to the author, January 4, 2013.

18. Ibid.

19. Ibid.

20. Michael Denneny, telephone interview, November 23, 2011.

21. Ibid.; Linda Alband, email to the author, January 4, 2013.

22. Michael Denneny, telephone interview, November 23, 2011.

23. A. Witt, "Gay Rights: Clearing the Path of Prejudice," *Virginian-Pilot*, April 5, 1991, B1.

24. George Stephanopoulos, *All Too Human: A Political Education* (New York: Little, Brown, 1999).

25. Randy Shilts, "Proposed Bill Would End Ban on Gays in Armed Services," *San Francisco Chronicle*, May 20, 1992, A8.

26. D. Tuller, "What Schwarzkopf Said about Gay Ban," *San Francisco Chronicle*, April 9, 1993, A1.

27. Shilts, *Conduct Unbecoming*, 105.

28. Terry Gross, producer and interviewer, transcript of interview with Randy Shilts, *Fresh Air*, April 23, 1993, American Public Radio via WHYY.

29. P. Holt, "Behind the Tragedy of AIDS," *San Francisco Chronicle*, October 18, 1987, B1.

30. Gross, transcript of interview.

## Chapter 13. Disclosing HIV

1. Bettijane Levine, "Explosive Look at Gays and Military," *St. Louis (MO) Post-Dispatch*, March 31, 1993, 67, https://www.newspapers.com/image/141632129/?terms=%22Randy%2BShilts%2Bsays%22.

2. Garry Wills, "Randy Shilts: The *Rolling Stone* Interview," *Rolling Stone*, September 30, 1993.

3. Patricia Holt, "The 'Outing' of Historical Leaders," *San Francisco Chronicle*, August 15, 1993, A6.

4. Wills, "Randy Shilts."

5. David Ellis, "Writer of Wrongs," *People*, April 26, 1993, 73–76.

6. Tempo, *Chicago Tribune*, November 1, 1987, 1.

7. C. Bercaw, "Shilts Gets Grip on His Being, Then Worldwide Epidemic," *Aurora (IL) Beacon-News*, November 15, 1987, A1, 8.

8. D. Romine, "About the Author: Gay Reporter Randy Shilts Finds Fame by Exposing Fear and Ignorance," *Charlotte (NC) Observer*, November 8, 1987, 1E.

9. Robert Reinhold, "Book About Epidemic Indicts Many, Praises Few," *New York Times*, November 26, 1987.

10. Jeffrey Schmalz, "Randy Shilts: Writing against Time, Valiantly," *New York Times*, April 22, 1993.

11. Randy Shilts, "A New Plague on Our House: Gastro-Intestinal Diseases," *Advocate*, April 10, 1977, 8–9.

12. William F. Buckley Jr., "Sexual Integration Is Illusive," *Colorado Springs Gazette*, April 29, 1993, A6.

13. Wills, "Randy Shilts."

14. "Randy Shilts Public Statement Regarding HIV Status," news release, *San Francisco Chronicle,* February 16, 1993.

15. Cleve Jones, personal communication, October 4, 2011.

16. Leah Garchik, "Reporter, Author Randy Shilts Reveals That He Has AIDS," *San Francisco Chronicle*, February 16, 1992, 2; J. Stanley, "A Look at the Ethical Challenges of an Epidemic," *San Francisco Chronicle*, December 17, 1989, A1.

17. "Randy Shilts Public Statement."

18. Wills, "Randy Shilts."

19. C. Sgueglia, producer, and Charlie Rose, host, *The Charlie Rose Show*, April 14, 1993, PBS Television.

20. Ibid.

21. Ibid.

22. Ibid.

23. Ibid.

24. Terry Gross, producer and interviewer, transcript of interview with Randy Shilts, *Fresh Air*, April 23, 1993, American Public Radio via WHYY.

25. Ibid.

26. J. M. Adams, "Randy Shilts Fights On: As He Exposes Military Hounding of Gays, He Faces the Personal Enemy of AIDS," *Boston Globe*, May 4, 1993, B1.

27. J. Auchmutey, "The Battles of Randy Shilts: His Own Illness, Anti-gay Bias," *Atlanta Journal-Constitution*, April 25, 1993, B1.

28. Steve Newman, personal communication, November 30, 2012.

29. Schmalz, "Randy Shilts."

30. Ibid.

31. Ibid.

## Chapter 14. Journalist versus Advocate

1. James Kinsella, *Covering the Plague: AIDS and the American Media* (New Brunswick, NJ: Rutgers University Press, 1989), 183.

2. Randy Shilts, *Conduct Unbecoming: Gays and Lesbians in the U.S. Military* (New York: St. Martin's Press, 1992), 5.

3. Ibid., 144.

4. Ibid., 414.

5. Ibid., 6–7, 293.

6. Ibid., 96–97, 445, 548.

7. R. J. Sheppard, book review, *Time*, October 11, 1993, 76–77.

8. John D'Emilio, "All That You Can Be," *Nation*, June 7, 1993.

9. Timothy Cahill, "The Uniform in the Closet," book review, *Boston Globe*, May 16, 1993, B39, 41.

10. Michael Denneny, telephone interview, November 23, 2011.

11. Jessea Greenman, "More to the Shilts Story," in *The Columbia Reader on Lesbians and Gays in the Media, Society and Politics*, ed. Larry Gross and Lillian Faderman (New York: Columbia University Press, 1999), 411.

12. Ibid., 412.

13. Michelangelo Signorile, *Queer in America: Sex, the Media and the Closets of Power* (Madison: University of Wisconsin Press, 1993), 149, 151.

14. Marianna Patrona, "Journalists on the News: The Structured Panel Discussion as a Form of Broadcast Talk," *Discourse Society* 23, no. 2 (2012): 159.

15. A. Witt, "Gay Rights: Clearing the Path of Prejudice," *Virginian-Pilot*, April 5, 1991, B1.

16. Randy Alfred, producer and interviewer, *The Gay Life with Randy Alfred*, May 10, 1980, KSAN-AM, retrieved from Gayback Archive, GLBT History Center.

17. Ibid.

18. E. Alwood, *Straight News: Gays, Lesbians and the News Media* (New York: Columbia University Press, 1998), 185–86.

19. Alfred, *The Gay Life*.

20. Michelangelo Signorile, *Queer in America: Sex, the Media and the Closets of Power* (Madison: University of Wisconsin Press, 1993), xviii.

21. Witt, "Gay Rights," B1.

22. Randy Shilts, interview by Eric Marcus, March 1989.

23. J. Weir, "Reading Randy," *Out*, August–September 1993, 46.

24. Randy Shilts, "Johnson Disclosure Renews the Focus on AIDS Epidemic," *San Francisco Chronicle*, November 8, 1991, A22; R. W. Stevenson, "Magic Johnson Ends His Career, Saying He Has AIDS Infection," *New York Times*, November 8, 1991, 1.

25. Randy Shilts, "Question Isn't Good AIDS, Bad AIDS; All Are Victims," *New York Times*, November 13, 1991.

## Chapter 15. Unfinished Work

1. Steve Kroft, producer, "Randy Shilts," CBS News, *60 Minutes*, February 20, 1994.

2. Linda Alband, email to the author, January 4, 2013.

3. Kroft, "Randy Shilts."

4. Randy Shilts, "Happy Endings," letters, *Advocate*, January 25, 1994, 3.

5. Linda Alband, "Randy Shilts Ongoing Considerations," typewritten memorandum, December 6, 1993, GLBT History Center Archive.

6. Susan Sward, "The Price of Freedom," *San Francisco Chronicle*, March 6, 1994, A12.

7. Lori Olszewski and David Tuller, "Writer Randy Shilts Dies at 42; Pioneer in Coverage of AIDS," *San Francisco Chronicle*, February 18, 1994, A1.

8. Keith Power, "Reporter Driven by His Mission," *San Francisco Chronicle*, February 18, 1994, D6.

9. Jennifer Warren and Richard C. Paddock, "Randy Shilts: Chronicler of AIDS Epidemic, Dies at 42," *New York Times*, February 18, 1994, A12.

10. Power, "Reporter Driven," D6.

11. S. Solis Espinosa, "Health Chief Lauds Shilts' Works on AIDS," *San Francisco Chronicle*, February 21, 1994, A13.

12. Glide Memorial Church DVD of Randy Shilts's memorial service, February 22, 1994, Glide Memorial Church Archive.

13. Westboro Baptist Church news release, February 19, 1994, Glide Memorial Church Archive.

14. D. Tuller and S. Espinosa Solis, "SF Farewell to Randy Shilts: Reporter Eulogized, Anti-gay Protest Fizzles," *San Francisco Chronicle*, February 23, 1994, A1.

15. Glide Memorial Church DVD.

16. *Aurora Beacon-News*, June 17, 2012.

17. Susan Sward, "The Price of Freedom," *San Francisco Chronicle*, March 6, 1994, A12.

18. Paul Newman to Randy Shilts beneficiaries, May 12, 1994, GLBT History Center Archive.

19. Last Will and Testament of Randy Shilts, November 11, 1993, GLBT History Center Archive.

20. Betsy Bourbon, "Randy Shilts' Partner Talks about Love, Grief, and Survival," *Russian River News*, May 25–31, 1994.

21. Ibid., 1, 7.

## Conclusion

1. Michael Worobey et al., "1970s and 'Patient O' HIV-1 Genomes Illuminate Early HIV/ AIDS History in North America," *Nature*, October 26, 2016, https://www.ncbi.nlm.nih.gov/pmc/articles/PMC5257289/.

2. Donald C. McNeil Jr., "HIV Arrived in the U.S. Long before 'Patient Zero,'" *New York Times*, October 26, 2016.

3. Ariana Eunjung Cha, "New Research Provides AIDS 'Patient Zero' Is Not How Virus Entered U.S.," *Washington Post*, October 27, 2016.

4. White House remarks by President Barack Obama, December 22, 2010, https://www.whitehouse.gov/the-press-office/2010/12/22/remarks-president-and-vice-president-signing-dont-ask-dont-tell-repeal-a.

5. Steve Kroft, producer, "Randy Shilts," CBS News, *60 Minutes*, February 20, 1994.

# Index

ANDREW E. STONER is an assistant professor of communication studies at California State University, Sacramento. His books include *Campaign Crossroads: Presidential Politics in Indiana from Lincoln to Obama.*

The University of Illinois Press
is a founding member of the
Association of American University Presses.

———————————————

Composed in 10.75/14 Arno Pro
with Courier Std display
by Kirsten Dennison
at the University of Illinois Press
Cover designed by Dustin J. Hubbart
Cover illustration: Randy Shilts, in the *San Francisco Chronicle*
newsroom. (Scott Sommerdorf, *San Francisco Chronicle*)
Manufactured by Sheridan Books, Inc.

University of Illinois Press
1325 South Oak Street
Champaign, IL 61820-6903
www.press.uillinois.edu